Using
QuickBooks Pro®
FOR ACCOUNTING
2004

Glenn Owen

Allan Hancock College

University of California
at Santa Barbara

THOMSON
SOUTH-WESTERN

Australia · Canada · Mexico · Singapore · Spain · United Kingdom · United States

Manuel Arias

BOA

THOMSON
SOUTH-WESTERN

Using QuickBooks Pro® 2004 for Accounting
Glenn Owen

VP/Editorial Director:
Jack W. Calhoun

Team Leader:
Melissa Acuña

Acquisitions Editor:
Julie Moulton

Developmental Editor:
Erin Joyner

Marketing Manager:
Chip Kislack

Production Editor:
Stephanie Blydenburgh

Manufacturing Coordinator:
Doug Wilke

Production House/Compositor:
DPS Associates, Inc.

Printer:
Globus Printing
Minster, OH

Art Director:
Stacy Jenkins Shirley

Cover Designer:
Stacy Jenkins Shirley and Kathy Heming

Cover Photos:
PhotoDisc, Inc.

Brief Contents

Contents

What if you could integrate a popular computerized accounting program into your classroom without using confusing and complicated manuals? What if your students could use this program and reinforce basic accounting concepts in an online and interactive case setting? What if you could accomplish both without spending a fortune and a vast amount of time preparing examples, cases, and illustrations? In fact, *Using QuickBooks® Pro 2004 for Accounting* by Owen is a textbook that fulfills and expands upon all three of these "what ifs."

WHY IS THIS TEXTBOOK NEEDED?

The first course in accounting has evolved significantly over the last several years. Educators are responding to the demand of accounting and nonaccounting faculty who rely on this course to lay a foundation for other courses. Moreover, the accounting profession relies on this course to attract the "best and the brightest" to become accounting majors. The evolution of this course has also put pressure on instructors to integrate computers into the classroom and, in doing so, develop students' skills in intelligently using and interpreting accounting information.

Faculty often want to incorporate computerized accounting into the first course, but are reluctant to invest the time and effort necessary to accomplish this laudable goal. Existing materials are often "preparer" driven in that they focus on the creation of financial reports only. Students are often discouraged in their use of computers in the first accounting course because of the complicated and confusing accounting software manuals that concentrate on accounting mechanics.

This text responds to all of these needs. It provides a self-paced, step-by-step environment in which students use *QuickBooks® Pro 2004* or *QuickBooks® Basic 2004* to create financial statements and other financial reports, to reinforce the concepts they learn in their first course, and to see how computer software can be used to make business decisions.

WHAT ARE THE NEW FEATURES
IN THIS VERSION OF QUICKBOOKS?

You can e-mail more forms and reports right from QuickBooks. In addition to invoices, statements, and estimates, you can now e-mail purchase orders, sales orders, sales receipts, credit memos, and reports—all right from QuickBooks. You can save forms and reports in a PDF format, so they'll look professional when your customers, vendors, or accountant views or prints them.

You can also now import Microsoft Excel data into QuickBooks, including customer lists, vendor lists, item lists, and other important information. Just assign each column in your Excel spreadsheet to a corresponding QuickBooks "field," such as inventory item, phone number, or price. You can also save import settings to use again. In addition you can now easily export QuickBooks reports to any Microsoft Excel worksheet. Just indicate a specific worksheet, and QuickBooks will export your report to that sheet, replacing any existing data with your updated report data.

QuickBooks now lets you customize prices for different groups of customers, such as corporate, loyal, or high-volume, with more price levels (up to 100). Plus, you can attach percentage discounts or markups in pricing to each customer group, so you can automatically reduce or raise prices.

In addition, you can now put an end to surprise cash flow crunches. QuickBooks helps you predict your cash flow for the next six weeks, using your QuickBooks data and your answers to simple questions. Easily view your projected "available to spend" weekly cash balance in a printable report.

WHAT ARE THE GOALS OF THIS TEXTBOOK?

This textbook takes a user perspective by illustrating how accounting information is both used and created. QuickBooks is extremely user friendly and provides point and click simplicity with excellent and sophisticated accounting reporting and analysis tools. The textbook uses a proven and successful pedagogy to demonstrate the software's features and elicit student interaction.

The text's first and foremost goal is to help students learn or review fundamental accounting concepts and principles through the use of QuickBooks and the analysis of business events. The content complements the first course in accounting and, therefore, should be used in conjunction with a core text on accounting.

A second goal is to enable students to view financial statements from a user perspective. After an initial tour of QuickBooks, students learn how to use QuickBooks to understand and interpret financial statements.

A third goal of the text is to provide students a means to investigate the underlying source documents that generate most financial accounting information, such as purchase orders, sales invoices, and so on. Students will experience this process by entering a few business events for later inclusion in financial reports.

A fourth goal is to provide students a means of exploring some managerial aspects of accounting by performing financial analysis and comparisons. Budgets are created and compared to actual operating results, and receivables and payables are aged for analysis of cash management and cash flow projections.

A fifth goal of this text is to reduce the administrative burdens of accounting faculty by providing a self-paced environment, data sets, cases, and a correlation table describing how this text might be used with a variety of popular accounting texts.

WHAT ARE THE KEY FEATURES OF THIS TEXTBOOK?

The key features of this book are outlined below.

- This book will work with either *QuickBooks® Pro 2004* or *QuickBooks® Basic 2004*. However, only QuickBooks Pro includes the export to Excel feature covered briefly in Chapter 7. The basic version of QuickBooks does not include that feature.

- The chapters incorporate a continuing, interesting, realistic case— Phoenix Systems Consulting, Inc.—that helps students apply QuickBooks's features and key accounting concepts.

- A tested, proven step-by-step methodology keeps students on track. Students enter data, analyze information, and make decisions all within the context of the case. The text constantly guides students, letting them know where they are in the course of completing their accounting tasks.

- Numerous screen shots include callouts that direct students' attention to what they should look at on the screen. On almost every page in the book, you will find examples of how steps, screen shots, and callouts work together.

- **trouble?** paragraphs anticipate the mistakes that students are likely to make or problems they are likely to encounter, and help students recover and continue with the chapter. This feature facilitates independent learning and frees you to focus on accounting concepts rather than on computer skills.

- With very few exceptions, QuickBooks does not require the user to record journal entries to record business events. An appendix on traditional accounting records gives you the flexibility to teach journal entries at your discretion. It provides the information necessary for students to make journal entries to record the events described in Chapters 2 through 7.

- Questions begin the end-of-chapter material. They are intended to test students' recall of what they learned in the chapter.

- Chapter Assignments follow the Questions and provide students additional hands-on practice with QuickBooks skills. Some Chapter Assignments are designated by the icon shown here as Internet Assignments. These are optional.

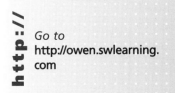

http://

Go to
http://owen.swlearning.
com

- A continuing Case Problem—OCEAN VIEW FLOWERS, a wholesale flower distributor, is included in Chapters 2 through 7. This is a series case which needs to be completed for each chapter before the following chapter's case can be performed. Unlike the JENNINGS & ASSOCIATES Case (see below), there are no data files for this case. This initial file, created in Chapter 2, is used in each successive chapter. The Case Problems ask the students to apply the same QuickBooks skills they learned in the chapter to this entirely new case.

- A continuing assignment, CENTRAL COAST CELLULAR, a retail cellular phone sales and consulting service, is included in Chapters 2 through 7. Like OCEAN VIEW, there are no data files in this case. The original QuickBooks file created in Chapter 2 is used in each successive chapter once again asking the students to apply the same skills they learned in the chapter to this new case.

- A continuing Case Problem—JENNINGS & ASSOCIATES, an advertising firm—concludes each chapter. This case has approximately the same scope as the Phoenix chapter case.

- Comprehensive problems appear at the end of Chapters 3 and 7. These problems provide an opportunity for students to demonstrate their comprehensive understanding of QuickBooks procedures.

- The Instructor's Package contains an *Instructor's Manual*, including solutions to end-of-chapter materials, and a master copy of the Student Disk, which contains backups of the practice data files students need to work through the materials.

- Comprehensive problems appear at the end of Chapters 3 and 7. These problems provide an opportunity for students to demonstrate their comprehensive understanding of QuickBooks procedures.

ABOUT THE AUTHOR

Glenn Owen is a tenured member of Allan Hancock College's Accounting and Business faculty, where he has lectured on accounting and information systems since 1995. In addition, he is a lecturer at the University of California at Santa Barbara, where he has been teaching accounting and information systems courses since 1980. His professional experience includes a position at Deloitte & Touche and vice-president of finance positions at Westpac Resources, Inc., and Expertelligence, Inc. He has authored many Internet-related books and accounting course supplements and is currently developing online accounting instruction modules for his Internet-based financial accounting courses. Mr. Owen has recently published another text, *Excel and Access in Accounting*, which gives accounting students specific, self-paced instruction on the use of spreadsheets (Excel) and database applications (Access) in accounting. His innovative teaching style emphasizes the decision-maker's perspective and encourages students to think creatively. His graduate studies in educational psychology and his 30 years of business experience combine for a balanced blend of theory and practice.

Note to Student and Instructor

QUICKBOOKS VERSION AND PAYROLL TAX TABLES

The text and related data files created for this text were constructed using *QuickBooks® Pro 2004* release R1P. To check your release number, open *QuickBooks® Pro 2004* and type **Ctrl 1**. If your release is less than number R1P, use the QuickBooks Update Service under the Online menu to update your version. This is a free service to version 2004 Pro users and requires an Internet connection. The files accompanying this text can be used in any *QuickBooks® Pro 2004* release R1P or higher.

In this version of QuickBooks, Intuit continues its use of a basic payroll service. This is a requirement in order to use the QuickBooks payroll features that automatically calculate taxes due to federal or state agencies. Initially, QuickBooks comes with the current tax tables; however, they become out of date, which can occur within a month of purchase, and the payroll feature is disabled unless the user subscribes to the payroll service.

Some previous versions of this text utilized whatever tax tables were in effect at the time of publication. Users who had different tax tables often noted differences in solutions as a result. This new requirement solves that problem. The author decided to utilize the manual payroll tax feature, which requires that students manually enter the tax deductions. This alleviates the discrepancies between the solutions manual and the students' data entry and lifts the burden of having to purchase the tax table service for each copy of QuickBooks installed in a lab environment. Instructions on how to set up payroll for manual calculation of payroll taxes are provided in the text. For more information, see your QuickBooks documentation.

All reports have a default feature which identifies the basis in which the report was created, such as accrual or cash, and the date and time the report was printed. The date and time shown on your report will of course be different from that shown in this text.

Getting Started with QuickBooks

In this chapter you will:

- ■ Take an interactive tour of QuickBooks

- ■ Create a balance sheet and modify its presentation

- ■ Create an income statement and modify its presentation

- ■ Create a statement of cash flows and modify its presentation

- ■ Create supporting reports and modify their presentation

This chapter is designed to help you navigate through QuickBooks. It provides a foundation for the chapters that follow by showing you how to create a new QuickBooks file and record a variety of operating, investing, and financing transactions.

This chapter is divided into five sessions—each with its own set of questions, assignments, and case problems. Session 1 of Chapter 1 gives you a quick interactive tour of QuickBooks, in which you will create your Working Disk and become familiar with QuickBooks's essential features. Sessions 2, 3, 4, and 5 introduce you to creating and preparing the balance sheet, the income statement, the statement of cash flows, and supporting reports.

1

An Interactive Tour of QuickBooks

Learning Objectives

In this session you will:

- Make your QuickBooks Working Disk
- Launch and exit QuickBooks in Windows
- Identify the major components of the QuickBooks window and the major menu commands
- Open and close a QuickBooks file
- Correct mistakes and use the Undo and Revert commands
- Use QuickBooks Help
- View and print a set of financial statements

CASE: ROCK CASTLE CONSTRUCTION COMPANY

You've been working in a part-time job at a restaurant, and today you decide that you've served your last hamburger. You want a new part-time job—one that's more directly related to your future career in business. As you skim the want ads, you see an ad for an administrative assistant at Rock Castle Construction Company. Rock Castle specializes in remodeling existing homes and is well known in town for its quality construction and timely completion of projects. The ad says that job candidates must have earned or be earning a business degree, have some computer skills, and be willing to learn on the job. This looks promising. And then you see the line "Send a résumé to Jim Reed." You know Jim Reed! He was in one of your marketing classes two years ago; he graduated last year with a degree in accounting. You decide to send your résumé to Jim right away.

A few days later you're delighted to hear Jim's voice on the phone. He remembers you well. He explains that he wants to hire someone to help him with clerical and other administrative tasks in support of his job as Rock Castle's accountant. He asks if you could start right away. When you say yes, he offers you the job on the spot! You start next Monday.

When you arrive Monday morning, Jim explains that the first thing he needs you to learn is how to use a software package called QuickBooks. You quickly remind Jim that you're not an accounting major. Jim laughs as he assures you you'll have no problem with QuickBooks because it is so user oriented. He chose QuickBooks exactly for that reason and has been using it for about six months. Many of the Rock Castle managers want accurate, useful, and timely financial information to help them make sound business decisions, and they're not accountants.

Jim explains that on May 31, 2007 he started using QuickBooks by entering opening balances. Since then, he has recorded all transactions in QuickBooks. But he's becoming so busy at Rock Castle that he now needs someone else in the office who can enter transactions, generate reports for the managers, and so on. So he says that today he will give you a tour of QuickBooks and teach you some of the basic features and functions of this package. You tell him that you're familiar with Windows and you're ready to start.

USING THIS TEXT EFFECTIVELY

Before you begin the tour of QuickBooks, note that this textbook assumes you are familiar with the basics of Windows: how to control windows, how to choose menu commands, how to complete dialog boxes, and how to select directories, drives, and files. If you do not understand these concepts, please consult your instructor. Also note that this book is designed to be used with your instructor's and/or another textbook's discussion of essential accounting concepts.

The best way to work through this textbook is to carefully read the text and complete the numbered steps, which appear on a shaded background, as you work at your computer. Read each step carefully and completely before you try it.

As you work, compare your screen with the figures in the chapter to verify your results. You can use QuickBooks with any Windows operating system. The screen shots you will see in this book were captured in a Windows XP Professional environment. So if you are using Windows 98, 2000, ME, or XP you may see some minor differences between your screens and the screens in this book. Any significant differences that result from using the different operating systems with QuickBooks will be explained.

Don't worry about making mistakes—that's part of the learning process. The **trouble?** paragraphs identify common problems and explain how to correct them or get back on track. Follow the suggestions *only* if you are having the specific problem described.

After you complete a chapter, you can do the questions, assignments, and case problems found at the end of each chapter. They are carefully structured so that you will review what you have learned and then apply your knowledge to new situations.

DATA FILES CD

To complete the chapters and exercises in this book, you must have access to data files. The CD located inside the front cover of this book contains backups of all the practice files you need for the chapters, the assignments, and the case problems.

You will need to restore the backup files to their original format. The files on your Data Files CD are named to correspond to chapters and sessions in this book.

To restore a backup file (file with a .qbb extension) to its original format (file with a .qbw extension):

1. Insert your Data Files CD into your CD drive.
2. Launch QuickBooks.
3. Click **File**, then click **Restore**.
4. Click the **Browse** button in the Get Company Backup From: section of the Restore Company Backup window and then locate the backup file you want to restore on your Data Files CD.
5. Next, click the **Browse** button in the Restore Company Backup To: section of the Restore Company Backup window to change the location of where you want the file to be restored on your computer's hard drive. Be sure to note its location for future use. See the example in Figure 1.1.

Figure 1.1
Restore Company Backup
Window

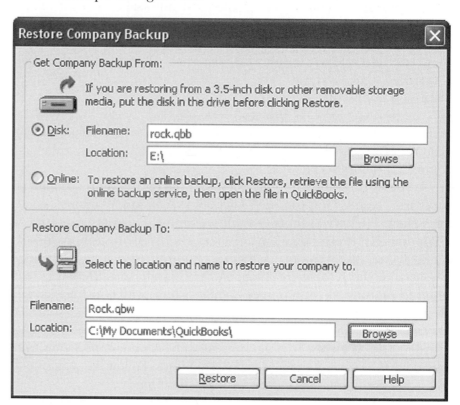

6. Click **Restore** in the Restore Company Backup window.
7. Click **OK** in the QuickBooks Information window, which should indicate that your data was restored successfully.
8. Continue this process for all the backup files on your Data Files CD as you need them.
9. Click **OK** in the QuickBooks Information window, which should indicate that your data was restored successfully.

Working from your computer's hard drive is the most efficient way to use the QuickBooks program. However, if you are in a lab environment and want to take your file with you when you leave, you'll need to make a backup copy of the file and save it to a removable disk.

To create a backup file (file labeled with a .qbb extension) from one in an original format (file labeled with a .qbw extension):

1. Insert a blank formatted disk into your disk drive (usually drive A:).
2. Launch QuickBooks (if not already running).
3. Open the file you want to back up (once again, only if it is not already open).
4. Click **File**, then click **Back Up**.
5. Change the backup location to your disk. See the example in Figure 1.2.

Figure 1.2
QuickBooks Backup Window

6. Click **OK** to begin the backup process.
7. Click **OK** once again in the QuickBooks information window, which should indicate that your data was backed up successfully.

To restore the .qbb file you just created to a different computer:

1. Insert your backup disk into drive A:.
2. Launch QuickBooks.
3. Click **File**, then click **Restore**.
4. Change the location of the Get Company Backup From: section of the Restore Company Backup window to A:\ (assuming you want to restore the file from the disk located in drive A:)

5. Change the location of the Restore Company Backup To: section of the Restore Company Backup window to a location on your computer's hard drive, being sure to note its location for future use.
6. Click **Restore**.
7. Click **OK** in the QuickBooks Information window, which should indicate that your data was restored correctly.

WHAT IS QUICKBOOKS?

Jim is excited about using QuickBooks since it is the best selling small business accounting software on the market today. He explains that **QuickBooks** is an automated accounting information system that describes an entity's financial position and operating results and that helps managers make more effective business decisions. He also likes QuickBooks's reports and graphs, which quickly and easily organize and summarize all the data he enters.

Jim says he especially likes QuickBooks because it can handle all of Rock Castle's needs to invoice customers and maintain receivables, as well as pay bills and maintain payables. It can track inventory and create purchase orders using Rock Castle's on-screen forms—all without calculating, posting, or closing. Jim can correct all transactions he's recorded at any time, while an audit trail feature automatically keeps a record of any changes he makes.

Jim explains further that QuickBooks has four basic features that, when combined, help manage the financial activity of a company. The four features—lists, forms, registers, and reports and graphs—work together to create an accounting information system. Let's take a closer look at each of these four features.

Lists

Lists are groups of names, such as customers, vendors, employees, inventory items, and accounts, and information about those names. Lists are created and edited either from a list window or while completing a form, such as an invoice, bill, or time sheet. Figure 1.3 shows a list of Rock Castle's customer names with jobs for each of these customers, balances owed for each job, and any explanatory notes.

Forms

Forms are QuickBooks's electronic representations of the paper documents used to record business activities, such as customer invoices, a vendor's bill for goods purchased, or a check written to a vendor. The customer invoice form in Figure 1.4 contains many **fields**, or areas on the form that you can fill in.

If you fill in a field, such as the Customer:Job field, QuickBooks often automatically fills in several other fields with relevant information to speed up data entry. In Figure 1.4, for example, the BILL TO, TERMS, and Tax fields are filled in as soon as the Customer:Job field is entered.

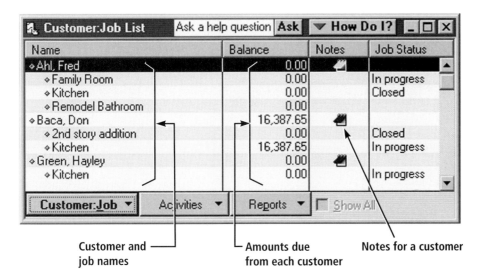

Figure 1.3
A Customer List from Rock Castle
Construction

Customer and
job names

Amounts due
from each customer

Notes for a customer

Also, filling in a field is made easier through the use of drop-down lists. Whenever you see an arrow next to or in a field, that field is a drop-down list.

Registers

A QuickBooks **register** contains all financial activity for a specified balance sheet account. Examples of registers include checking (cash), accounts receivable, inventory, and accounts payable. The checking register in

Your screen may show the words Print, Send, Ship, and Find if your Create Invoice window is expanded. QuickBooks automatically removes words to save space when the window size is reduced.

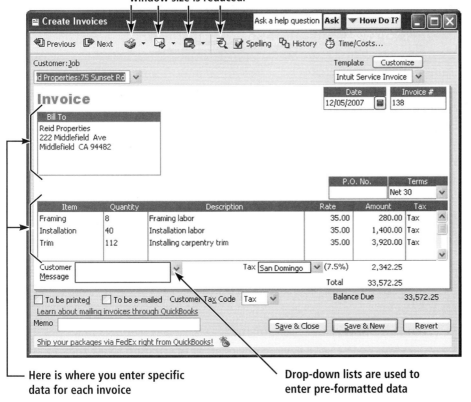

Figure 1.4
An Invoice Form for Rock Castle
Construction

Here is where you enter specific
data for each invoice

Drop-down lists are used to
enter pre-formatted data

Figure 1.5

A Section of the Checking
Register from Rock Castle
Construction

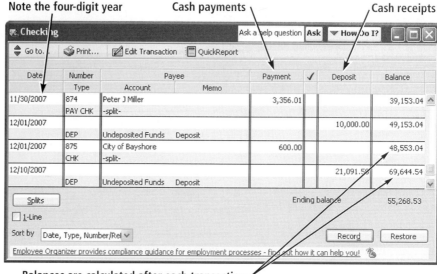

Figure 1.5 shows some of Rock Castle's cash payments and cash receipts, and provides cash balances after each transaction.

The financial effects of business transactions may be entered directly into the register or into the forms that automatically record the effects of these transactions in the relevant register. For example, if an owner's cash contribution is recorded on a Deposit form, the increases in both the checking account and relevant owner's equity account are simultaneously recorded in the Checking register and Contributed Capital register.

Reports and Graphs

QuickBooks **reports** and **graphs** present the financial position and the operating results of a company in a way that makes business decision making easier. The Profit and Loss report in Figure 1.6 shows the revenues and expenses of Rock Castle Construction for a specific period of time. Note that QuickBooks uses the title "Profit and Loss," but the generally accepted accounting title for this report is "Income Statement." Titles for this and other reports are all changeable using QuickBooks's Header/Footer tab. You can modify reports in many other ways, such as by comparing monthly periods, comparing this year with prior years, or examining year-to-date activity.

QuickBooks can also graph data to illustrate a company's financial position and operating results. For example, the bar chart in Figure 1.7 illustrates sales by month and the pie chart illustrates sales by construction category.

LAUNCHING QUICKBOOKS

Now that you know about lists, forms, registers, and reports and graphs, you are ready to launch QuickBooks. Jim invites you to join him in his office and use his large-screen monitor to start your tour. You open Windows, and Jim tells you how to launch QuickBooks.

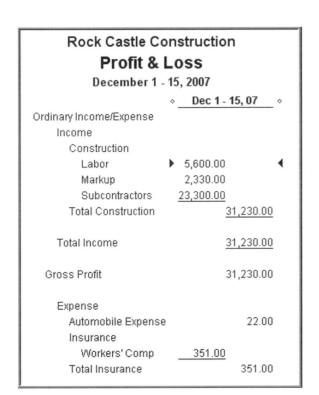

Figure 1.6

A Profit and Loss Report (Income Statement) from Rock Castle Construction

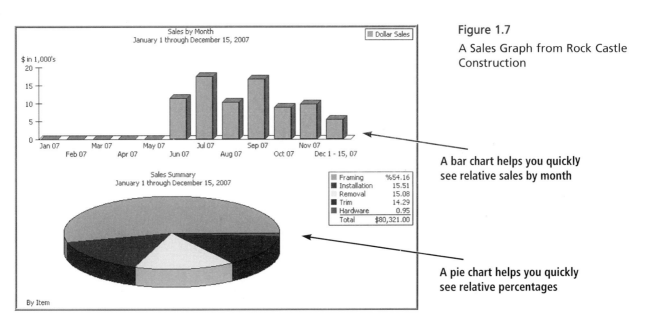

Figure 1.7

A Sales Graph from Rock Castle Construction

A bar chart helps you quickly see relative sales by month

A pie chart helps you quickly see relative percentages

To launch QuickBooks in Windows:

1 Click the **Start** button.

2 Select the **Programs** menu and look down the list for QuickBooks.

3 Once you've located the QuickBooks program, click and release the QuickBooks icon or name.

trouble? If, when QuickBooks was last used, the file being worked on was closed, you will see a No Company Open window.

If, however, a QuickBooks file is open, click **File**, then click **Close Company**. Be sure to close any open files before you proceed to the next set of steps.

Now that you have launched QuickBooks, you can begin to learn how to use it.

RESTORING AND OPENING A QUICKBOOKS FILE

Jim hands you a disk and tells you to open a file called Rock.qbw. (You will find a backup of this file included on your Data Files CD).

To restore and open the Rock Castle Construction Company file:

1 Insert your Data Files CD into your CD ROM drive.

2 Launch QuickBooks.

3 Click **File**, then click **Restore**. You should see a window like Figure 1.8.

Figure 1.8

Restore Company Backup Window

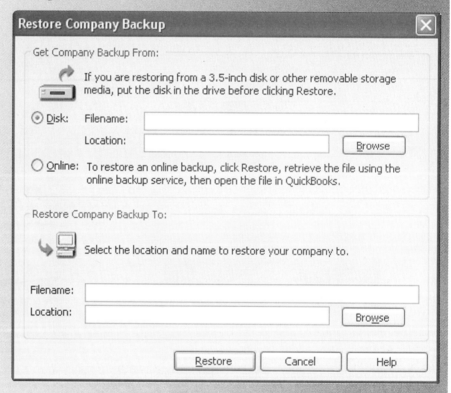

4 Change the location of the Get Company Backup From section of the Restore Company Backup window to E:\ (assuming drive E is your CD ROM drive).

5 Change the location of the Restore Company Backup To section of the Restore Company Backup window to a location on your computer's hard drive, being sure to note its location for future use, perhaps as shown in Figure 1.9.

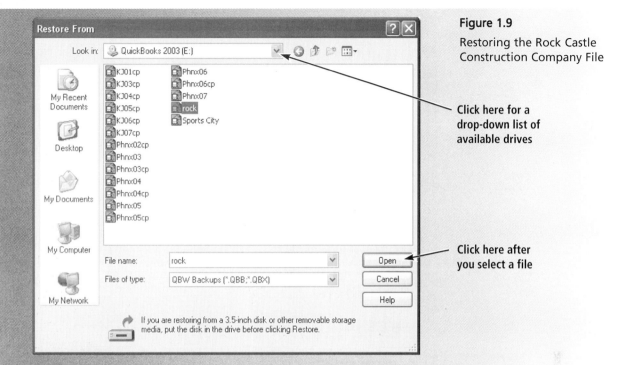

Figure 1.9
Restoring the Rock Castle
Construction Company File

Click here for a
drop-down list of
available drives

Click here after
you select a file

6 Click **Restore**.

7 The QuickBooks Information window appears as shown in Figure 1.10. Note that Rock.qbw is a modified version of the QuickBooks sample file, and it will assume a system date of December 15, 2007. Click **OK**.

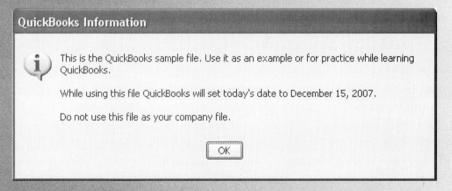

Figure 1.10
QuickBooks Information Window

8 Click **OK** in the QuickBooks Information window, which should indicate that your data was restored correctly.

9 Click the **OK** button. The New Features window may appear. Let's skip this for now and click **Close box**. The Company Navigator window should appear. See Figure 1.11. QuickBooks automatically opens this window every time you open a file. You will learn more about this later. If it does not appear, click **Company** listed as the first Navigator in the Open Windows list on the far left of the screen.

trouble? If your QuickBooks Application window does not already fill the desktop, click the Application window Maximize button, located next to the Close button.

Figure 1.11

Company Navigator Window

THE QUICKBOOKS WINDOW

Jim explains that QuickBooks operates like most other Windows programs, so most of the QuickBooks window controls will be familiar to you if you have used other Windows programs. He reaches for the mouse and quickly clicks a few times until his screen looks like Figure 1.12. The main components of the QuickBooks window are shown in this figure. Let's take a look at these components so you are familiar with their location and use.

The **title bar** at the top of the window tells you that you are in the QuickBooks program and identifies the company file currently open. The **menu bar** contains the **command menus**, which open windows within QuickBooks. The File, Edit, View, and Help menus are similar to other Windows programs in that they allow you to perform such common tasks as open, save, copy, paste, find, and get help.

The Lists menu gives you access to all lists, including the chart of accounts, customers, vendors, employees, and inventory items, to name a few. The Company, Customers, Vendors, Employees, and Banking menus provide easy access to the previously mentioned centers as well as common tasks unique to that menu. For instance, in the Customers menu you can create invoices, enter cash sales, create credit memos, receive payments, etc. The Reports menu will give you quick

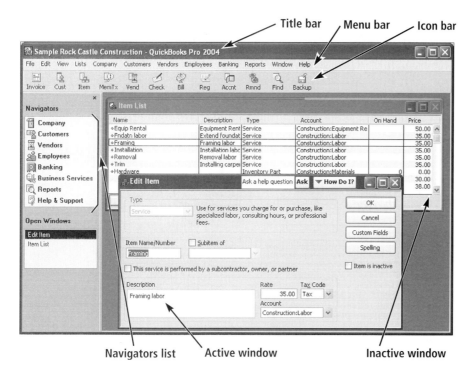

Figure 1.12

Components of the QuickBooks Window

access to common reports and graphs for easy creation. The Window menu allows you to choose the format for window displays, such as cascade or tile vertically. Finally, the Help menu will give you immediate access to an index of help topics.

The **icon bar** includes icons representing tasks you do on a daily basis, such as entering and paying bills, creating invoices, and receiving payments. If you use QuickBooks payroll system, you might consider adding icons for your payroll forms. Icons can be added, removed, or reordered to fit your needs. Use the View menu to hide or display the icon bar and make any changes. As an alternative, or in addition to the icon bar, you can display a vertical shortcut list. The **shortcut list** includes shortcuts to frequently used windows. Shortcuts and navigators are grouped by area of QuickBooks.

QuickBooks is preset to display the icon bar instead of the shortcut list. However, if you prefer the vertical shortcut list, you can display it instead of, or in addition to, the icon bar. Like the icon bar, the shortcut list can be customized to include the features and reports you use most.

The **Open Windows list** gives you quick access to the navigator features in QuickBooks. These navigators can help you find tasks and information related to the major areas of QuickBooks, such as customers, vendors, employees, banking, etc. It also gives you a peek at what other QuickBooks windows might be open. Use the View menu to hide or display this feature.

The **active window** is the window in which you can enter or edit data, and it is identified by a solid window title bar. Only one window may be active at a time. Other windows may be open, but they are inactive. If the active window is closed, or if a window behind it is selected, it becomes **inactive**, and the window selected becomes active.

SAVING AND CLOSING A QUICKBOOKS FILE

Now that you have seen the components of the QuickBooks screen, Jim wants to show you how to close a file, so that you will always be able to save your work and exit QuickBooks. He explains that to close a QuickBooks file, you can do one of three things:

- Exit QuickBooks using the Exit command on the File menu.

- Open another company file using the Open Company command.

- Close the file using the Close Company command on the File menu.

To close the Rock Castle Construction Company's file:

1 Click **File**.

2 Click **Exit**. The Rock Castle Construction Company file is automatically saved and closed. A dialog box might display the message "Intuit highly recommends backing up your data to avoid any accidental loss. Would you like to back up now?" Another message about QuickBooks Update Service might also appear. Close this message window for now. See Figure 1.13.

Figure 1.13

Closing Files

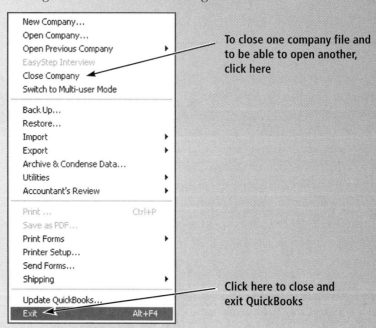

To close one company file and to be able to open another, click here

Click here to close and exit QuickBooks

3 Click **No** to exit QuickBooks and return to Windows.

Then Jim tells you something very unusual. He says that unlike other Windows programs, QuickBooks *does not have a Save command.* In other words, in QuickBooks you cannot save a file whenever you want. You stare at Jim in disbelief and ask how that can be possible. Jim explains that *QuickBooks automatically saves all of the data you input and the changes you make as soon as you make them and click OK.* Jim admits that when he first used QuickBooks, he was uneasy about exiting the program until he could find a way to save his work. But he discovered that there are no Save or Save As commands on the QuickBooks File menu as there are on most other Windows programs. He reassures you that as unsettling as this is, you'll get used to it when you become more familiar with QuickBooks.

CORRECTING MISTAKES: THE BACKSPACE KEY, THE UNDO COMMAND, AND THE CLEAR COMMAND

Another skill you must have when you start using a program that's new to you is how to correct mistakes. Jim explains that, as with many other programs, one of the easiest ways to correct a mistake while entering data into QuickBooks is to use the Backspace key. Whenever you are typing and need to correct a mistake, you can press the Backspace key to back up the cursor and delete one or more characters. To demonstrate this error correction method, let's use Rock.qbw again and intentionally make a mistake when entering a cash sale.

To correct a mistake as you are typing:

1 Open Rock.qbw as you have done before.

2 Click **Customers** on the menu bar and scroll to **Enter Sales Receipts**. The Enter Sales Receipts window appears. (You might get a Merchant's Account Service Message. Click on **do not display this message in the future** or click on **No**.)

3 Move the cursor to the SOLD TO field. Type **United Ari** in the SOLD TO field to make the intentional error, as shown in Figure 1.14, *but don't press [Enter]*.

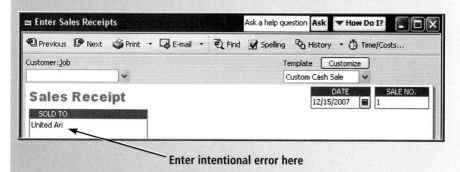

Figure 1.14

Correcting Mistakes Using the Backspace Key

Enter intentional error here

4 Press **[Backspace]** twice to delete the "ri".

5 Type **irlines** and press **[Enter]** to make the correction.

The correct customer name is now entered in the SOLD TO field of the Sales Receipt form, and the cursor is positioned to enter the customer's address.

Two other useful ways to correct mistakes are to use the Undo command and the Clear command. Both of these are located on the Edit menu. The Undo command is so called because it "undoes" all typing since the last Enter command. The Clear command causes the form to revert back to the form's initial appearance. To demonstrate how to use these commands, let's continue filling in the form for Sample Company and enter an address for United Airlines.

To correct a mistake after typing several words:

1 Type **10000 Skyway Blvd.** under United Airlines in the SOLD TO field, *but don't press [Enter]*. You think that this is the correct address for United Airlines.

2 You then discover that this is not the correct address. Click **Edit**, then click **Undo Typing** to delete the entire entry. See Figure 1.15.

Figure 1.15
Correcting Mistakes Using the
Undo and Clear Commands

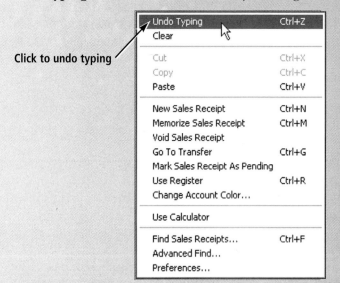

Click to undo typing

3 Type **United Airlines** and press **[Enter]**. Then type **1234 Airline Way**, the correct address, and press **[Enter]**.

4 Type **Chicago, Illinois 30021** and press **[Enter]**.

5 Now suppose that the United Airlines purchasing agent changes her mind, and you don't have a reason to enter this cash sale at all. Click **Edit**, then click **Clear**. The form returns or "reverts" to its original appearance.

Let's completely cancel this transaction. Close the Enter Sales Receipts window to leave this form without entering any data into the United Airlines' account.

QUICKBOOKS'S MENUS AND SHORTCUT LIST

Jim explains that to enter sales receipts, create invoices, pay bills, receive payments, and so on, you use QuickBooks menu commands. Some of these functions are also available from buttons on the QuickBooks icon bar.

Some QuickBooks menus are dynamic; in other words the options on the menu change depending upon what form, list, register, or report with which you are working. For instance, when you enter sales receipts information, the File and Edit menus change to include menu commands to print the sales receipts, or to edit, delete, memorize, or void the sales receipts.

The shortcut list, selected in the View menu, is a drop-down list of frequently used windows. It provides fast access to the areas of QuickBooks you use the most. You can customize this feature by clicking on the Customize button located at the bottom of the shortcut list. The Customize Shortcut List window appears as shown in Figure 1.16. This customization process can add a window such as Pay Sales Tax or remove a window such as Products & Services by first selecting the title of the window from either the Select windows to add list or the current shortcut list as appropriate.

Because this is all new to you, Jim suggests that first you become familiar with how managers at Rock Castle use QuickBooks to make business decisions.

USING QUICKBOOKS TO MAKE BUSINESS DECISIONS: AN EXAMPLE AT ROCK CASTLE

Once transactions are entered into the QuickBooks accounting information system, they can be accessed, revised, organized, and reported in

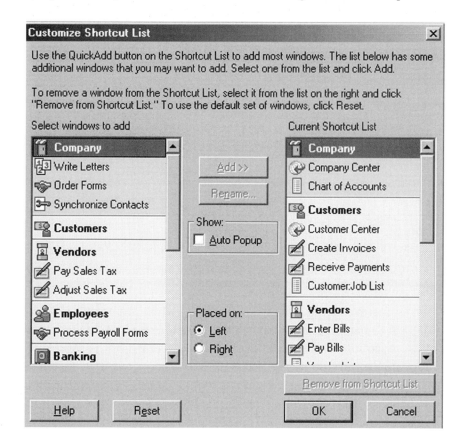

Figure 1.16

Customizing the Shortcut List

many ways to aid business decision making. This ability is what makes a computerized accounting information system so valuable to managers.

While you're sitting with Jim, he receives a phone call from Susan Guttmann, the manager of Rock Castle Construction's credit department. Susan needs some information to help her decide if any past due accounts should be turned over to a collection agency. You know from your accounting course that Susan is really asking for information about Rock Castle's **accounts receivable**, or amounts due from customers from previously recorded sales. Susan wants to know how much is due from customers and how current those receivables are; specifically, which customers owe Rock Castle and when their payments were due. Jim tells Susan he'll look into this immediately and call her right back.

To identify the customers who owe Rock Castle money and the total amount of receivables due from these customers:

1 Click **Reports**, click **Customers & Receivables**, and then click **A/R Aging Detail**. The report in Figure 1.17 appears. Notice that the report on your screen shows a date "As of December 15, 2007." The Rock.qbw file will always assume a system date of December 15, 2007 even if you may be working on your computer on March 20, 2005.

trouble? The report you see might be slightly different from the one shown in Figure 1.17. Some column widths have been altered. Use the scroll bars to view this report both vertically and horizontally.

Click here to refresh the report for the change you make in the report date

Figure 1.17
Accounts Receivable Detail

Purchase order column resized to view the entire width of the report

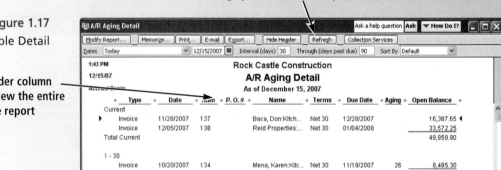

Scroll down to view additional information

2 Scroll down this summary report, and note that three customers owe Rock Castle a total of $118,445.20.

3 Jim wants to see a graphic illustration of this information. From the Menu bar, click **Reports**, click **Customers & Receivables**, then click **Accounts Receivable Graph**. The graphic in Figure 1.18 appears on the following page.

Jim calls Susan back and tells her that $118,445.20 is due from three customers: Don Baca, Karen Mena, and Reid Properties. The $49,959.90

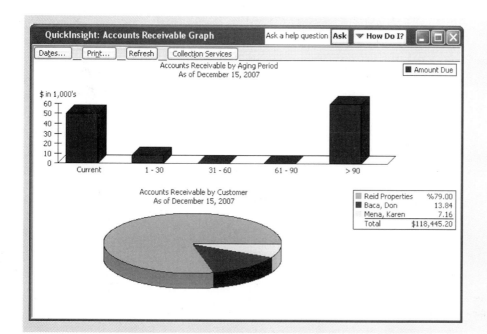

Figure 1.18

Accounts Receivable by Aging Period and Customer

due from Baca and Reid is current, while $8,485.30 due from Mena and $60,000.00 due from Reid are past due. Susan says that only Mena concerns her as she's already working on the Reid past due amount. She'd like to know specifically when invoices were sent to Mena, when Mena made payments, and in what amounts. Jim knows he can easily get this information by accessing the Customer Balance Detail for Mena.

To access the Customer Balance Detail for Mena:

1 From the Menu bar, click **Reports**, click **Customers & Receivables**, then click **Customer Balance Detail**.

2 Scroll down the report to **Karen Mena's** detailed information shown in Figure 1.19. This report describes the two invoices that billed Karen Mena for construction services rendered. It also shows the cash payments received to date from Mena.

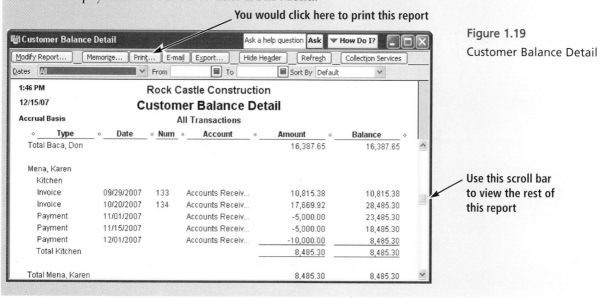

Figure 1.19

Customer Balance Detail

Jim calls Susan back and tells her that the invoice dates are 9/29/2007 and 10/20/2007, and that the dates of the most recent payments are 11/01/2007, 11/15/2007, and 12/01/2007. He has quickly and easily accessed financial information from the company's QuickBooks data file and Susan thanks him. She is grateful for his quick response so she can make her decision. She asks if, before the end of the day, he would print out a copy of this information and leave it on her desk. Jim is happy to oblige.

PRINTING IN QUICKBOOKS

Jim suddenly remembers a meeting he must attend. But before exiting QuickBooks you remind him that he promised to print a Customer Balance Detail report for Susan.

To print a Customer Balance Detail report:

1 If you have closed the Customer Balance Detail report, click **Reports**, click **Customers & Receivables**, then click **Customer Balance Detail**.

2 Click the **Print** button located on the button bar. See Figure 1.19.

3 Click **Print** in the Print Reports dialog box. The report prints out. **trouble?** You might have to set up a printer before printing. If necessary, click **Cancel** in the Print Report dialog box. Then select Printer Setup from the File menu. QuickBooks allows you to set up different printers for different functions. Click the Settings tab and select the printer you would like to use from the printer name drop-down list.

4 You've opened several windows and not closed them. Click the **Windows** menu, and then click **Close All** to close all open windows and return to the QuickBooks opening window.

Since you may have modified the settings for one or more reports, a Memorized Reports window may appear. Since we don't plan to use this report again, click **No**.

Jim asks you to drop this report off at Susan's desk sometime after lunch.

Figure 1.20

The Help Menu

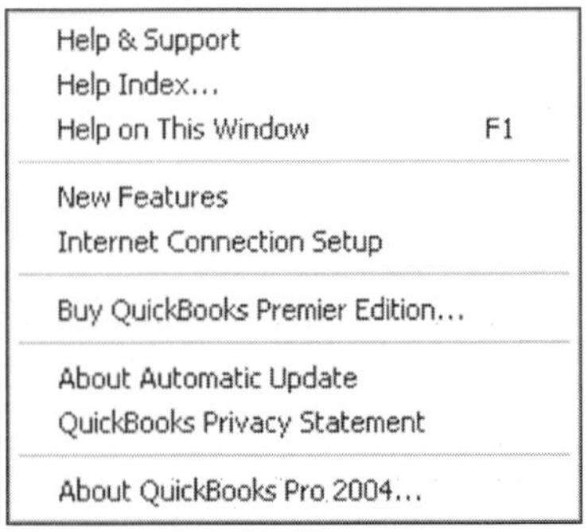

Help & Support	
Help Index...	
Help on This Window	F1
New Features	
Internet Connection Setup	
Buy QuickBooks Premier Edition...	
About Automatic Update	
QuickBooks Privacy Statement	
About QuickBooks Pro 2004...	

USING QUICKBOOKS HELP

Jim suggests you explore QuickBooks's Help features while he is at his meeting. He tells you that QuickBooks Help has the standard features and functions of Windows Help, and, in addition, has other help features specific to QuickBooks. These other features are listed in the main Help menu shown in Figure 1.20.

As with other Windows programs, you can access Help by clicking on the Help menu or pressing F1. QuickBooks Help is context sensitive—

that is, different help screens appear depending on where you are in the program. You can get help for a specific topic by choosing the Help Index menu item.

You decide to follow up on Jim's suggestion to look at a help feature he finds very useful, the Help Index. You are specifically interested in how QuickBooks uses accounts.

To use the Help Index:

1 Click **Help** from the menu bar. Then click **Help Index** on the menu.

2 Type the word **accounts** as a keyword.

3 Double-click **adding** under the caption accounts (managing) to view the QuickBooks Help window shown in Figure 1.21.

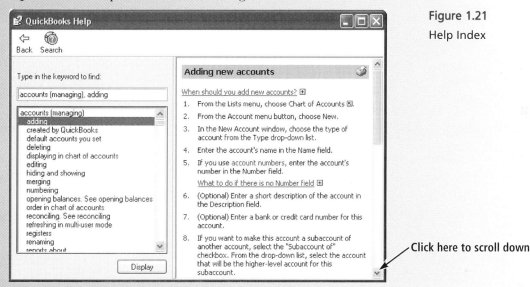

Figure 1.21

Help Index

Click here to scroll down

4 Click the **Print** button, then click **OK** to print this screen.

5 Close this window.

You will have an opportunity to use most of these options in this and later chapters.

ASK BUTTON

Jim returns from his meeting. He asks if you've tried the Ask button as he's found this an effective way to quickly access the QuickBooks Help feature. The Ask button appears on the title bar of most windows in QuickBooks.

To see how the Ask button can help you use QuickBooks:

1 Click the **Check** icon in the icon bar.

2 Type **How do I pay a bill with a check** in the Ask edit box, then click **Ask**.

3 Click once on the first topic shown in the QuickBooks Help window (**Paying a bill with a check**) to reveal the window shown in Figure 1.22.

Figure 1.22

QuickBooks Help

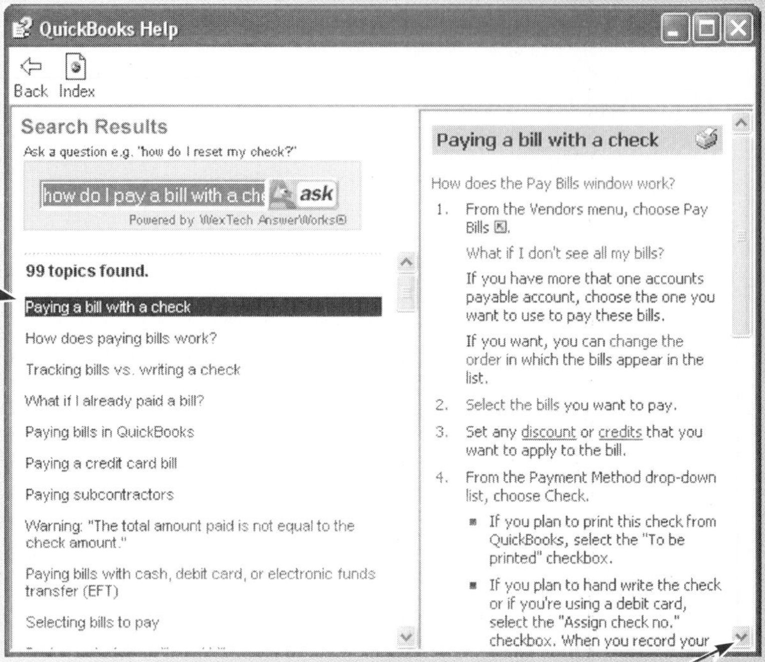

4 Close all windows.

HOW DO I BUTTONS

Jim then asks if you've discovered the How Do I button. He finds all of QuickBooks's features very useful, but he particularly recommends that you use the How Do I feature as you begin to work with QuickBooks. The How Do I button provides a drop-down menu for context sensitive help. Jim offers to demonstrate this unique feature of QuickBooks.

The How Do I button appears on the title bar of every window in QuickBooks. The drop-down menus provide access to various sections of QuickBooks Help including step-by-step procedures and other context-sensitive help.

To see how the How Do I button can help you use QuickBooks:

1 Click **Customers**, then click **Create invoices**.

2 Click on the **How Do I** button to reveal a drop-down menu.

3 Move the cursor over the words **Create invoices**, then move the cursor over the words **Create an invoice**. Your screen should look similar to Figure 1.23 on the following page.

4 Click on the words **Create an invoice** to reveal the twelve steps necessary to create an invoice.

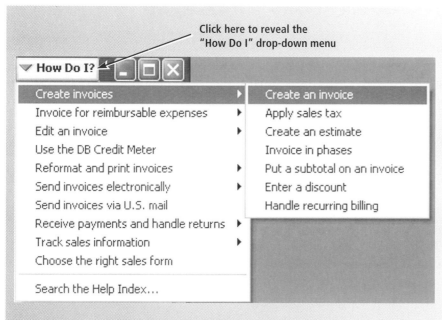

Click here to reveal the
"How Do I" drop-down menu

Figure 1.23

How Do I as a Help Feature

5 Close all windows.

QUICKBOOKS BUSINESS RESOURCES ONLINE SERVICE

QuickBooks has an online feature which, if your computer has Internet access, you might find helpful. Jim's computer is currently connected to the Internet via a company-wide network.

Jim offers to demonstrate the online support service to you by searching the online knowledge base for information on charging sales tax.

To access QuickBooks online support to better understand how you charge sales tax:

1 Open your browser (Internet Explorer or Netscape Navigator) and type **http://www.quickbooks.com** in the Address box.

2 Click **Support** located in the Related Links section.

3 Click the **Knowledge Base** button.

4 Select **Basics & Pro** from the drop-down edit box for Step 1 and **2004 for Windows** for Step 2, then click **Continue**.

5 Type **paying bills** in the Guided search text box, and then click the **Go** button.

6 Click the text **Paying bills in QuickBooks** from the list of results and review the resulting screen.

7 Close all windows.

THE QUICKBOOKS NAVIGATOR
. . . .

Besides How Do I, Jim explains, there is another feature—QuickBooks Navigator—that you might find useful. He tells you to think of it as your starting point to find lists, forms, registers, or reports. As you saw earlier, when you launched QuickBooks, the QuickBooks Company Navigators may have appeared in the center of the main QuickBooks window. If you choose to hide it, QuickBooks Navigators list appears on the left side of the screen, and you can redisplay the Company Navigators at any time by clicking Company.

To view QuickBooks Company Navigator:

1 Be sure that no companies are open, then open Rock.qbw as you have done before. If necessary, click **Open Window List** from the View menu to view the list of Navigators available. See Figure 1.24.

2 Click **Vendors** from the Navigators list as shown in Figure 1.24.

Figure 1.24

Navigator List

3 Most navigators contain a flow chart that shows the activities of this section, as shown in Figure 1.25 on the following page. Click the **Purchase Orders** icon. A purchase order form appears. Close this window.

4 Double-click the **A/P Aging Summary** and view the report.

5 Close the report and the Vendor Navigator window.

After you have learned the basics about QuickBooks in this course, you might decide to use the QuickBooks Navigators more often. But for now, follow the steps as they are written in this text. Close all windows.

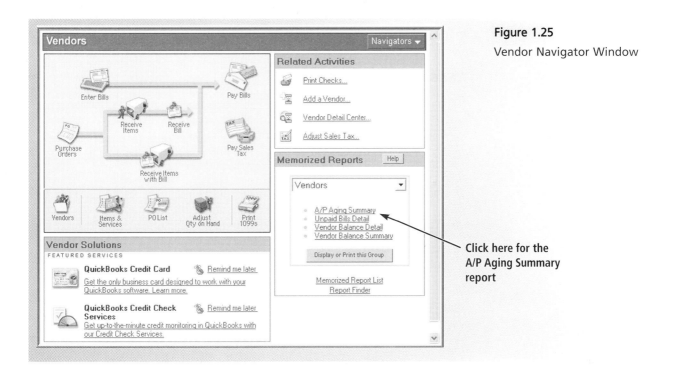

Figure 1.25
Vendor Navigator Window

EXITING QUICKBOOKS

You thank Jim for taking the time to introduce you to QuickBooks as he rushes off to yet another meeting. You know you can probably exit QuickBooks on your own, using standard Windows commands. You choose to use the Exit command on the File menu.

To exit QuickBooks:

1 Click **File** on the QuickBooks menu bar to display the File menu.

2 Click **Exit**. Once again a dialog box might display the message "Intuit highly recommends backing up your data to avoid any accidental data loss. Would you like to back up now?"

3 Click **No** to exit QuickBooks and return to Windows. Good accounting practice encourages backing up data files, but backup is not necessary now with these sample files.

END NOTE

Jim has shown you some of the features of QuickBooks, how to navigate these features, and how business decisions can be aided by the reporting and analysis of accounting information afforded by QuickBooks. You are impressed by the speed at which information is made available and are anxious to learn more.

practice

Session 1 Questions

1 Describe, in your own words, the various uses of QuickBooks.

2 List the four basic features of QuickBooks.

3 Describe how lists are used in QuickBooks.

4 Describe how forms are used in QuickBooks.

5 Name three forms used in QuickBooks.

6 Describe how registers are used in QuickBooks.

7 Describe how reports and graphs are used in QuickBooks.

8 Describe the function of the navigators in QuickBooks.

9 Describe how to print a report in QuickBooks.

10 Describe two of the Help features available in QuickBooks.

Session 1 Assignments

1 *Working with Files: Opening, Closing, and Printing*

Use the Rock Castle Construction Company file to practice opening, closing, and printing.

    a. Open the Rock.qbw file.
    b. Create a report of Open Invoices from the Customers & Receivables menu item on the Reports menu. Be sure the date 12/15/2007 is specified.
    c. Print the Open Invoices report.

2 *Practice Using the QuickBooks Help Menu*

Use the QuickBooks Help menu to learn more about QuickBooks's features.

    a. From the Help menu, select **Help Index**. Find the index section on reports. View the section for creating reports and print this topic.
    b. Find the index section on customer types. Print the section titled "Editing a list entry."
    c. Click **Chart of Accounts** from the Company menu. Press **F1**, then print the topic.

3 *Using the QuickBooks Knowledge Base*

 a. Navigate your browser to the QuickBooks website (http://www. QuickBooks.com).

 b. Use the Search feature to find information on manually calculating payroll.

 c. Print the first page of the resulting information found about this topic.

  trouble? Don't be surprised if your search comes up empty. Intuit is constantly updating its knowledge base and may have renamed some files.

> More information about QuickBooks Software can be found at **http://www.QuickBooks. com/**

4 *Using the South-Western Home Page for More Assignments or Cases*

If you have Internet access, go to the home page for this textbook at the address on the right.

 Click **Additional Problem Sets**, and then select the **Chapter 1: Session 1** section, and complete the problem(s) your instructor assigns.

> Go to **http://owen.swlearning. com**

Session 1 Case Problems: ROCK CASTLE CONSTRUCTION COMPANY

1 *Accessing Inventory Data*

Jim Reed, Rock Castle's accountant, wants to know the amount and nature of inventory on hand as of December 15, 2007. Use Rock.qbw to obtain this inventory information. Write your responses to Questions *c* through *e*, and print the Inventory Valuation Summary report.

 a. Open Rock.qbw.

 b. Open an Inventory Valuation Summary report as of December 15, 2007.

 c. What items of inventory were on hand on that date?

 d. How many of each item were on hand on that date?

 e. What was the average cost of those items on that date?

 f. Print the Inventory Valuation Summary report in landscape orientation.

2 *Accessing Sales Data*

Jim Reed also wants to know the company's sales for the period December 1 through December 15, 2007. Use Rock.qbw to obtain this sales information. Write your responses to Questions *c* through *f*, and print the Sales by Customer Detail report.

a. Open Rock.qbw.
b. Open the Sales by Customer Detail report for the period December 1 through December 15, 2007.
c. What customer was billed in this period?
d. What items are included on this invoice?
e. At what rate per hour was this customer billed?
f. What is the total amount of this invoice?
g. Print the Sales by Customer Detail report.

Preparing a Balance Sheet Using QuickBooks

Learning Objectives

In this session you will:

- Create a comparative balance sheet and a summary balance sheet
- Investigate detail supporting balance sheet items
- Use the Balance Sheet Report button bar
- Create a balance sheet as of a specific date other than the system date
- Print a balance sheet

CASE: ROCK CASTLE CONSTRUCTION COMPANY

It's your second day at your new job, and you arrive early. Jim is already hard at work at the computer. He tells you he is preparing for Rock Castle's fiscal year end on December 31, 2007. Since this is the first time he will prepare financial statements using QuickBooks, he's a little nervous. So he's decided to practice for the year-end closing by preparing a preliminary balance sheet as of December 15, 2007.

You recall from your accounting course that a balance sheet reports the assets, liabilities, and owners' equity of a company at a specific point in time. As part of your continued training on QuickBooks, Jim asks you to watch what he does as he prepares the preliminary balance sheet. He explains that his immediate goals are to familiarize himself with how to prepare a balance sheet using QuickBooks, and to examine some of the valuable features QuickBooks provides to help managers analyze and interpret financial information.

CREATING A BALANCE SHEET

You know from your business courses that the information on a balance sheet can be presented in many ways. Jim tells you that QuickBooks provides four preset ways to present a balance sheet; QuickBooks also allows him to customize the way he presents the information. He decides to examine one of the preset balance sheets first. He chooses what QuickBooks calls the Standard balance sheet report.

To create a Standard Balance Sheet report:

1 Open Rock.qbw.

2 Click **Reports**, click **Company & Financial**, then click **Balance Sheet Standard**. QuickBooks's Standard balance sheet appears. See Figure 1.26.

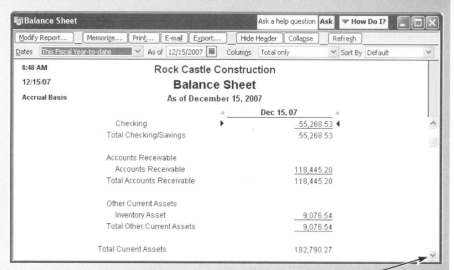

Scroll down to see the rest of the Balance Sheet

3 Scroll down the Rock Castle Construction Company Balance Sheet. Notice that this report shows the balance in each account, with subtotals for assets, liabilities, and owners' equity. Unlike standard accounting practice, QuickBooks displays net income for the year to date as part of owners' equity. In particular, take note of the current assets, fixed assets, current liabilities, long-term liabilities, and owners' equity. Note that QuickBooks refers to "owners' equity" as simply "equity."

4 Close this window.

trouble? On many of these reports, when you change the size of a column, then close the window, a "Memorized Report" window pops up asking if you want to memorize these new settings ("Would you like to memorize this report?") I suggest at this point that you just click **No**.

Jim is amazed at how rapidly QuickBooks created this balance sheet compared to how long it's taken him to create one manually in the past. As you both look over this balance sheet, Jim comments that because he generated this information so quickly with so little effort, he might now be able to add information to balance sheets that he didn't have time to include before. For example, he has always wanted to include comparative information on balance sheets to help Rock Castle's managers make better business decisions.

CREATING A COMPARATIVE BALANCE SHEET

By using the search function of QuickBooks Help, Jim discovers that QuickBooks has a built-in feature for preparing comparative balance sheets. He learns from Help that as long as the comparative information has already been entered in the QuickBooks file, he can easily create a comparative balance sheet. He tells you he entered the opening balances and transactions from December 15, 2006. When he sees how easily he can create a comparative balance sheet, he decides to create one comparing the balance sheet of December 15, 2007 with the one of December 15, 2006.

To create a Comparative Balance Sheet report:

1 Click **Reports**, click **Company & Financial**, and then click **Balance Sheet Prev Year Comparison**. Figure 1.27 appears.

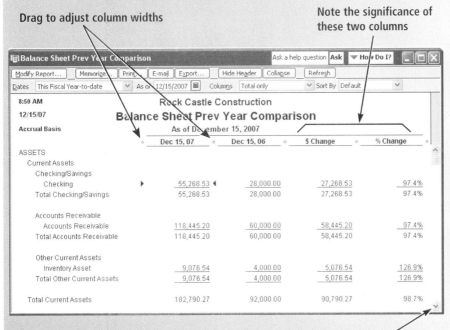

Figure 1.27

QuickBooks's Comparison Balance Sheet Report for Rock Castle as of December 15, 2007 and December 15, 2006

2 Scroll down and across this balance sheet. Note that this report is similar to the Standard report, except that the columns compare the amounts for this year to date and last year to date, and show the change in dollar amount and percent.

trouble? The balance sheet on your screen might not be the same as Figure 1.27 because the column widths are different. To change the column widths on any QuickBooks report, click and hold the mouse over the small diamond-shaped symbols to the right or left of any column. Drag to the right or left to increase or decrease each column's width. A dialog box might appear asking if you want to make all columns the same width. You may answer yes or no.

3 Close this window.

CREATING A SUMMARY BALANCE SHEET

Jim wonders if QuickBooks has a preset report that summarizes balance sheet information—in other words, one that provides no detail, only totals. In annual reports, such a summary is useful to external financial statement users, who usually do not have much interest in detailed balance sheet information. Jim again consults Help and learns that QuickBooks has a Summary balance sheet preset report.

To create a Summary Balance Sheet report:

1 Click **Reports**, click **Company & Financial**, and then click **Balance Sheet Summary**. See Figure 1.28.

Figure 1.28
QuickBooks's Summary Balance Sheet Report for Rock Castle

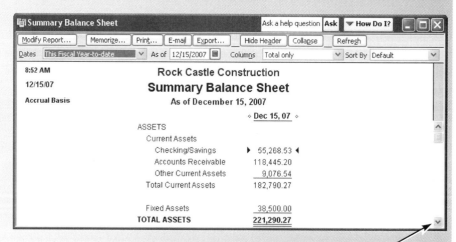

Scroll down to see more of this balance sheet

2 Scroll down the summary balance sheet. Note that it is a brief version of the Standard balance sheet; it shows amounts for each account type, such as Other Current Assets, but not for individual accounts within each account type.

INVESTIGATING THE BALANCE SHEET USING QUICKZOOM

Now that Jim knows he can generate the type of reports he wants, he decides to investigate QuickZoom—a feature he has heard QuickBooks provides for most reports. He tells you that QuickZoom shows you what transaction or transactions underlie any amount found in a report. You know that this is a helpful feature because managers often need to be able to quickly explain report balances; thus, knowledge of the underlying detailed transactions is essential.

Jim decides to practice using QuickZoom by analyzing the transactions that make up the Accounts Receivable balance.

To use QuickZoom:

1 Place the cursor over the Accounts Receivable balance of **118,445.20**. A cursor shaped like a magnifying glass and containing a "Z" appears. This cursor indicates that a QuickZoom report is available for this amount. See Figure 1.29.

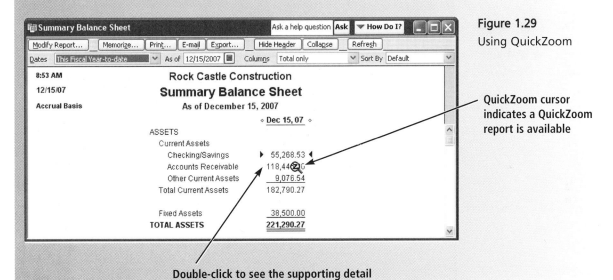

Figure 1.29
Using QuickZoom

QuickZoom cursor indicates a QuickZoom report is available

Double-click to see the supporting detail

2 Double-click the amount **118,445.20**. A transaction detail report, called Transactions by Account, appears. See Figure 1.30. The items listed in the Type column of this report—invoices and payments (that is, collections from customers)—represent the transactions that increased or decreased Accounts Receivable during the period from 1/01/07 to 12/15/07.

3 Double-click **129** in the Num column to examine one of the actual invoices. Invoice number 129 appears. See Figure 1.31. This invoice to Don Baca for a total of $31,568.25 is dated 7/26/2007.

Transactions are listed for 1/1/2007 through 12/15/2007

Figure 1.30
Viewing Transactions by Account

Transactions are listed in date order

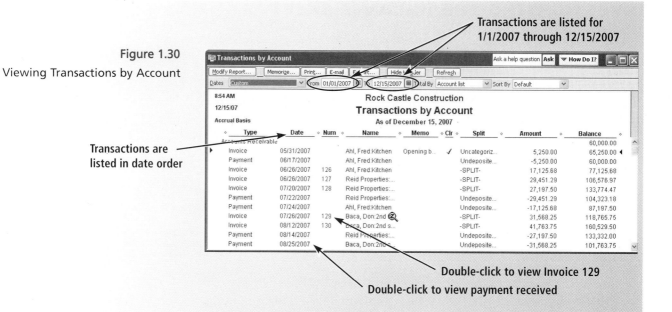

Double-click to view Invoice 129

Double-click to view payment received

Figure 1.31

Examining Invoice Number 129 for Don Baca

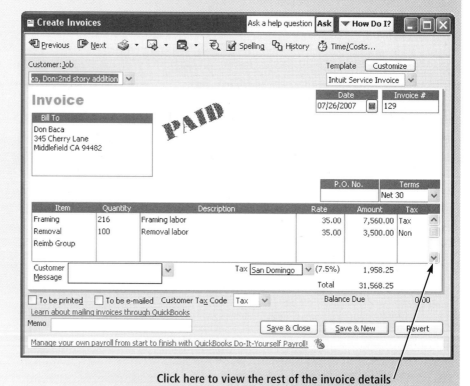

Click here to view the rest of the invoice details

4 Close the Create Invoices window. The Transactions by Account report, which was hidden while you examined Invoice number 129, reappears.

trouble? If the transactions report does not reappear, activate the Transactions by Account report by clicking Transactions by Account on the Window menu; or, if you closed the window, repeat Steps 1 through 4 above as necessary.

5 Double-click anywhere on the row containing the payment made by Don Baca posted 8/25/2007. A Receive Payments window appears. See Figure 1.32. Note that this payment is for Invoice 129.

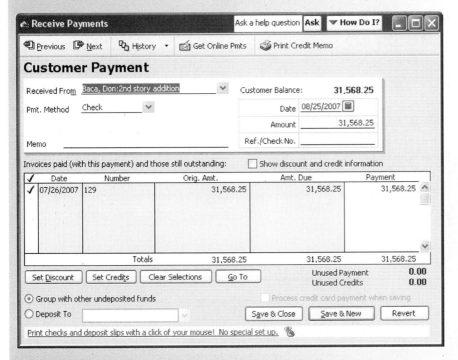

Figure 1.32

Customer Payment Received from Don Baca on 8/25/2007

6 Close the Receive Payments window.

7 Close the Transactions by Account window.

Jim is pleased with the QuickZoom feature of QuickBooks because it allows him to quickly and easily investigate any of the balances reported.

MODIFYING BALANCE SHEET REPORTS

The balance sheet report, like all other reports created in QuickBooks, can be modified using the report button bar, located on the menu bar. Jim decides that since this summary balance sheet is for internal use, he wants to change the heading, include the previous year's balances, report the numbers in thousands, and make a few other appropriate cosmetic changes.

To modify the Summary balance sheet report:

1 Click the **Modify Report** button on the report button bar. (*Note:* The summary balance sheet should still be open. If not, recreate it.)

2 Click the **Display** tab if it is not already active; then click the **Previous Year** check box as shown in Figure 1.33 to display the previous year's figures on the balance sheet.

Figure 1.33
The Modify Report Dialog Box
Display Tab

Click the
Fonts & Numbers
tab

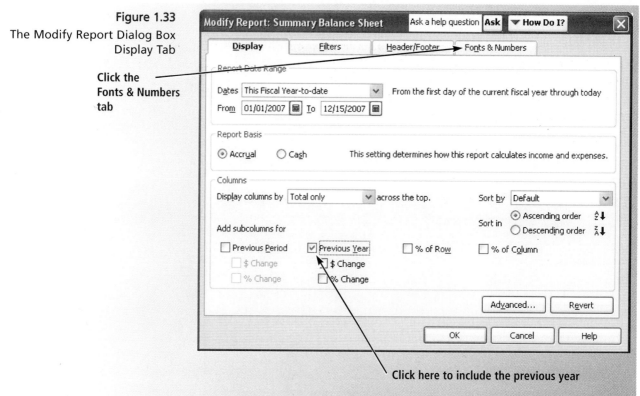

Click here to include the previous year

3 Click the **Fonts & Numbers** tab as shown in Figure 1.33.

4 Click the **Divided By 1000** and **Without Cents** checkboxes under the Show All Numbers section of the Modify Report dialog box. See Figure 1.34.

Figure 1.34
The Modify Report Dialog Box
Fonts & Numbers Tab

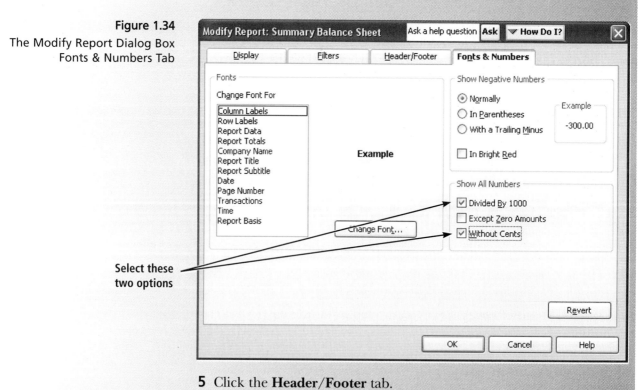

Select these
two options

5 Click the **Header/Footer** tab.

6 Click inside the Report Title edit box. Change the name of the report from Summary Balance Sheet to Preliminary Balance Sheet by deleting the word "Summary" and typing **Preliminary** as shown in Figure 1.35. (*Note:* To properly identify this report as yours, you may want to type your name in the Extra Footer Line of the Header/Footer tab.)

Change the name of the report title

Header/Footer tab

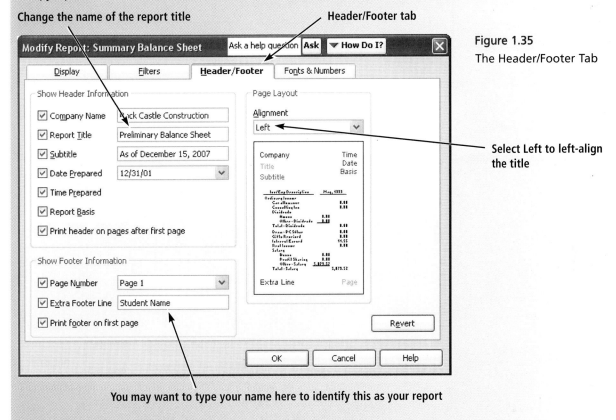

Figure 1.35
The Header/Footer Tab

Select Left to left-align the title

You may want to type your name here to identify this as your report

7 Change the alignment by clicking the **Down Arrow** in the Page Layout section and clicking **Left**. This changes the alignment of the title text to a left alignment.

8 Click **OK** to close the Modify Report window. The resulting report is shown in Figure 1.36 on the next page.

Jim knows that this modified balance sheet will help Rock Castle's managers analyze the financial information more easily and quickly. You will have an opportunity to explore other report modification features available in QuickBooks in the chapter assignments.

CREATING A BALANCE SHEET AS OF A SPECIFIC DATE

Jim receives a phone call from Frances Wu, an accountant with Rock Castle's CPA firm of Stoddard & Wong. Frances says that she's trying to determine Rock Castle's allowance for uncollectibles and she'd like Jim to fax her a balance sheet for Rock Castle as of the end of the third quarter 2007.

Figure 1.36

Jim's Customized Preliminary
Balance Sheet

Comparative data for 2006 is now displayed

Dollar amounts are
now in thousands

Although this adds up
to 183 on screen, the
difference is attributed
to rounding

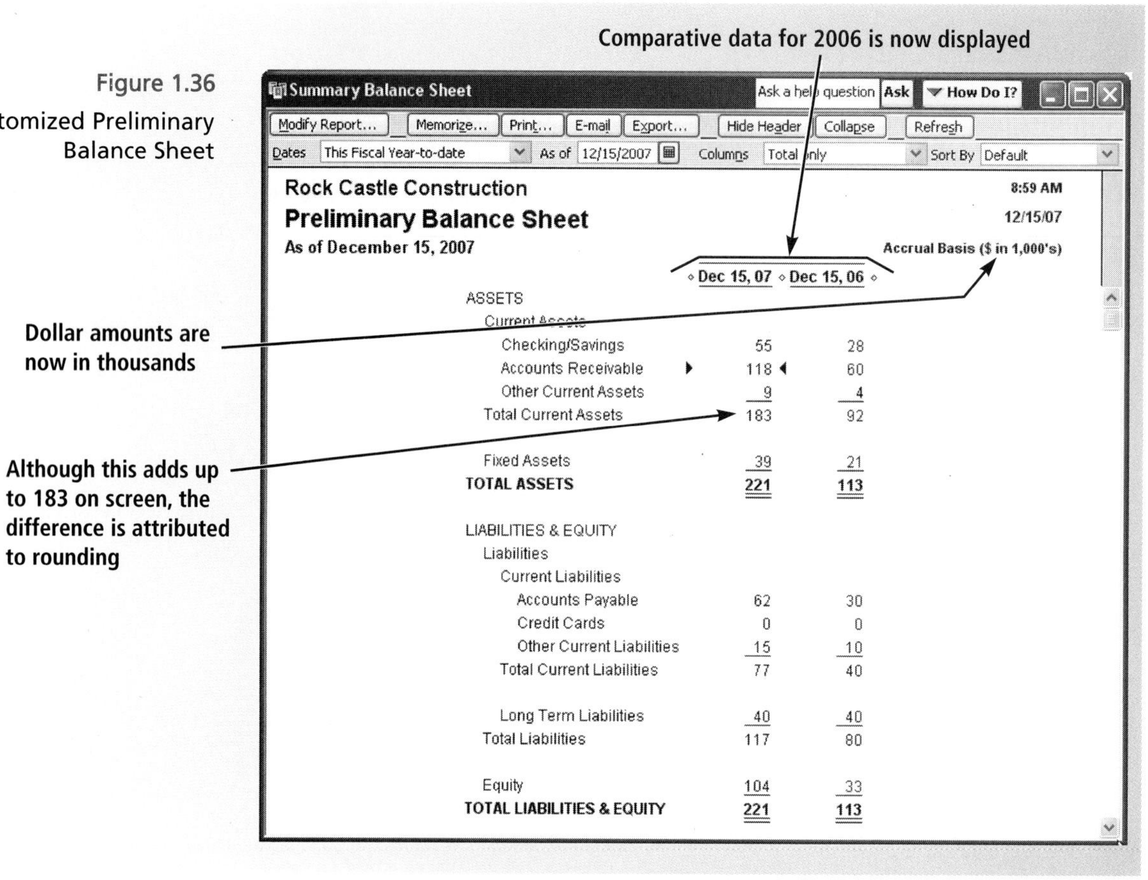

As Jim hangs up the phone, he mentions Frances's request. He explains that in QuickBooks the default setting produces a balance sheet as of the system date, the date according to the computer. But Frances wants a balance sheet as of October 31, 2007. You ask Jim how to change the default date. He explains that you do this by specifying the date you want in the balance sheet's "as of" field.

To modify the preliminary balance sheet report:

1 Click the **As of** box, which appears directly below the E-mail button. Delete 12/15/2007 and type **10/31/2007**.

Click **Refresh**, and the balance sheet as of 10/31/2007 appears along with a column of zeros for the 10/31/2006 balance sheet.

2 Click the **Modify Report** button on the report button bar.

3 Unclick the **Previous Year** check box you saw in Figure 1.33 to hide the previous year's figures on the balance sheet, then click **OK**. See Figure 1.37 on the next page for the modified report.

Jim now wants to print this balance sheet as of October 31, 2007 so he can fax it to Frances.

Date has changed in the "As of" box

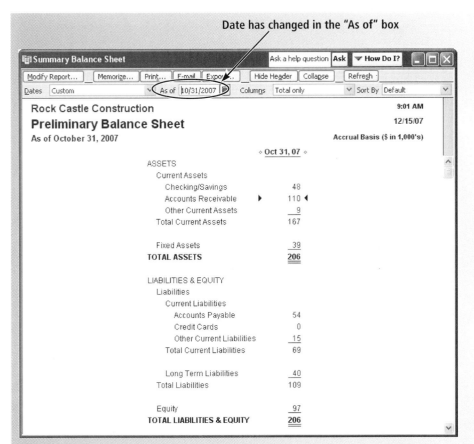

Figure 1.37

Preliminary Balance Sheet as of 10/31/2007

PRINTING THE BALANCE SHEET

You print a balance sheet just as you print any other report in QuickBooks.

To print the Preliminary balance sheet report:

1 Click **Print** on the Summary balance sheet button bar.

2 Click **Preview** in the Print Reports dialog box to preview the report. See Figure 1.38 on the next page.

3 Click the **Zoom In** button to see what the report will look like when printed. (Alternatively, you could have clicked anywhere on the screen to zoom in on the report.)

4 Click the **Print** button if you would like to print the report.

5 Close all windows and, if you are not proceeding to Session 3, exit QuickBooks. If a Memorized Report window appears, click in the checkbox next to Do not display this message in the future, then click **No**.

Jim feels much more confident about creating the year-end balance sheet in a couple of weeks. And you are quickly becoming more comfortable with QuickBooks.

Figure 1.38
Preview of the Preliminary
Balance Sheet

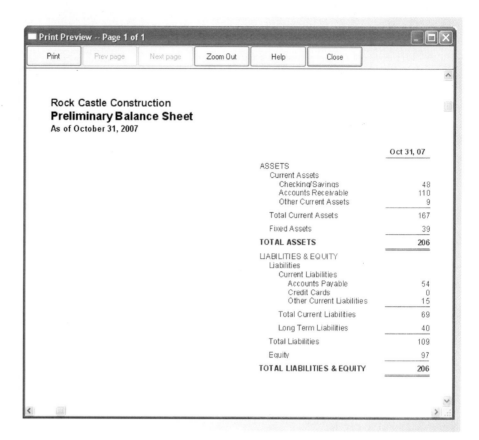

In the next session, you will expand your QuickBooks knowledge to include the creation, modification, and printing of another useful financial statement—the income statement.

practice

Session 2 Questions

1 List the preset ways in which QuickBooks can present a balance sheet.

2 What time period alternatives does QuickBooks provide for a balance sheet?

3 List the steps you would take to create a balance sheet for a date other than the current system date.

4 Describe the steps to generate a balance sheet in QuickBooks.

5 Describe the steps to resize the columns of a comparative balance sheet.

6 Describe the different types of transactions you might find in a transactions by account report on accounts receivable.

7 Describe how QuickZoom gives you more information about a balance sheet.

8 How might a manager use QuickZoom to analyze a business' financial position as reported in a balance sheet?

9 List five ways you can customize a QuickBooks report.

10 Suppose you wanted to include a column in a balance sheet that described what percentage each asset, liability, and owners' equity account was of the total assets amount. How would you do this in QuickBooks?

Session 2 Assignments

1 *Creating a Customized Summary Balance Sheet for Rock Castle*

Jim Reed asks you to help him prepare a balance sheet. (Be sure to type your name in the Extra Footer line of this report.)

a. He asks you to prepare and print a customized summary balance sheet as of November 30, 2007. He wants the amounts represented in thousands. Don't click the without cents checkbox and make sure to select the summary balance sheet and not standard.

b. Jim also asks you to prepare and print a summary balance sheet for Rock Castle Construction Company as of July 31, 2007. He wants amounts to be displayed without cents and the page layout left-aligned.

2   Investigating the Rock Castle Balance Sheet Using QuickZoom

Jim Reed asks you to help him investigate the Accounts Receivable balance as of December 15, 2007.

   a. Create a summary balance sheet as of December 15, 2007.
   b. Investigate the Accounts Receivable balance.
   c. Examine and print a copy of invoice 133.
   d. What was the invoice date and invoice number related to the September 9, 2007 customer payment?

3   *Using the South-Western Home Page for More Assignments or Cases*

If you have Internet access, go to the home page for this textbook at **http://owen.swlearning.com**.

Select the **Chapter 1: Session 2** section from Additional Problem Sets, and complete the problem(s) your instructor assigns.

4   *Customizing a Balance Sheet*

Modify the balance sheet you created in Assignment 1a to include columns reporting each asset, liability, and owners' equity account as a percentage of total assets. Change the report title and format the page as shown in Figure 1.39. (***Hint:*** Use the Modify Reports button.) Print the report with your name in the Extra Footer line in portrait orientation.

Figure 1.39
Customized Balance Sheet for November 30, 2007

9:23 AM	Rock Castle Construction	
12/15/07	**Statement of Financial Position**	
Accrual Basis ($ in 1,000's)	As of November 30, 2007	
	Nov 30, 07	% of Column
ASSETS		
Current Assets		
Checking/Savings	39	19%
Accounts Receivable	116	57%
Other Current Assets	9	4%
Total Current Assets	164	81%
Fixed Assets	39	19%
TOTAL ASSETS	**203**	**100%**
LIABILITIES & EQUITY		
Liabilities		
Current Liabilities		
Accounts Payable	59	29%
Other Current Liabilities	15	7%
Total Current Liabilities	73	36%
Long Term Liabilities	40	20%
Total Liabilities	113	56%
Equity	89	44%
TOTAL LIABILITIES & EQUITY	**203**	**100%**

Go to http://owen.swlearning.com

Session 2 Case Problem: JENNINGS & ASSOCIATES

Kelly Jennings has just started working full-time in her new business—an advertising agency named Jennings & Associates located in San Martin, California. Like many eager entrepreneurs, she started her business while working full-time for another firm. At first, her billings were quite small. But as her client base and her billings grew, she decided to leave her job and set out on her own. Two of her colleagues and friends—Cheryl Boudreau and Diane Murphy—see Kelly's eagerness and dedication, and decide the time is right for them too. They ask Kelly if they can join her sole proprietorship as employees, and so together they leave the traditional corporate agency environment.

Kelly knows that one of the first tasks she must accomplish is to set up an accounting system for Jennings & Associates. Also, she has just received a request from her banker to submit a balance sheet as documentation for a business loan. As a close, personal friend, you recommend she use QuickBooks, and you volunteer to help her get started.

Kelly tells you that in 2003 she borrowed $5,000 to start the business. Now she is applying for a loan to help expand the business. She also reminds you that although she did conduct some business in 2003, her first full-time month was January 2004.

Prepare and print the following reports using Kj01cp.qbw (include your name in the Extra Footer line of each report where possible):

1   A standard balance sheet as of December 31, 2003.

2   A standard balance sheet as of January 31, 2004.

3   Page 1 of the Transaction Detail by Account report for the month of January 2004. Be sure to specify a page range from 1 to 1. (***Hint:*** The report is listed in the Report menu item labeled Accountant & Taxes.)

4   A summary balance sheet as of January 31, 2004 formatted in thousands and without cents.

5   A report of those transactions recorded in January 2004 that affected accounts payable. (***Hint:*** Create a summary balance sheet and double-click accounts payable.)

Preparing an Income Statement Using QuickBooks

session

Learning Objectives

In this session you will:

- Change the way dates are formatted in QuickBooks
- create income statements for different time periods
- Create an income statement with year-to-date comparative information
- Investigate the detail underlying income statement items
- Use the Income Statement Report button bars
- Print an income statement

CASE: ROCK CASTLE CONSTRUCTION COMPANY

Now that Jim has created a preliminary balance sheet, he wants to practice for the year-end closing by creating a preliminary income statement for the period January 1, 2007 through December 15, 2007. You recall from your accounting course that the income statement reports revenues and expenses for a specific period.

Again, as part of your training with QuickBooks, Jim asks you to watch how he prepares the preliminary income statement. He expects to use many of the same functions and features to prepare an income statement that he used to prepare the balance sheet.

DATE FORMATS

Several users of Rock Castle's accounting information have mentioned to Jim that the default four-digit year format in QuickBooks (12/15/2007) seems a bit excessive, and they have requested that he return to the more standard date format (12/15/07).

Jim agrees and decides to show you the steps necessary to change the date preferences.

To change date preferences, open the Rock.qbw file, then:

1 Click **Edit**, then click **Preferences**. (Alternatively, you could click the Preferences icon in the Company Navigator.)

2 Click the **General** icon on the left of the Preferences window, then click the **Company Preferences** tab.

3 Uncheck the **Always show years as 4 digits (1999)** checkbox.

4 Click **OK** to save the changes and close the Preferences window.

5 To restore the Company Navigator, click **Company** in the Open Windows list.

Jim explains that now dates in QuickBooks registers, report windows, etc., will be in the standard format of a two-digit year (12/15/07).

CREATING AN INCOME STATEMENT

As with the Balance Sheet and other reports available in QuickBooks, the income statement can be presented in preset ways and can be customized. Jim decides to examine one of the preset income statement formats first—the format called Standard.

Before he does, he calls your attention to the fact that QuickBooks does not use the traditional name for this report. Instead of calling it the income statement, QuickBooks refers to this report as the "Profit and Loss" report. Jim prefers the name "income statement" because it is really the most accurate name for this report. And he says that although he cannot change the report title on the menu, he'll show you later how you can change the title on the report itself.

To create a standard income statement:

1 Open Rock.qbw.

2 Click **Reports**, click **Company & Financial** and then click **Profit and Loss Standard**. (Alternatively, you could click Profit & Loss in the Memorized Reports section of the Company Navigator.) The report shown in Figure 1.40 should appear.

3 Scroll down the Rock Castle Construction Company income statement. This report summarizes revenues and expenses for this month-to-date. Notice that QuickBooks does not use the standard accounting term "revenue," but instead uses the term "income." Note that subtotals are included for revenues and expenses. Note also the period specified for this particular report is December 1–15, 2007, the period for this report period.

Figure 1.40

A Rock Castle Income Statement for the Period December 1, 2007 to December 15, 2007

Called "Income Statement" in traditional accounting

Note that now the From and To dates are formatted to two digits

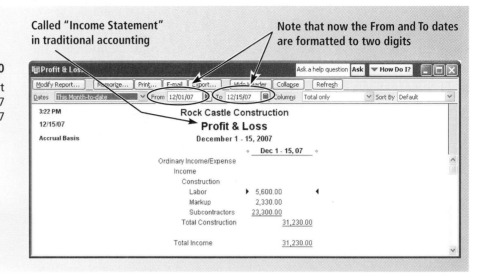

Jim tells you that this report is too limited. He wants a year-to-date statement for his preliminary income statement.

CREATING AN INCOME STATEMENT FOR A SPECIFIED PERIOD

As you have just seen, the default setting for QuickBooks creates an income statement for the current month with the period ending as of the system date. In the example files for Rock Castle, the current month and date were December 2007. But you will rarely need an income statement for the month ending with the system date. Thus you will often need to change the date specified in the income statement's From and To fields to the dates you want. Jim decides to revise the report to make it a year-to-date income statement for the period January 1, 2007 through December 15, 2007. He also wants to show you how to change the report title from "Profit and Loss" to the more accurate "Income Statement." For this title change you will modify the header, a function you already learned how to perform with the balance sheet.

To revise the period of time and the report title:

1 Move the cursor to the From field, which appears directly below the E-mail button on the Report button bar. Delete 12 and type **01**. Click **Refresh**. The revised report appears. See Figure 1.41.

2 To change the report title, click **Modify Report**, then click **Header/ Footer**. The Header/Footer tab appears. See Figure 1.42.

3 Move the cursor to the Report Title edit box and delete Profit and Loss. Type **Income Statement**. (*Note:* To properly identify this report as yours, you may want to type your name in the Extra Footer Line of the Header/Footer tab.)

Changed date to 01/01/07

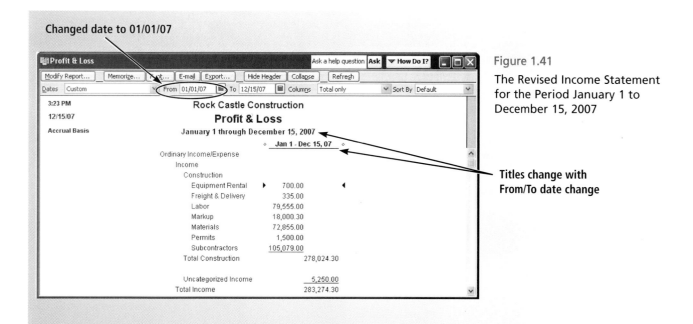

Figure 1.41

The Revised Income Statement for the Period January 1 to December 15, 2007

Titles change with From/To date change

Type "Income Statement" in this edit box

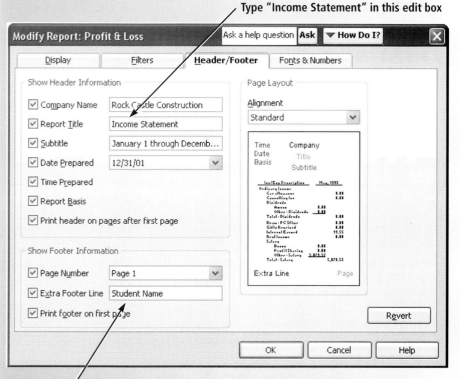

Figure 1.42

Header/Footer Tab

You may want to type your name here to identify this as your report

4 Click **OK** to view the revised report. See Figure 1.43.

5 When you have finished viewing the revised report, close this window.

Figure 1.43

Revised Rock Castle Income
Statement with Corrected Title

New title

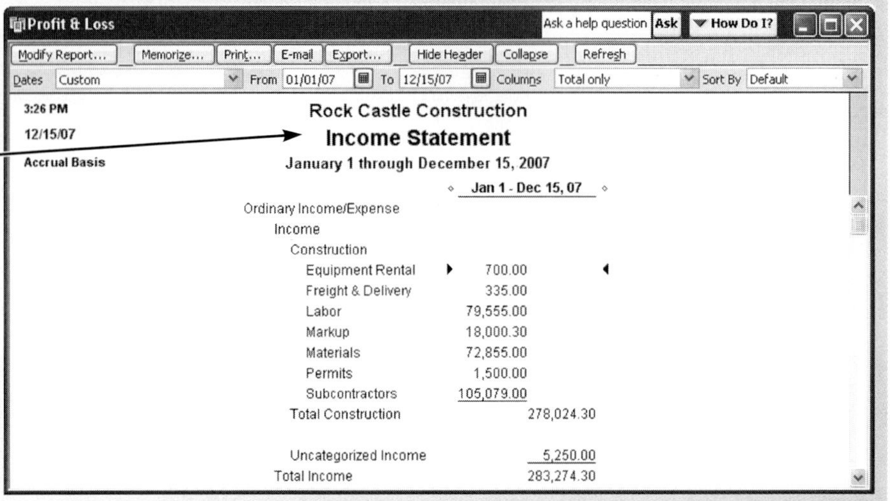

Figure 1.43

Revised Rock Castle Income
Statement with Corrected Title

Once again Jim comments on how remarkably fast this process is
compared to creating income statements manually. As with the balance
sheet, he decides to create a year-to-date comparison—this time with the
income statement.

CREATING A COMPARATIVE INCOME STATEMENT

QuickBooks has a built-in feature to prepare comparative income statements easily and quickly if the comparative data has already been
entered into a QuickBooks file. Jim entered last year's income statement
data when he first created Rock.qbw, so he is ready to create the comparative income statement. You guess that the process will be very similar to how you already prepared the comparative balance sheet.

To create a comparative income statement for the year-to-date period
ended December 15, 2007:

1 Click **Reports**, **Company & Financial**, and then click **Profit and Loss
Prev Year Comparison**. Note that the standard accounting term is
"comparative" income statement not "comparison," the term
QuickBooks uses.

trouble? If your screen does not look the same as Figure 1.44,
the column widths are probably not the same. As you learned in
Session 2, you can change the column widths by dragging the small
diamond-shaped symbols that divide the columns. If a dialog box
appears asking if you want to make all columns the same width, you
may answer yes or no.

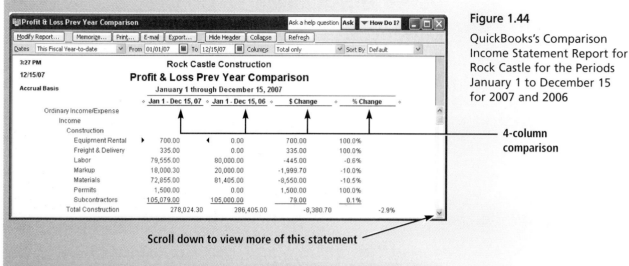

Figure 1.44

QuickBooks's Comparison Income Statement Report for Rock Castle for the Periods January 1 to December 15 for 2007 and 2006

4-column comparison

Scroll down to view more of this statement

2 Scroll down and across this comparative income statement. Note that it includes four columns. The first two columns compare amounts for 2007 with 2006, respectively, for the current period. The other two columns show the change in dollar amount and percent.

trouble? If the first two column headings omit the years 2007 and 2006 it's probably because you have changed the column widths in such a way that the complete column heading is not displayed. The first column is for 2007 and the second is for 2006.

Now Jim wants to change the title of the report to conform to standard accounting terminology.

To change the title of the report:

1 Click **Modify Report**, then click **Header/Footer**. The Modify Report Header/Footer window appears.

2 Delete "Profit & Loss Prev Year Comparison" in the Report Title edit box, and type **Comparative Income Statement**. (*Note:* Once again, you may want to type your name in the Extra Footer Line.)

3 Click **OK** to view the revised report. See Figure 1.45.

Changed title

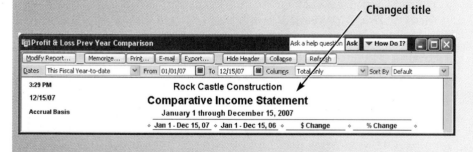

Figure 1.45

Comparative Year-to-Date Income Statement with Corrected Title

USING QUICKZOOM WITH THE INCOME STATEMENT

You ask Jim if QuickZoom can be used with the income statement just as it was with the balance sheet. He suggests you see for yourself.

To use QuickZoom with an income statement:

1 Scroll down the income statement until you find the Job Expenses category. Under that category look for the account titled Job Materials. Place the cursor over the 75,841.15 amount as shown in Figure 1.46.

Figure 1.46

Using QuickZoom to View the Job Materials Expense for 2007

Expense category

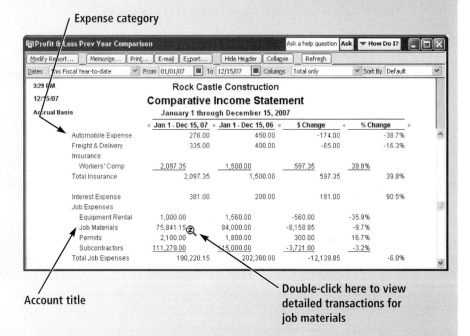

Account title

Double-click here to view detailed transactions for job materials

2 Double-click the **75,841.15** amount. A report appears that provides the details of transactions by account. See Figure 1.47 on the following page. This particular report displays the transactions that increased the job materials expense from 1/01/07 to 12/15/07.

3 Double-click **Cabinets** in the first transaction listed, or any other word in this row. Figure 1.48 appears as shown on the following page. It is a bill dated 06/09/07 from Sarvis Kitchen & Bath for a total of $3,630.

4 After you view this bill, close all windows.

You have now seen that the QuickZoom feature of QuickBooks is available with the income statement as well as with the balance sheet and that it provides background detail relating to revenues and expenses.

Double-click here to view the detail of this transaction

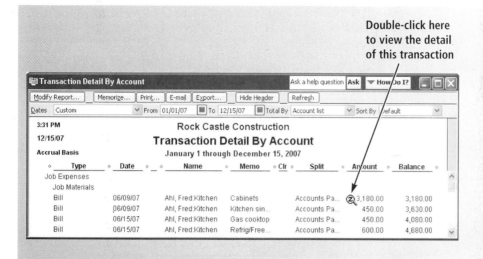

Figure 1.47

Transactions Detail for the Job Materials Account in 2007

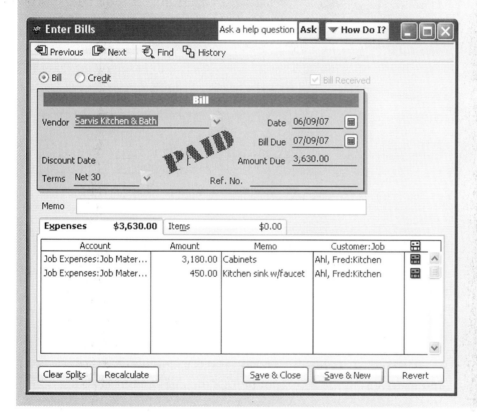

Figure 1.48

Sarvis Kitchen and Bath Bill

MODIFYING THE INCOME STATEMENT REPORT

The Income Statement report, like all other reports created in QuickBooks, can be modified using the Report button bar. Jim knows from experience that when he works with income statements in the future he will definitely need to add columns, change report dates, use different number formats, modify headings, and so on. So he decides to explore the ways he can modify an income statement. He decides first to add percentage of net income columns and change the report dates.

To add percentage of net income columns and to change the dates on an Income Statement report:

1 Click **Reports**, click **Company & Financial**, and then click **Profit and Loss Standard**.

2 Click the **Modify Report** button on the Report button bar, then select the **Display** tab if it is not already selected.

3 Click the **Down Arrow** of the **Columns** drop-down edit box, and select **Month** to report monthly columns. See Figure 1.49.

Change to these dates to customize the report

Figure 1.49
The Modify Report Window

Click on the calendar icons to view the calendar for changing dates

Change this to "Month" to modify column configuration

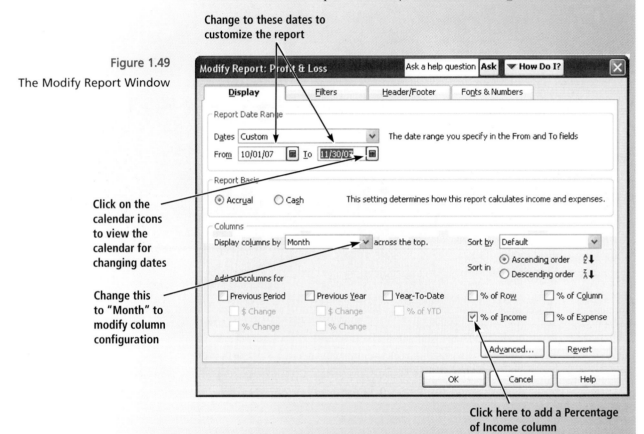

Click here to add a Percentage of Income column

4 Click the **% of Income** checkbox in the Columns section to report monthly amounts as a percent of total income—actually a percent of total revenue. See Figure 1.49.

5 Click the **From** edit box and change the date from 12/01/07 to **10/01/07**.

6 Click the **To** edit box and change the date from 12/15/07 to **11/30/07**. See Figure 1.49. These two changes customize the report so it reports on the months of October and November only. (Alternatively, you can select the calendar icons and click the arrows and specific dates.)

7 Click **OK** to accept these changes. A revised report appears. See Figure 1.50. Adjust the column widths if necessary to view more of the report.

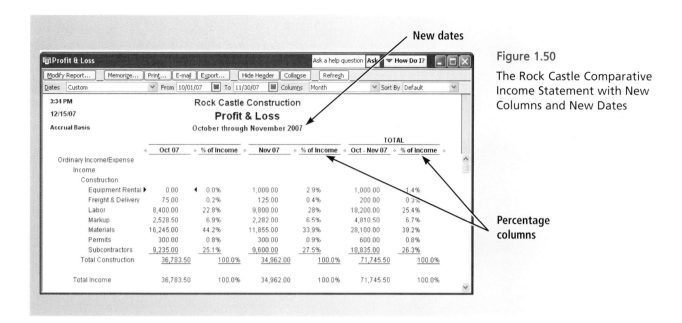

Figure 1.50

The Rock Castle Comparative Income Statement with New Columns and New Dates

Jim decides that he wants to report the numbers without cents.

To report the amounts without cents:

1 Click **Modify Report** on the Report button bar, then click the **Font & Numbers** tab.

2 Click the **Without Cents** checkbox under the Show All Numbers section of the Format Report window. A check mark appears in the box.

3 Click **OK** to accept these changes. The revised report appears. See Figure 1.51.

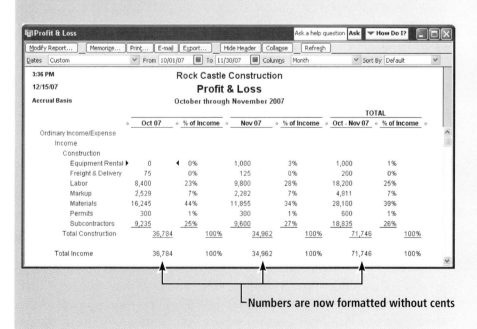

Figure 1.51

The Rock Castle Comparative Income Statement with Numbers Reported without Cents

As Jim looks over the latest version of the income statement, he sees that again he must correct the report title. Also, he decides the title would look better if it appeared on the right side of the report.

To modify the title and its layout:

1. Click **Modify Report**, on the Report button bar, then click the **Header/Footer** tab.
2. Click inside the **Report Title** edit box, and change the name of the report from Profit and Loss to **Income Statement** as you have done before.
3. Change the title alignment by clicking the **Down Arrow** in the Page Layout section and changing the selection from Standard to **Right**.
4. Before you accept these changes, look at the Subtitle edit box. Notice that QuickBooks had changed the subtitle of this report. QuickBooks does this automatically for you whenever you change the dates in the To and From edit boxes. (***Note:*** Once again, you may want to type your name in the Extra Footer Line.
5. Click **OK** to accept the changes. The modified income statement appears. See Figure 1.52.

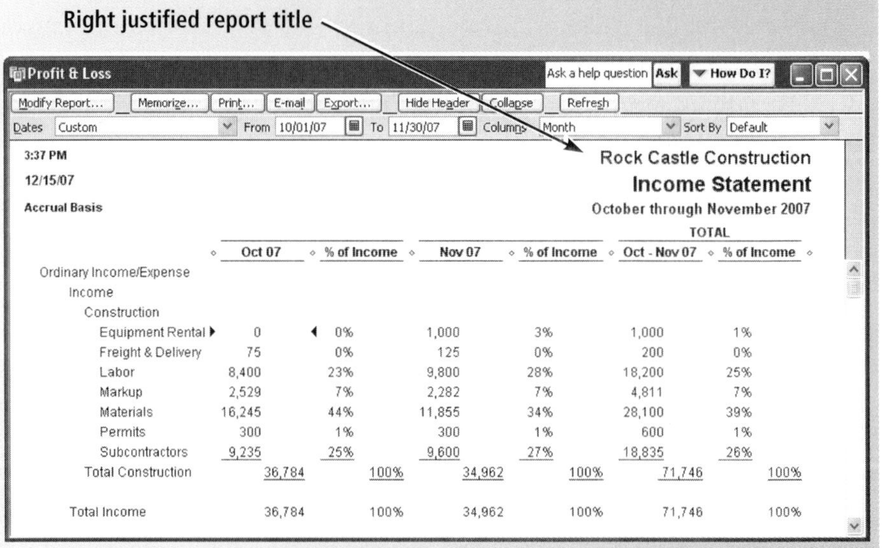

	Oct 07	% of Income	Nov 07	% of Income	Oct - Nov 07 (TOTAL)	% of Income (TOTAL)
Ordinary Income/Expense						
Income						
Construction						
Equipment Rental	0	0%	1,000	3%	1,000	1%
Freight & Delivery	75	0%	125	0%	200	0%
Labor	8,400	23%	9,800	28%	18,200	25%
Markup	2,529	7%	2,282	7%	4,811	7%
Materials	16,245	44%	11,855	34%	28,100	39%
Permits	300	1%	300	1%	600	1%
Subcontractors	9,235	25%	9,600	27%	18,835	26%
Total Construction	36,784	100%	34,962	100%	71,746	100%
Total Income	36,784	100%	34,962	100%	71,746	100%

Figure 1.52

The Modified Income Statement Report with New Title and Right Page Layout

QuickBooks provides many other ways to modify a report—grouping and subtotaling data, sorting transactions, and specifying which columns appear in a report, to name just a few. Jim encourages you to explore these additional options when you generate reports in the future.

PRINTING THE INCOME STATEMENT

Jim would like to print this modified report so he can show some of the managers at Rock Castle an example of the type of reports he can generate for them. He'd like this example to fit on one piece of 8½″ × 11″ paper—both to save paper and to make analysis of the report easier. He decides to use QuickBooks's preview option to preview the report and see if it will fit onto one piece of paper.

To preview the modified income statement:

1 Click **Print** on the Report button bar.

2 Click **Preview** in the Print Reports window. A miniature reproduction of the report appears. See Figure 1.53. (Do not resize the columns.) The heading "Page 1 of 2" may appear at the top of the window. This indicates how many pages the report contains and which page you are previewing.

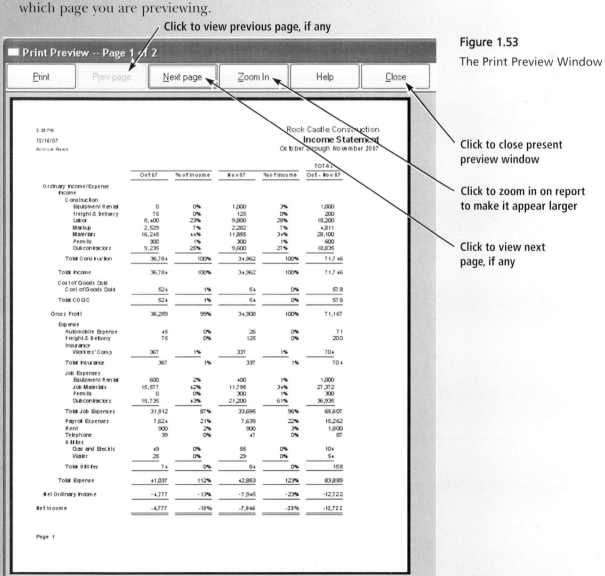

Click to view previous page, if any

Figure 1.53
The Print Preview Window

Click to close present preview window

Click to zoom in on report to make it appear larger

Click to view next page, if any

trouble? Your screen may indicate Page 1 of 1 depending on your computer and printer settings. If so, skip to Step 4, but continue reading so that you are familiar with the options that can help fit a long report on one page.

3 Notice the Next page and Prev page buttons below the window heading. The Prev page button is grayed out, which indicates that there is no previous page. But the Next page button is not grayed out. Click **Next page** to preview Page 2 of the report.

4 After previewing the statement, click the **Close** button on the button bar, and then click **Cancel** in the Print Reports window. The report reappears.

Jim has seen that the report is not much more than one page and so it might fit onto one page if he reduces the size of the type font.

To reduce the font size of the type in a report:

1 Click **Modify Report** on the Report button bar, then click the **Fonts & Numbers** tab. See Figure 1.54.

Figure 1.54
The Modify Report Window

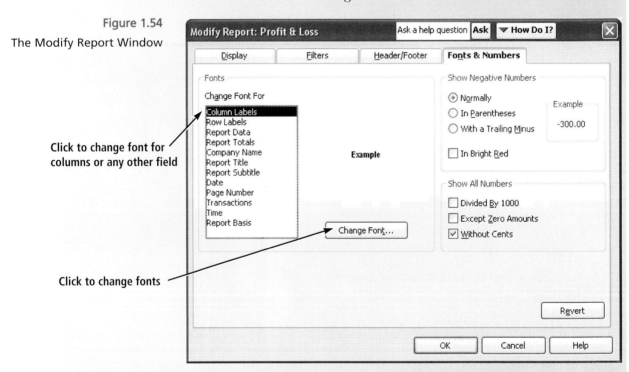

Click to change font for columns or any other field

Click to change fonts

2 Click the **Change Font** button located in the bottom center of the window. The Column Labels window appears. See Figure 1.55.

3 Click the **Size** edit box. Delete 9 and type (or click on) **8** to reduce the font size by one. Then click the **Font** edit box and choose **Arial Narrow**, if available, or choose another font that is small enough to accomplish your goal.

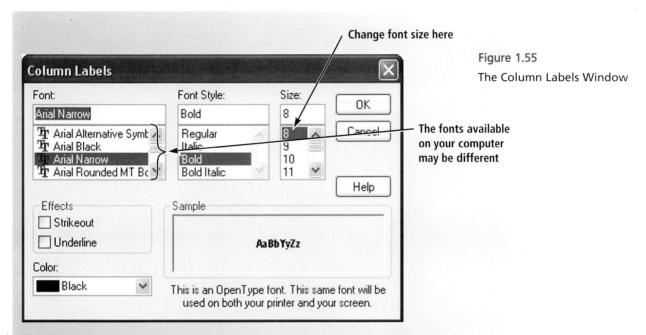

Change font size here

Figure 1.55
The Column Labels Window

The fonts available on your computer may be different

4 Click **OK** to accept this new size. A Changing Font window will appear asking if you want to make the change to all related fonts. Click **Yes**. Then click **OK** again. The revised report appears—now in Size 8 font.

Jim hopes that this change will make the example report now fit on one page. To see if it worked, he again previews the report. If it fits on one page, he'll print it.

To preview the modified income statement again:

1 Click **Print** on the Report button bar.

2 Click **Preview**. The Print Preview window appears. Notice that the heading for this window may still include the words "Page 1 of 2." The change of font size has reduced the report size but not adequately to fit the report on one page.

3 Click **Close**, and then click **Cancel** in the Print Reports window.

Suddenly Jim realizes there might be another way to fit the report on one page. He decides to change the orientation of the page from portrait—a vertical orientation—which is the default setting, to landscape—a horizontal orientation.

To change a document from portrait to landscape orientation:

1 Click **Print** on the Report button bar to view the Print Reports window. See Figure 1.56.

Figure 1.56

The Print Reports Window

Select landscape orientation

Click to reduce the report to one page wide

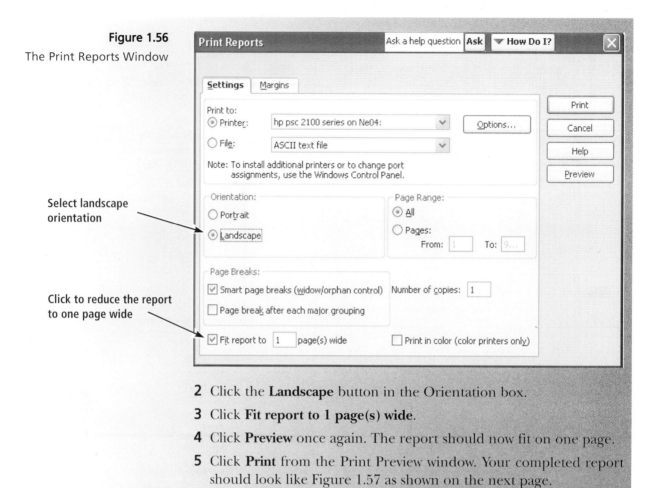

2 Click the **Landscape** button in the Orientation box.

3 Click **Fit report to 1 page(s) wide**.

4 Click **Preview** once again. The report should now fit on one page.

5 Click **Print** from the Print Preview window. Your completed report should look like Figure 1.57 as shown on the next page.

trouble? If your printer still prints this document on two pages consult with your lab personnel. Different printers may result in different output.

6 Close all windows and exit QuickBooks as you have done before.

Now that you have completed Sessions 2 and 3 of Chapter 1, you see how easily QuickBooks creates the two financial reports most commonly used to communicate accounting information to external users—the balance sheet and the income statement. In Session 4 of Chapter 1, you will continue your quick overview of QuickBooks by creating a statement of cash flows.

Figure 1.57 Jim's Modified Example Income Statement on One Page

Rock Castle Construction
Income Statement
October through November 2007

Ordinary Income/Expense	Oct '07	% of Income	Nov '07	% of Income	TOTAL Oct-Nov '07	% of Income
Income						
Construction						
Equipment Rental	0	0%	1,000	3%	1,000	1%
Freight & Delivery	75	0%	125	0%	200	0%
Labor	8,400	23%	9,800	28%	18,200	25%
Markup	2,528	7%	2,282	7%	4,811	7%
Materials	16,245	44%	11,855	34%	28,100	39%
Permits	300	1%	300	1%	600	1%
Subcontractors	9,235	25%	9,600	27%	18,835	26%
Total Construction	36,784	100%	34,962	100%	71,746	100%
Total Income	36,784	100%	34,962	100%	71,746	100%
Cost of Goods Sold						
Cost of Goods Sold	524	1%	54	0%	578	1%
Total COGS	524	1%	54	0%	578	1%
Gross Profit	36,259	99%	34,908	100%	71,167	99%
Expense						
Automobile Expense	45	0%	26	0%	71	0%
Freight & Delivery	75	0%	125	0%	200	0%
Insurance						
Workers' Comp	367	1%	337	1%	704	1%
Total Insurance	367	1%	337	1%	704	1%
Job Expenses						
Equipment Rental	600	2%	400	1%	1,000	1%
Job Materials	15,577	42%	11,795	34%	27,372	38%
Permits	0	0%	300	1%	300	0%
Subcontractors	15,735	43%	21,200	61%	36,935	51%
Total Job Expenses	31,912	87%	33,695	96%	65,607	91%
Payroll Expenses	7,624	21%	7,639	22%	15,262	21%
Rent	900	2%	900	3%	1,800	3%
Telephone	39	0%	47	0%	87	0%
Utilities						
Gas and Electric	49	0%	55	0%	104	0%
Water	25	0%	29	0%	54	0%
Total Utilities	74	0%	84	0%	158	0%
Total Expense	41,037	112%	42,853	123%	83,889	117%
Net Ordinary Income	-4,777	-13%	-7,945	-23%	-12,722	-18%
Net Income	**-4,777**	**-13%**	**-7,945**	**-23%**	**-12,722**	**-18%**

practice

session 3

Session 3 Questions

1 List at least three of the preset formats QuickBooks provides for an income statement.

2 Identify the different periods of time that QuickBooks provides for an income statement.

3 Describe the steps necessary to create an income statement for a period other than one ending with the current system date of the computer.

4 Describe the steps necessary to generate an income statement in QuickBooks.

5 Describe the steps necessary to reformat the columns of a comparative income statement.

6 Describe the steps necessary to modify an income statement to include comparative information.

7 How does QuickZoom help you further investigate an income statement?

8 How could a manager use QuickZoom to access underlying information as reported in an income statement?

9 List five report modification features that QuickBooks provides with an income statement.

10 How would you modify an income statement to include a column describing the percentage relationship between expenses and total revenues?

Session 3 Assignments

1 *Preparing an Income Statement for Rock Castle*

Jim Reed has asked you to help him prepare Rock Castle's income statement. Include your name in the Extra Footer Line of all reports printed.

a. First he asks you to prepare and print a modified income statement that includes operating information for August and September 2007. He wants the income statement to include amounts (without cents) and columns reflecting the dollar change and percentage change between periods. (**Hint:** Set the dates to reflect September only, and be sure the Previous Period box, $ Change, and % Change boxes are also checked in the Modify Report window.) He asks you to change the title to "Comparative Income Statement." Finally, he wants you to format the page layout to the left.

　　b. Next, Jim asks you to prepare and print a standard income statement for Rock Castle Construction Company for the month of July, 2007 in a format different from what you used in *a* above.

2　*Investigating the Rock Castle Income Statement Using QuickZoom*

Jim Reed asks you to help him investigate the $111,279 Job Expense:Subcontractors balance shown on a standard income statement created for the fiscal year ended December 15, 2007.

　　a. Investigate the $111,279 Job Expense:Subcontractors. **trouble?** Remember to change the From/To dates on the income statement to reflect the fiscal year-to-date amounts.

　　b. Examine the bill received on June 1, 2007.

　　c. Which vendor performed the work?

　　d. Has the bill been paid?

3　*Using the South-Western Home Page for More Assignments or Cases*

If you have Internet access, go to the home page for this textbook at **http://owen.swlearning.com**.

　　Select the **Chapter 1: Session 3** section of Additional Problem Sets, and complete the problem(s) that your instructor assigns.

Go to
http://owen.swlearning.
com

http://

4　*Modifying an Income Statement*

Modify the income statement created in Chapter Assignment 1 as follows. Include your name in the Extra Footer Line of all reports printed.

　　a. Change the To/From dates to include amounts from October 1 through December 15, 2007.

　　b. Change the columns to no longer reflect comparative information.

　　c. Change the columns to include year-to-date amounts and year-to-date percentages. *Hint:* Customize the report by checking the Year-to-Date and % of YTD boxes.

　　d. Print this customized income statement.

Session 3 Case Problem: JENNINGS & ASSOCIATES

As you learned in Session 2, Kelly Jennings prepared a balance sheet to submit to her banker with her application for a business loan. When she delivered the balance sheet to the banker, he told her that he also needed information about her operations. In other words, her banker needed an income statement.

　　Kelly asks you to help her prepare and print three versions of the income statement, one of which she will include with her application. She gives you a QuickBooks file named Kj01cp.qbw. Include your name in the Extra Footer Line of all reports printed.

1   Open Kj01cp.qbw.

2   Prepare a standard income statement for the month of January 2004.

3   Prepare a standard income statement for the month of January 2004 without cents, formatted with a left layout, and with the title "Income Statement."

4   Modify the income statement you prepared for 3 above by adding a % of Income column.

Preparing a Statement of Cash Flows Using QuickBooks

4

session

Learning Objectives

In this session you will:

- Create and customize a statement of cash flows for a specified period
- Investigate the detail underlying statement of cash flow items
- Format and print a statement of cash flows

CASE: ROCK CASTLE CONSTRUCTION COMPANY

One of the main financial statements used by businesses is the statement of cash flows. Your previous experience with this statement has not always been good so the thought of the computer preparing this one for you is quite enticing. You recall that this statement reports cash flow from operating, investing, and financing activities for a specific period.

Once again, as a part of your training with QuickBooks, Jim asks you to work with him as he prepares a preliminary statement of cash flows for the period January 1, 2007 through December 15, 2007.

CREATING A STATEMENT OF CASH FLOWS

Unlike both the balance sheet and income statement, the statement of cash flows in QuickBooks is presented in only one format, although it can be modified after it is created. There is another report for cash flows called Forecast which creates a forecast of future cash flows based on the current period's cash flow and is not addressed in this text. Jim decides to create the statement of cash flows and modify it later.

To create a statement of cash flows:

1 Open Rock.qbw.

2 Click **Reports**, click **Company & Financial**, then click **Statement of Cash Flows**. (Alternatively, you could click Statement of Cash Flows from the Memorized Reports section of the Company Navigator.)

3 Scroll down this report as shown in Figure 1.58 and notice the three sections: operating activities, investing activities, and financing activities. Notice at the bottom of the statement the net cash increase for the period is reported. It is then added to the cash at the beginning of the period to yield cash at the end of the period.

Make sure you've changed the From and To dates

Click here to modify the layout of the statement of cash flows

Figure 1.58
A Rock Castle Statement of Cash Flows for the Period January 1, 2007 through December 15, 2007

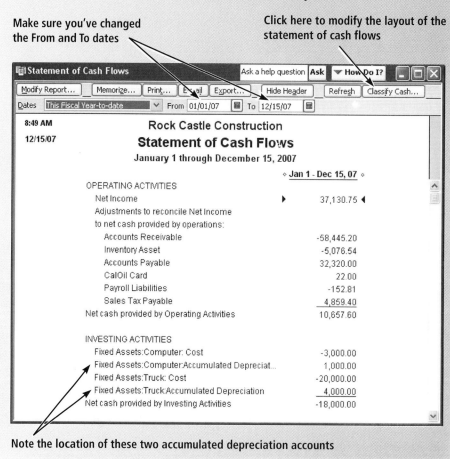

Note the location of these two accumulated depreciation accounts

In your examination of the Statement of Cash Flows, you notice in the operating activities section that several adjustments are made to reconcile net income to net cash provided by operations. Jim points out that one of the more common adjustments should be depreciation expense, since it reduces income but does not use cash. However, depreciation is not shown in this reconciliation. Instead, Jim finds that changes in accumulated depreciation (which of course usually result from depreciation expense) are shown in the investing activities section of the statement.

"We need to modify this statement's layout to properly reflect changes in accumulated depreciation as adjustments to net income in the operating activities section, not as line items in the investing activities section," he says. To do this he uses the Classify Cash button on the Statement of Cash Flows window.

To modify the layout of the statement of cash flows:

1 Click **Classify Cash** to open the Preferences window with the Reports and Graphs icon selected and the Company Preferences tab selected as shown in Figure 1.59.

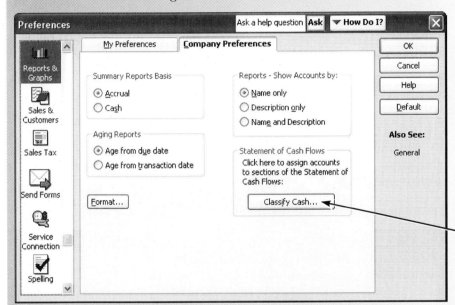

Figure 1.59
Company Preferences

Click here to modify the Statement of Cash Flows

2 Click **Classify Cash** in the Preferences window to view the Classify Cash window as shown in Figure 1.60.

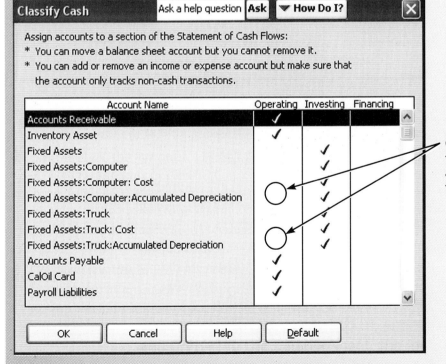

Figure 1.60
Classify Cash Window for Modifying the Statement of Cash Flows Layout

Click in these two locations to reclassify changes in accumulated depreciation to Operating Activities

3 Click in the Operating column next to **Fixed Assets: Computer: Accumulated Depreciation** to move the change in accumulated depreciation from an investing activity to an operating activity as shown in Figure 1.60.

4 Click in the Operating column next to **Fixed Assets: Truck: Accumulated Depreciation** to move the change in accumulated depreciation from an investing activity to an operating activity as shown in Figure 1.60, then click **OK** to record your changes.

trouble? If you accidentally click in the wrong column, simply click the correct column for the item you accidentally reclassified.

5 Click **OK** in the Preferences window to close it. A Report needs to be refreshed window may appear indicating that the changes you made require refreshing of the report. Click **Yes** to refresh the report. Note how the report has been adjusted to reflect changes in accumulated depreciation (depreciation expense) as an adjustment to operating activities and not an investing activity. See Figure 1.61.

Figure 1.61

Statement of Cash Flows after Changes in Types of Accounts

Note the changes

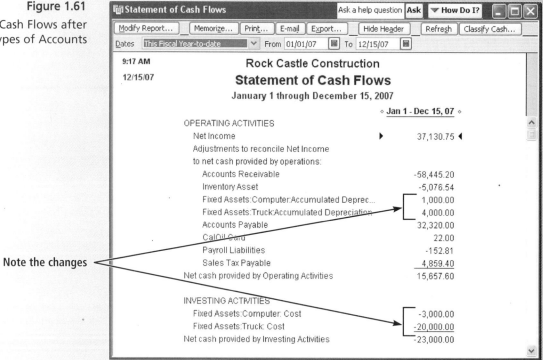

"How about modifying the Statement of Cash Flows to reflect comparative amounts like prior years? Isn't there a previous year comparative report available like we saw for the income statement?" you ask.

"Well, no." Jim explains. "Not only is there no present comparative report in QuickBooks, but there is no way to modify the report to show percentage changes or year-to-date amounts like we can do for the income statement. Maybe in the next version."

USING QUICKZOOM WITH THE STATEMENT OF CASH FLOWS

You then ask about the QuickZoom feature you found so helpful in examining information on the income statement. Jim responds with a big smile. "Let's check it out!"

To use QuickZoom with the statement of cash flows:

1 Double-click the **32,320.00** amount on the report reflecting changes in Accounts Payable to open a Transactions Detail by Account window as shown in Figure 1.62.

Double-click here to view the detail of this transaction

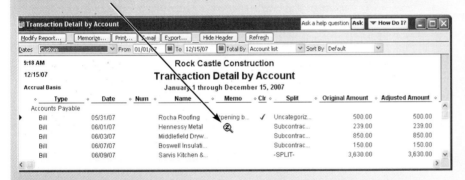

Figure 1.62

Transaction Detail for Accounts Payable in the Statement of Cash Flows

2 Double-click **Hennessy Metal** to view the bill creating this transaction.

3 Close both the Hennessy Metal bill and the Transaction Detail by Account window.

You have now seen that the QuickZoom feature works for the balance sheet, income statement, and statement of cash flows. However, the QuickZoom feature in the statement of cash flows does not necessarily provide much help. In the case above, the accounts payable amount in the statement of cash flows reflects the changes in accounts payable, an increase in this case, which needs to be added to net income to reconcile to cash provided by operating activities. Thus it is the change, in this case an increase, which is being analyzed, not the underlying transactions.

FORMATTING AND PRINTING THE STATEMENT OF CASH FLOWS

Jim would like to print this statement of cash flows in a format without cents.

To modify and print the statement of cash flows:

1 Click **Modify Report** on the Report button bar, then click the **Fonts & Numbers** tab.

2 Click in the **Without Cents** check box, then click **OK** to close the window.

3 Click **Print** on the Report button bar to reveal the Print Reports window.

4 Click **Print** in the Print Reports window to print the report.

5 Close all remaining windows.

You've now seen how all three of the key financial statements, the balance sheet, income statement, and statement of cash flows, can be easily created, modified, and printed from within QuickBooks. In Session 5 of Chapter 1, you will complete your overview of QuickBooks by creating supporting reports for accounts receivable, inventory, and accounts payable.

practice

Session 4 Questions

1 List the reports available for reporting cash flows.

2 Describe the steps necessary to create a statement of cash flows.

3 What additional steps are necessary to create a statement of cash flows for a period other than one ending with the current system date of the computer?

4 Identify three different periods of time that QuickBooks provides for a statement of cash flows.

5 List the three sections of the statement of cash flows.

6 Describe the statement of cash flow operating section created by QuickBooks.

7 Describe the one adjustment necessary to reconcile net income to cash provided by operations that was not initially a part of the Rock Castle statement of cash flows until you made some changes in the reports layout.

8 Describe the steps necessary to make changes in the statement of cash flows report layout to properly reflect the adjustments necessary to reconcile net income to cash provided by operations.

9 Describe how the QuickZoom feature of QuickBooks does or does not provide the same help in the statement of cash flows as it does in the income statement.

10 Describe the steps necessary to format and print a statement of cash flows different from the software provided Statement of Cash Flows header.

Session 4 Assignments

1 *Preparing a Statement of Cash Flows for Rock Castle*

Jim Reed has asked you to prepare and print a customized statement of cash flows for the period April 1, 2007 to June 30, 2007. He wants the statement to include amounts (without cents), with a left page layout, and with a report subtitle of "2nd quarter 2007". *Hint:* Be sure accumulated depreciation is classified correctly. Include your name in the Extra Footer Line of all reports printed.

http://

Go to
http://owen.swlearning.
com

2 *Using the South-Western Home Page for More Assignments or Cases*

If you have Internet access, go to the home page for this textbook at **http://owen.swlearning.com**.

Select the **Chapter 1: Session 4** section of Additional Problem Sets, and complete the problem(s) your instructor assigns.

Session 4 Case Problem: JENNINGS & ASSOCIATES

Continuing your work from Session 3, Kelly has asked you to prepare two versions of the statement of cash flows, one of which she will include with her application. She gives you a QuickBooks file named Kj01cp.qbw. Include your name in the Extra Footer Line of all reports printed.

1 Open Kj01cp.qbw.

2 Prepare a statement of cash flows for the period 1/1/04 to 1/31/04. *Hint:* Be sure accumulated depreciation accounts are properly classified.

3 Prepare a statement of cash flows for the same period 1/1/04 to 1/31/04 but without cents and with a right page layout.

Creating Supporting Reports to Help Make Business Decisions

Learning Objectives

In this session you will:

- Create, print, and analyze an Accounts Receivable Aging report
- Create and print a Customer Account Balance Summary
- Create, print, and analyze an Inventory Valuation Summary
- Create, print, and analyze an Accounts Payable Aging report
- Create and print a Vendor Balance Summary

CASE: ROCK CASTLE CONSTRUCTION COMPANY

You arrive at work, and two phones are ringing. As Jim hangs up from one call and is about to answer another, he quickly explains what's happening—the managers at Rock Castle are preparing for the fiscal year end and are requesting up-to-the-minute information. You quickly answer a phone and write down the manager's request for some information on inventory. As you hang up from the call, Jim asks you to come into his office. You compare notes—he has requests for information on accounts receivable and accounts payable. You show him your note requesting information on Rock Castle's inventory.

Jim has shown you that QuickBooks can easily generate transaction reports, but you can see that the manager's requests require more detailed information. You remember from your accounting course that accountants frequently use what are called supporting schedules—reports that provide the underlying details of an account. You ask Jim if QuickBooks can help. He smiles and says, "You bet. QuickBooks calls these schedules 'reports,' but they are the same thing. Let's get to work."

CREATING AND PRINTING AN ACCOUNTS RECEIVABLE AGING REPORT

You know from your accounting course that accounts receivable represent amounts due from customers for goods or services they have received but for which they have not yet paid. QuickBooks provides several preset accounts receivable reports that anticipate the information managers most often need.

The first request for information is from Susan Guttmann, the manager in charge of accounts receivable. She wants information on a particular customer's past due account balance, and she wants to know the total amount due from customers as of today.

Jim tells you that the best way to get information on past due accounts is to create a schedule that QuickBooks calls an "Accounts Receivable Aging report"—but what you learned in your accounting course is usually called an "accounts receivable aging schedule." You remember that an aging schedule is a listing of how long each receivable has been uncollected.

To create an Accounts Receivable Aging report:

1 Open Rock.qbw.

2 Click **Reports**, click **Customers & Receivables**, then click **A/R Aging Summary**. (Alternatively, you could have selected A/R Aging Summary from the Memorized Reports section of the Customer Navigator.)

3 If necessary, resize the columns so you can view the entire report on your screen, as shown in Figure 1.63.

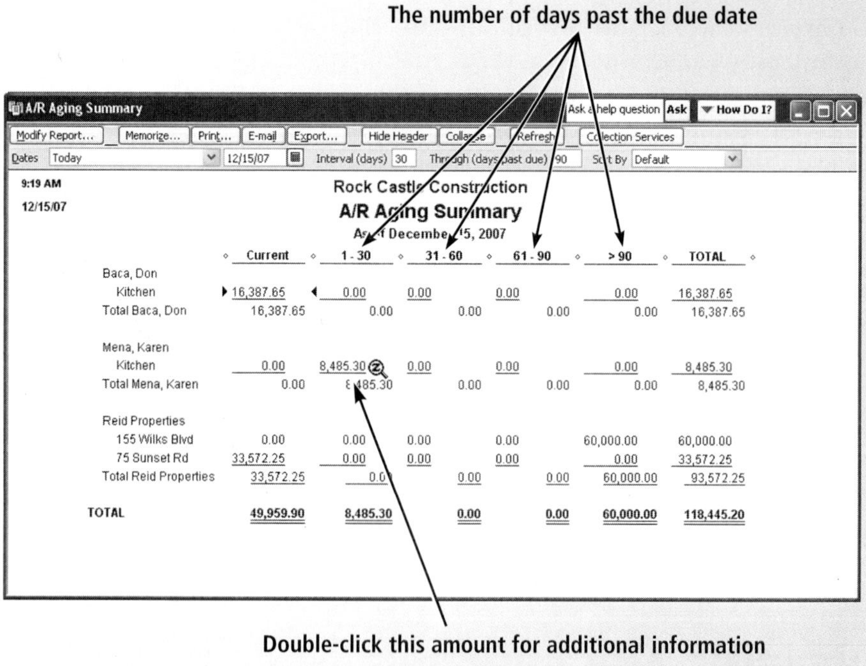

The number of days past the due date

Figure 1.63

Rock Castle's A/R Aging Summary as of 12/15/07

Double-click this amount for additional information

You can see that this report gives Susan an up-to-date listing of customers and their balances. It tells her how long each receivable has been uncollected so she can take appropriate action.

You ask Jim the name of the customer about whom Susan requested information. He says the customer's name is Karen Mena and that Susan wants to know the status of her account and her payment history. He says that, as you have done with other reports, you can use QuickZoom to gather this information.

To investigate a particular receivable on an Accounts Receivable Aging report:

1 Double-click the **8,485.30** balance owed by Karen Mena.

2 An A/R Aging QuickZoom report appears. See Figure 1.64. This report indicates that Invoice 134, dated 10/20/07, was due 11/19/07 and is presently 26 days late.

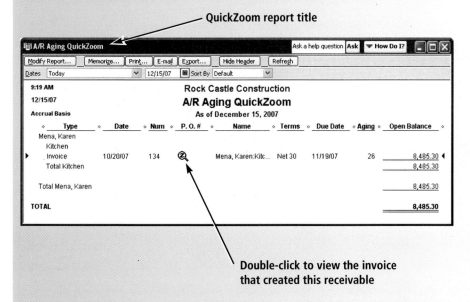

QuickZoom report title

Double-click to view the invoice that created this receivable

Figure 1.64

A/R Aging QuickZoom Report

3 Double-click **134** to investigate further. Invoice 134 appears. See Figure 1.65. Invoice 134 describes the framing labor, installation labor, and reimbursable expenses that Rock Castle billed Karen Mena. Adjust the size of your window if necessary to view the entire window.

4 Click the **Down Arrow** in the invoice's scroll box to view more of the invoice. Notice that the balance due—8,485.30—matches the receivable balance you are investigating. But notice also that Invoice 134 totals 17,669.92. How can that be?

5 Click the **History** button on the top of the window to help you investigate this difference. The transaction history of this invoice appears. See Figure 1.66. Notice that a payment of 9,184.62 was applied to this invoice on 12/01/07. This seems an unusual amount for a customer to pay; usually people pay in even amounts of money. Let's investigate further.

Figure 1.65

Invoice 134

Click to display payment history for this invoice

Click to scroll up or down to view the rest of the invoice data

Invoice total differs from balance due

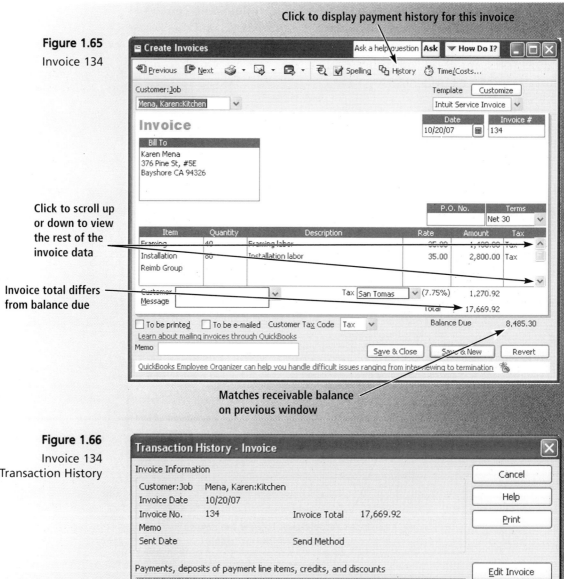

Matches receivable balance on previous window

Figure 1.66

Invoice 134 Transaction History

Details of the payment applied to Invoice 134

Click to display the Receive Payments window

6 Be sure that the 9,184.62 payment is highlighted. Then click **Go To** to examine the payment in more detail. The Receive Payments window appears. See Figure 1.67. Notice that a $10,000 check was received from Karen Mena on 12/01/07. Of this payment, $815.38 was applied to pay off Invoice 133. The balance of the $10,000.00— 9,184.62—was applied to Invoice 134. This explains why the balance due and the invoice amount were different.

7 Close all open windows.

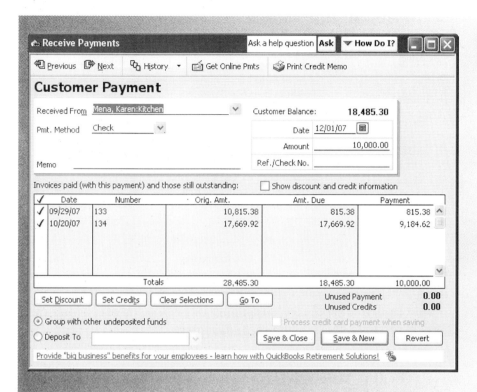

Figure 1.67

Receive Payments Window for Karen Mena

Jim has copied down the information Susan requested—Karen Mena is 26 days past due on Invoice 134, she owes $8,485.30 on that invoice, and Invoice 133 was paid off on 12/01/07. He is now ready to fulfill Susan's other request.

CREATING AND PRINTING A CUSTOMER BALANCE SUMMARY

Jim says that Susan's request for the total amount due from customers as of today is easy to fulfill because QuickBooks has a built-in feature that prepares a customer balance summary. He can provide Susan this information with only a few clicks of the mouse.

To create a Customer Balance Summary:

1 Click **Customer Balance Summary** from the Memorized Reports section of the Customer Navigator. See Figure 1.68.

   trouble? If the Customer Navigator is not open, click **Customers** in the Open Window list. Make sure your Open Windows list is open. If not, click **View**, and then click **Open Windows List.**

2 Notice that this is exactly the information Susan has requested—a list of the total amounts each customer owes Rock Castle as of December 15, 2007. When you have finished viewing this report, close this window.

Figure 1.68

Customer Balance Summary
for December 15, 2007

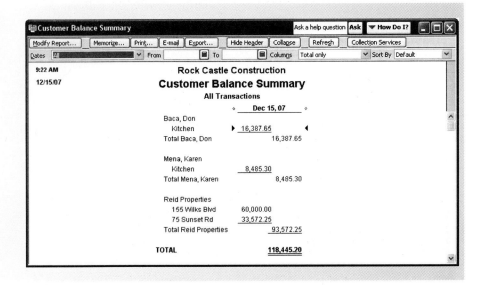

Jim prints this report for Susan and asks you to drop it by her desk later. He's ready to handle the second request.

CREATING AND PRINTING AN INVENTORY VALUATION SUMMARY REPORT

Jim asks you about the request you took on the phone. You show him your notes; you spoke to Kim Hui, who handles inventory for Rock Castle. Occasionally, when he finds good prices, Kim purchases inventory materials that Rock Castle routinely uses—such as doorknobs, locks, and nails—and he holds them for future jobs. For the fiscal-year-end planning and reporting, Kim wants to know what inventory Rock Castle has on hand, its acquisition cost, and recent sales.

Jim tells you that, again, QuickBooks has a report that anticipates many of the information needs of inventory managers. He says you can easily get the information Kim needs by creating what QuickBooks calls an Inventory Valuation Summary.

To create an Inventory Valuation Summary:

1 Click **Reports**, click **Inventory**, and then click **Inventory Valuation Summary** from the submenu. The Inventory Valuation Summary appears. See Figure 1.69. Resize the columns as necessary to view this report.

2 Scroll around this report to familiarize yourself with its contents. It describes the inventory on hand as of 12/15/07.

As you examine this report, you notice that the QuickZoom cursor appears every so often as it passes over certain items. You ask Jim to show you examples of the QuickZoom reports that QuickBooks provides for inventory.

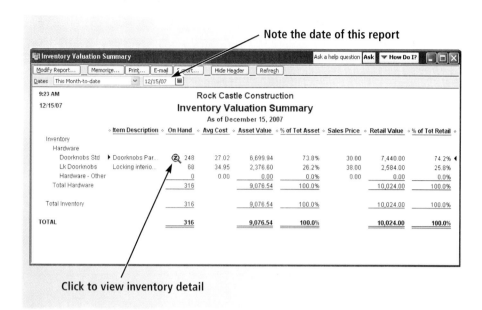

Figure 1.69

Inventory Valuation
Summary for Rock Castle

To view the underlying documentation of the Inventory Valuation Summary:

1 Double-click on the **248 Doorknobs Std** in the On Hand column. An Inventory Valuation Detail appears. By default, this report shows activity for the month-to-date only (12/01/07 to 12/15/07). But Kim wants to know the *total* inventory on hand and to see activity for the *entire* year. To find this information you need to change the From date to 1/1/07.

2 Delete the date in the From date edit box and type **1/1/07** in the box. Click once on the report itself. A new report appears. See Figure 1.70.

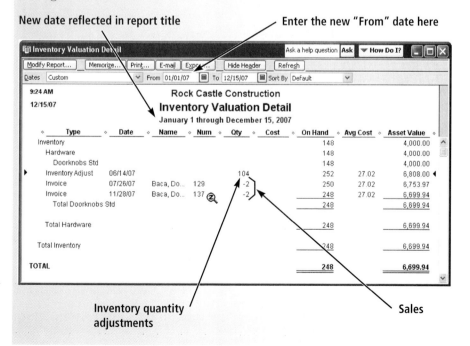

Figure 1.70

Inventory Valuation Detail
from January 1 through
December 15, 2007

Note that this report shows a beginning inventory of 148, an inventory adjustment of 104, and two invoices for sales of 2 units each.

You ask Jim if QuickZoom lets you view the actual invoices. "Sure does," he says. "Let's look at one."

To view an actual invoice:

1 Double-click anywhere in the row containing information on Invoice 137. The invoice appears as shown in Figure 1.71. Adjust your window size or scroll as necessary to view the entire invoice.

Figure 1.71

Invoice 137
Reduced Inventory

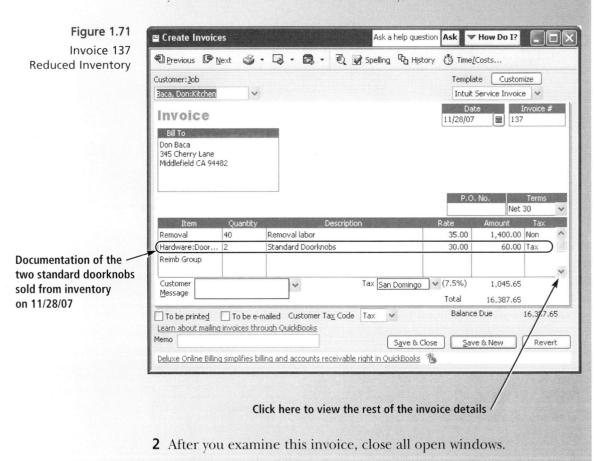

Documentation of the two standard doorknobs sold from inventory on 11/28/07

Click here to view the rest of the invoice details

2 After you examine this invoice, close all open windows.

Jim retrieves the Inventory Valuation Summary and prints it for Kim. He asks you to deliver this report to Kim when you deliver Susan's. He's now ready to fulfill the last request.

CREATING, PRINTING, AND ANALYZING AN ACCOUNTS PAYABLE AGING REPORT

The last request to which you and Jim need to respond is from Laura Valdez, accounts payable manager. She wants two reports so she can estimate how much money Rock Castle will owe its vendors at the end of the fiscal year.

You quickly ask if QuickBooks handles accounts payable aging the same way it handles accounts receivable aging. Jim smiles. "You catch on fast," he says. "Let's start with an Accounts Payable Aging report. It provides the detail Laura needs. Then we'll print her a Vendor Balance Summary."

To create an Accounts Payable Aging report:

1 Click **Reports**, click **Vendors & Payables**, and then click **A/P Aging Summary**. (Alternatively, you could have clicked **A/P Aging Summary** in the Memorized Reports section of the Vendor Navigator.) The A/P Aging Summary report appears. See Figure 1.72.

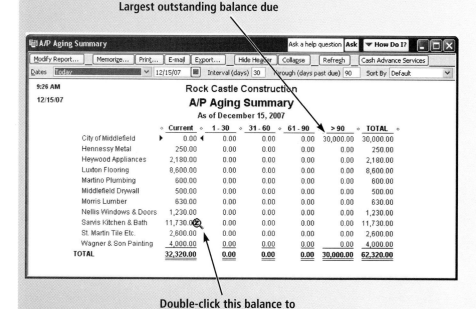

Largest outstanding balance due

Figure 1.72

Accounts Payable Aging Summary

Double-click this balance to view a QuickZoom report

2 Scroll through the A/P Aging Summary. If necessary change the column widths so the entire report displays on your screen.

After Jim prints this report for Laura Valdez, you look it over. You notice a large outstanding balance three months past due to the City of Middlefield, and you suggest using QuickZoom to investigate it further. Jim tells you that Rock Castle is disputing this bill in court and so it's already being handled. You both decide instead to investigate the next largest balance—the Sarvis Kitchen & Bath liability to whom Rock Castle owes $11,730.

To analyze the Sarvis Kitchen & Bath liability:

1 Double-click the Sarvis Kitchen & Bath liability balance of **11,730.00**. An A/P Aging report appears. See Figure 1.73. Notice that two bills are listed; their total is the amount owed to Sarvis as of 12/15/07.

Figure 1.73

A/P Aging QuickZoom Report for Sarvis Kitchen & Bath

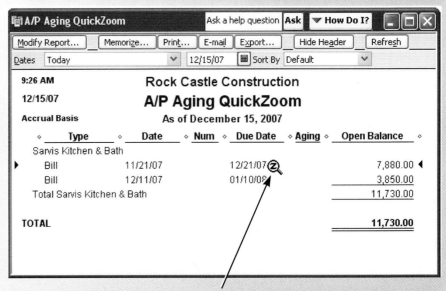

Double-click anywhere on this line to view the underlying bill supporting this entry

2 Double-click anywhere in the entry for the bill dated **11/21/07**. The details of this bill appear. See Figure 1.74. Notice that this bill documents materials expenses incurred in the Don Baca kitchen remodeling job.

Figure 1.74

Sarvis Kitchen & Bath Bill Dated 11/21/07

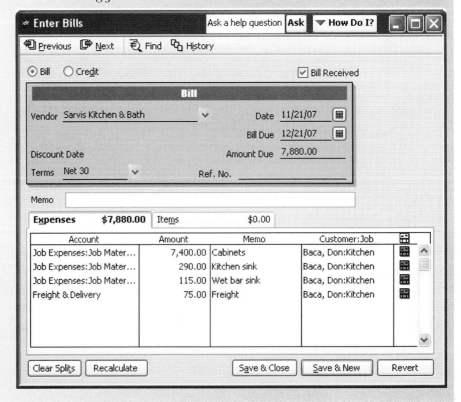

3 When you have finished viewing this bill, close all open windows.

CREATING AND PRINTING A VENDOR BALANCE SUMMARY

· ·

The final supporting report for Laura Valdez is a Vendor Balance Summary. This report is also a preset report available from the QuickBooks Reports menu. It will summarize for Laura all of the unpaid balances due to vendors and will be valuable information for her year-end reporting.

To create and print a Vendor Balance Summary:

1 Click **Reports**, then **Vendors & Payables**, and then **Vendor Balance Summary**. The Vendor Balance Summary appears. See Figure 1.75. Notice that the vendors are listed alphabetically.

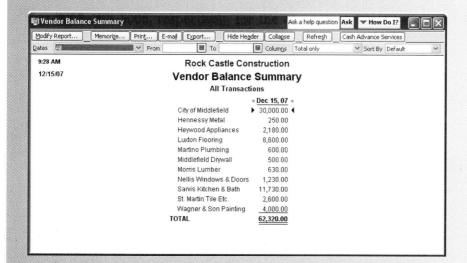

Figure 1.75

Vendor Balance Summary as of December 15, 2007

2 When you finish viewing this report, close this window.

Jim prints the Vendor Balance Summary for Laura, and looks at you. "Yes, I'll deliver this one too," you volunteer good naturedly.

END NOTE

· ·

As you gather the reports and set out to deliver them, you are struck by how easily and quickly Jim has been able to respond to the managers' requests. Within a short time, QuickBooks has generated accurate, up-to-the-minute financial information to help Rock Castle's managers. The many preset reports—summaries, details, and supporting documentation—anticipate the information that managers often need to make sound business decisions.

practice

Session 5 Questions

1 Which menu in QuickBooks provides you access to supporting reports?

2 What information does an Accounts Receivable Aging report provide?

3 What types of transactions might appear in a QuickZoom report created from an Accounts Receivable Aging report? Give two examples.

4 How might the payment history of an account receivable help you analyze the Accounts Receivable Aging report?

5 What information does an Inventory Valuation Summary provide?

6 What types of transactions might appear in a QuickZoom report created from an Inventory Summary? Give two examples.

7 What information does an Accounts Payable Aging report provide?

8 What types of transactions might appear in a QuickZoom report created from an Accounts Payable Aging report?

9 What options can you choose from the Print Reports dialog box to help you print a report?

10 How can you create a supporting report for a date other than the system date? Describe a situation for which you would want to do this.

Session 5 Assignments

1 *Creating Supporting Reports for Rock Castle*

Remember to include your name in the Extra Footer Line of all reports printed.

Jim Reed wants you to help him provide supporting reports. Use Rock.qbw on your Working Disk for this assignment. Create the reports Jim has requested, and write down the answers to the following questions:

a. Create and print a Customer Balance Summary as of 10/31/07. Other than the $60,000 receivable from Reid Properties, what is the amount of the largest customer receivable and what is the customer's name? What invoices support that receivable? What is the nature of each invoice?

b. Create and print an Aging Accounts Receivable report as of 10/31/07. Other than the $60,000 receivable from Reid Properties, list all past due invoices. When is each due? What is the nature of each invoice?

c. Create and print an Aging Accounts Payable report as of 10/31/07. Other than the $30,000 payable to the City of

Middlefield, what is the largest vendor liability? What bill makes up this liability? What is the nature of this bill?

d. Create and print an Inventory Valuation Summary as of 10/31/07. What inventory items are on hand? What is their average cost and retail value?

2 *Creating More Supporting Reports for Rock Castle*

Jim Reed wants you to help him provide more supporting reports. Create the reports Jim has requested, and write down the answers to the following questions:

a. Create and print a Customer Balance Summary as of 12/15/07 using All in the dates box and examine the QuickZoom reports for Don Baca. What invoice created this receivable? What was Don Baca invoiced for? What are the terms of this invoice?

b. Create and print an Aging Accounts Receivable report as of 12/15/07 and examine the QuickZoom reports for the Reid property located at 75 Sunset Road. What invoice is represented by this receivable? What was Reid Property invoiced for? What are the terms of this invoice?

c. Create and print an Aging Accounts Payable report as of 12/15/07 and examine the QuickZoom reports for Wagner & Son Painting. What bill is represented by this payable? What was Rock Castle billed for? What are the terms of this invoice?

d. Create and print an Inventory Valuation Summary as of 12/15/07 and examine the QuickZoom reports for Lk Doorknobs. Describe the two invoices in which these products were billed to customers; that is, which customers were billed, when were they billed, and so on.

trouble? Don't forget to change the Dates field to "This Fiscal Year-to-Date."

3 *Using the South-Western Home Page for More Assignments or Cases*

If you have Internet access, go to the home page for this textbook at **http://owen.swlearning.com**.

Select the **Chapter 1: Session 5** section in Additional Problem Sets, and complete the problem(s) your instructor assigns.

Go to
http://owen.swlearning.
com

4 *Customizing Supporting Reports*

Customize each of the reports you created in Assignment 1 as follows:

a. Modify the Customer Balance Summary by changing the To/From dates to include amounts from September 1 through December 15, 2007. Change the columns from totals only to monthly totals. Describe the changes in customer balance over this period. Print this report.

   b. Create two Accounts Receivable Aging reports, one as of 12/15/07 and one as of 11/30/07. Describe the differences in the two reports. Print both reports.

   c. Create two Accounts Payable Aging reports—one as of 12/15/07 and one as of 11/15/07. Describe the differences in the two reports. Print both reports.

   d. Create two Inventory Valuation Summaries—one as of 12/15/07 and one as of 9/30/07. Describe the differences in the two reports. Print both reports.

Session 5 Case Problem: JENNINGS & ASSOCIATES

Kelly Jennings created financial reports and submitted them to her banker to secure a loan. Today Kelly received a phone call from her banker. He told her that the balance sheet she submitted requires further explanation. He'd like to see some documentation to support her company's receivables, inventory, and payables balances.

Kelly asks you to prepare and print three supporting reports using her QuickBooks file Kj01cp.qbw.

1   Open Kj01cp.qbw.

2   Prepare an Accounts Receivable Aging report for January 31, 2004. Print this report. Write a brief paragraph in which you explain the status of the two largest balances—that is, how old they are, what was sold, and so on.

3   Prepare an Accounts Payable Aging report for January 31, 2004. Print this report. Write a brief paragraph in which you explain the status of the two largest balances—that is, how old they are, what was purchased, and so on.

4   Prepare an Inventory Valuation Summary for January 31, 2004. Print this summary. Write a brief paragraph in which you describe the most recent purchase of film. Be sure to include the date, vendor, amount, and cost per unit.

chapter 2

Setting Up Your Business's Accounting System

In this chapter you will:

- Create a new company file

- Add a new customer to the customer list

- Add a new vendor to the vendor list

- Add a new employee to the employee list

- Add a new account to the chart of accounts

- Add two new items to the item list

CASE: PHOENIX SYSTEMS CONSULTING, INC.

You hear the doorbell and go to the front door. You open it and see Casey Nicks, a friend you've known since third grade.

Casey worked his way through college helping businesses computerize their operations. After graduation he worked six years for a software development company, but he missed the type of work he did while he was going to school. Casey made a brave decision. He decided to leave his job and do what he enjoyed doing most—start a company that would sell and service business computer systems and software. Casey decided to name his new company Phoenix Systems Consulting, Inc.

The first thing Casey did after making this decision was to write a business plan. He spent a great deal of time thinking about what his company would do, how it would be different from similar companies, what unique goods and services it could provide, and so on. His plan was so well thought out and so well written, that New Endeavors, Inc., a venture capital firm well-known for its backing of high-tech start-up companies, decided to invest $50,000 in his company.

So Casey has come to your house to ask you for help. He must establish an accounting information system, and he hopes you can help.

"I don't know much about accounting," he says. "I'm worried that I won't be able to manage the financial details of the business. I'm confused about receivables and payables, and about debits and credits; and I don't know how I'll ever be able to create reports for New Endeavors or for my customers, not to mention my own decision making."

"Don't worry," you reassure him. "I can help you create an accounting information system quickly and easily. I learned how to use QuickBooks last year. It's an accounting software package specially designed for small businesses like yours. If you buy a copy and bring it over this weekend, I'll help you set up your accounting information system."

Casey is relieved, and he says he'll see you Saturday afternoon.

CREATING A NEW COMPANY FILE

When Casey returns on Saturday you install QuickBooks on his laptop computer, and you're ready to begin. You tell him that first you must create a new company file. There are two ways to do this. One is to use QuickBooks's EasyStep Interview—a step-by-step guided series of questions that you can answer to help you choose and set up various QuickBooks features. The second way is to skip the EasyStep Interview. This way is convenient if you prefer to add minimal information to get started. Casey says that since he hasn't conducted a lot of business yet, he'd like to skip the interview.

"Skipping the interview is probably a good idea," you agree. "Besides, no matter which method you use to set up your company on QuickBooks, you can always change the decisions you make during the setup later."

If you want to know more about the EasyStep Interview, you can read the section entitled "A Word About the EasyStep Interview" at the end of this chapter. Also you can work through an entire EasyStep Interview in Case Problem 1 at the end of this chapter.

To create a new company file:

1 Before you begin, close any previously created company files.

2 Click **File**, then click **New Company**. The EasyStep Interview window appears. See Figure 2.1. Notice that there are four section tabs and the Welcome tab is selected.

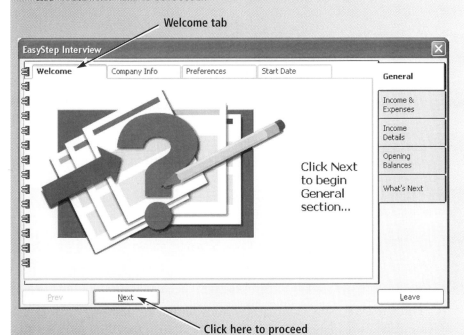

Figure 2.1
EasyStep Interview Window

trouble? When you first launch QuickBooks, the message "Welcome to QuickBooks Pro for Windows Version 2004" might appear. If this occurs click the Set up a new datafile button.

3 Click **Next** in the EasyStep window as shown in Figure 2.1. The next Welcome screen appears. This screen asks about help needed to set up QuickBooks.

4 Click **Next** and a screen appears asking if you're converting data from a Quicken file.

5 Click **Next** and a screen appears titled "Setting up a new QuickBooks company." Read this screen.

Casey reads this screen and reminds you that he wants to get started quickly. You decide to skip the interview.

To skip the EasyStep Interview:

Note: Before you proceed be sure you have time to complete all of the steps from here through page 93.

1 Click the **Skip Interview** button. The Creating New Company window appears. See Figure 2.2. This window contains blank spaces for you to fill in information about Phoenix Systems.

Figure 2.2

Filling Out the Creating New Company Window

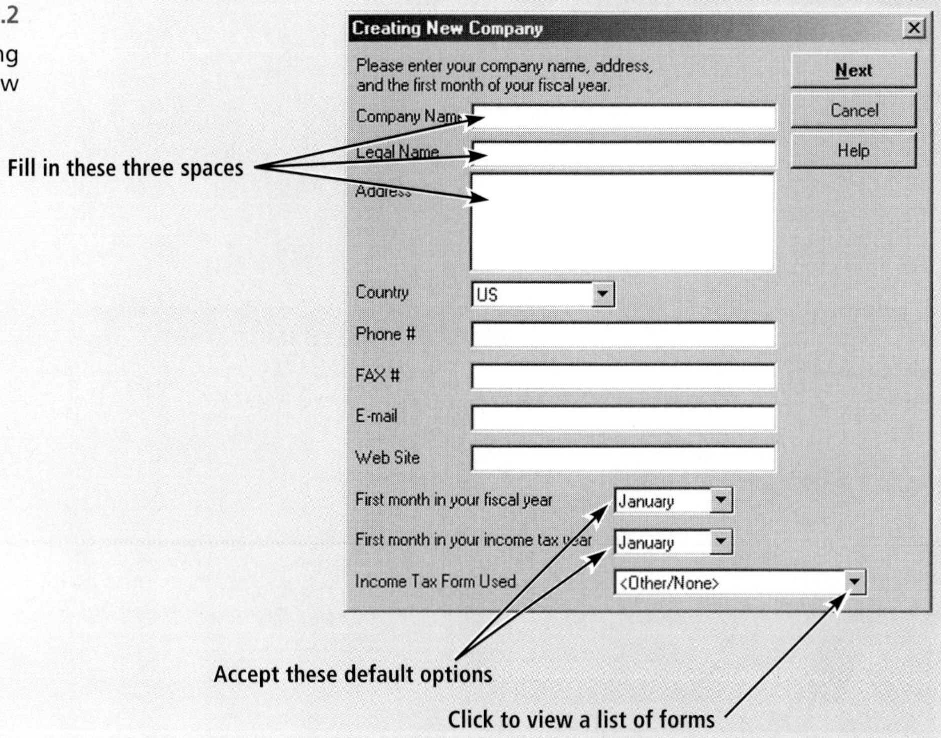

Fill in these three spaces

Accept these default options

Click to view a list of forms

The Creating New Company window and the following screens ask for minimal information about the new company. By filling in this information you will set up Phoenix Systems quickly and begin to use QuickBooks.

To create a new company:

1 Type **Phoenix Systems** in the Company Name edit box.

2 Press the **Down Arrow** key once. The words Phoenix Systems automatically appear in the Legal Name edit box.

3 Press the **Right Arrow** key once, press the **[Spacebar]** once, and then type **Consulting Inc.**

   trouble? If you press a key that causes this screen to disappear before you complete Step 5, click the **Prev** button, and repeat Step 3 as necessary.

4 Press the **Down Arrow** key once. Type the first line of the company's address in the Address edit box as **1234 State Street**. Press **[Enter]**. Type the second line as **Cupertino, CA 95014**.

5 Skip the phone, fax, e-mail, and website fields. The default country and the two default Januarys are correct, so press the **Down Arrow** key until the Income Tax Form Used edit box is highlighted.

6 Phoenix Systems Consulting, Inc. is a corporation. Click the **Down Arrow** on the drop-down list, and click **Form 1120 (Corporation)**.

Now you're ready to move to the next screen and select a chart of accounts.

To select a chart of accounts for a new company:

1 Click **Next** to move to the next screen. See Figure 2.3.

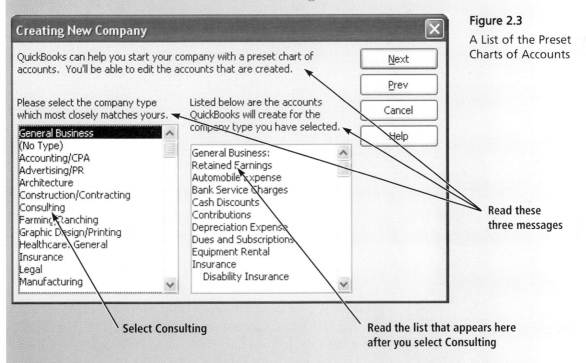

Figure 2.3
A List of the Preset Charts of Accounts

2 Read the information in this window about choosing a preset chart of accounts.

3 Select **Consulting** as the company type. Read through the account titles.

You are now ready to save your new company file, but first you must name it.

To name your new company file:

1 Click **Next**. The Filename for New Company window appears. See Figure 2.4. Notice that QuickBooks has automatically named your file Phoenix Systems.qbw. Save this file to your hard drive. (Alternatively, you may save this file to a disk.)

Figure 2.4

The Filename for New Company Window

Accept this name

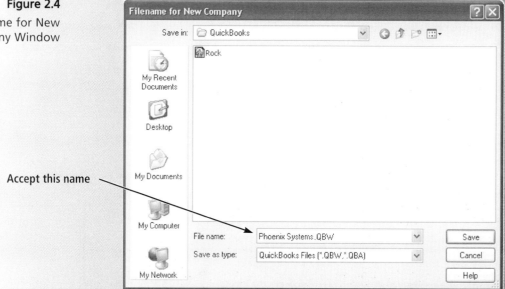

2 Click **OK** to save your file. Messages appear letting you know that QuickBooks is creating and saving your file.

3 An Industry-specific Documentation window may appear. If so, read this window for your information. Then click **No**.

4 Read the Getting Started window, then close it.

Now that Casey's new company file is established, it's imperative that you set certain preferences in QuickBooks to prepare for future activities. The next set of steps will establish preferences for the Enter key, the icon bar, sales tax information, inventory, purchase orders and payroll use, and fix federal and state tax identification numbers.

To set preferences:

1 Click **Preferences** from the Edit menu.

2 Click the **General** icon from the icon bar on the left, then click on the **My Preferences** tab. The first checkbox on the left is "Pressing Enter moves between fields." Select this checkbox; it will save you time in the future. It will allow you to move around in the window using the Enter key without closing the window.

3 Click on the **Company Preferences** tab, then uncheck the Always show years as 4 digits (1999) checkbox. This will allow dates to be shown in the familiar 2-digit year format (1/31/03).

4 Scroll down the Preferences icon bar, click the **Sales Tax** icon, then click **Yes** in the Save Changes window. Then click **OK** in the Warning window. (*Note:* This will close the Company Navigator.)

5 Click the **Company Preferences** tab, then click **Yes** under Do You Charge Sales Tax?

6 Click the drop-down arrow next to Most common sales tax, then click **<Add New>** to add a new sales tax, as shown in Figure 2.5.

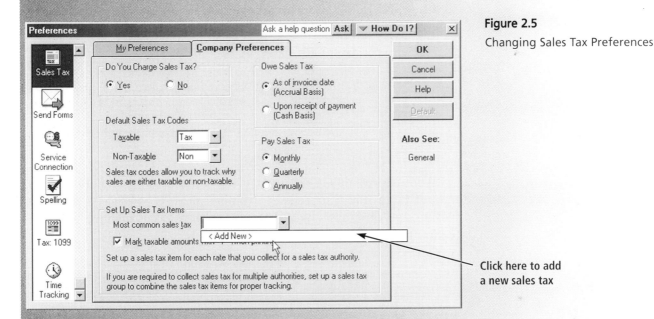

Figure 2.5

Changing Sales Tax Preferences

Click here to add a new sales tax

7 Next, a New Item window appears. Select **Sales Tax Item** from the drop-down listing of new item types. Enter **Sales Tax** as the Tax Name and tax description, **7.5%** as the Rate, and **State Board of Equalization** as the Tax Agency. Then click **OK**.

8 Click **Quick Add** in the Vendor Not Found window to add this vendor to the vendor list. Then click **OK** in the New Item window once again.

9 Next click the **Purchases & Vendors** icon from the Preferences icon bar. When the Save Changes window appears, click **Yes** to save changes in Sales Tax preferences. Then click **OK** in the Updating Sales Tax window to make all existing customers taxable and make all existing non-inventory and inventory parts taxable.

10 When the Purchases & Vendors Preferences window appears, click the checkbox labeled **Inventory and purchase orders are active**. Leave all other checkboxes as they are.

11 Scroll the Preferences icon bar, then click the **Payroll & Employees** icon. When the Save Changes window appears, click **Yes** to save changes in Purchases & Vendor preferences.

12 When the Payroll & Employees Preferences window appears, click the option button labeled **Full payroll features** if it is not already selected.

13 Next, click the **Reports & Graphs** icon. If the Save Changes window appears, click **Yes**.

14 Click the **My Preferences** tab, then click the **Refresh automatically** option button. Click **OK** to close the Preferences window.

15 Click **Multiple Windows** from the View menu.

16 Finally, to establish the Federal and State tax identification numbers, select **Company Information** from the Company menu. Then enter the Federal Employer Identification Number (FEIN) as **77-9999999**. Click **OK** in the Company Information window.

17 Click **Close Company** from the File menu.

Working with data files from a disk is a time consuming effort. Casey has indicated that a more effective alternative is to place QuickBooks files on the computer's hard drive and then use the backup and restore feature to keep a copy of the work.

To create a backup file:

1 From QuickBooks, open the file Phoenix Systems.qbw from your hard disk.

2 Click **Back Up** from the File menu.

3 Click the **Browse** button to change the location of the backup to A:, then click **Save**. (Be sure to have a disk in the A: drive.)

4 Click the **OK** button.

5 Click **OK** in the QuickBooks Information dialog box presented next.

6 Click **Close Company** from the File menu.

To restore a backup file to your hard drive while you work:

1 With no company open, click **Restore** from the File menu.

2 Click the first **Browse** button from the Get Company Backup From section in the Restore Company Backup window.

3 Select **3½ Floppy (A:)** from the Look in: edit box.

4 Select **Phoenix Systems**, then click **Open**.

5 Click the second **Browse** button from the Restore Company Backup To section in the Restore Company Backup window.

6 Select a hard drive and folder from the Restore To window. (***Note:*** The example shown in Figure 2.6 indicates the file restoring location is C:\My Documents\QuickBooks\. Your location may be different depending on where on your computer you would like to store this file. In a lab environment, you may want to save to a Temp folder.

7 Click **Save**. Your screen should look similar to Figure 2.6.

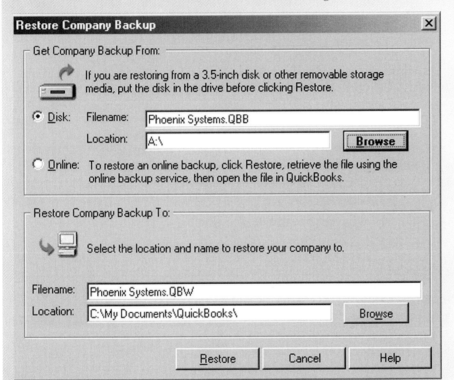

Figure 2.6
Restoring a Company File

8 Click **Restore** to restore your file to the hard disk location you specified. If you're restoring your backup to a location where your previous file was located, you will be asked if you want to overwrite the existing company file. Click **Yes** only if you're sure you want to replace that file. Type **Yes** to confirm and then click **OK**.

9 Click **OK** in the QuickBooks Information window which appears next indicating that your data has been successfully restored.

Casey is thrilled that you have set up QuickBooks for use with Phoenix Systems. But you tell him that he still has many decisions to make and more work to do before he can use all of QuickBooks's features and generate reports. Next you need to set up what QuickBooks calls company lists.

SETTING UP COMPANY LISTS
. . . .

QuickBooks uses lists to maintain information about customers, vendors, employees, items, and other significant business details. You decide to show Casey how to start creating lists for Phoenix Systems.

Customer List

A **customer list** helps expedite creating invoices, tracking receipts and balances owed, communicating with customers who have past due balances, and reporting sales by customer. Also, a customer list is necessary if customers pay at a time other than the time of sale. Casey has decided that Phoenix Systems customers will receive a standard 2% discount if they pay within 10 days of invoice. Otherwise, the balance due must be paid within 30 days. You help Casey start his customer list for Phoenix Systems by adding the first name to the list.

To add a new customer:

1 Open the file Phoenix Systems.qbw that you recently created, if it is not already open.

2 Click **Lists**, then click **Customer:Job List**. A blank Customer:Job List window appears.

3 Click the **Customer:Job** button and then click **New**. A New Customer window appears.

4 Fill in the New Customer window using the information provided in Figure 2.7. Note how QuickBooks duplicates appropriate information for you and that you can click the **Copy** button to copy the address from one window into the other.

Figure 2.7

Adding a New Customer

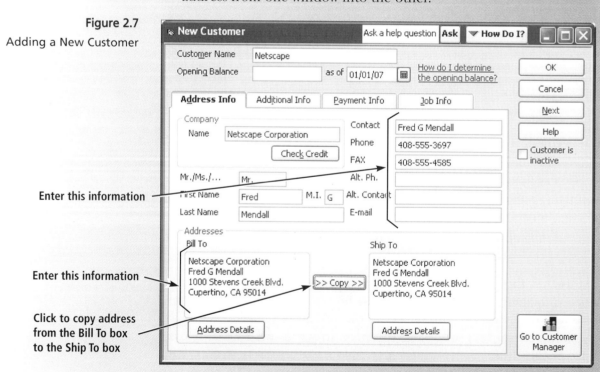

5 Click the **Additional Info** tab.

6 Select Type as **Commercial**.

7 Select Terms as **2% 10 Net 30**.

8 Verify that the Tax Item is specified as **Sales Tax** and that the Tax Code edit box is specified as **Tax**.

9 Click the **Payment Info** tab.

10 Type **15,000.00** as the Credit Limit.

11 If you wanted to enter additional customers at this time, you would click Next. Instead, click **OK** to accept this new customer record and close this window. The Customer:Job List window reappears now including the customer you just added.

12 Close this window.

Casey sees how easy it is to enter customers and says he'll be able to enter the rest of his current customers on his own. So now you'll help him add a vendor.

Vendor List

In QuickBooks, a **vendor list** helps managers expedite payments to vendors or suppliers, track bills and payments due, and report by vendor expenses, amounts owed, and items purchased. You tell Casey that he can use his vendor list to generate purchase orders, record inventory shipments, and pay vendor invoices.

To add a new vendor:

1 Click **Lists**, and then click **Vendor List**. A Vendor List window appears.

2 Click **Vendor**, then click **New**. A New Vendor window appears.

3 Fill in the New Vendor window using the information provided in Figure 2.8.

4 Click the **Additional Info** tab. See Figure 2.9. Enter the information provided in this figure.

5 If you wanted to enter additional vendors at this time, you would click Next. Instead click **OK** to record and close this window. The Vendor window appears, which now includes the vendor you just added.

6 Close this window.

As with the customer list, Casey is pleased with how easily you added the vendor to the vendor list. You tell him that the employee list is next.

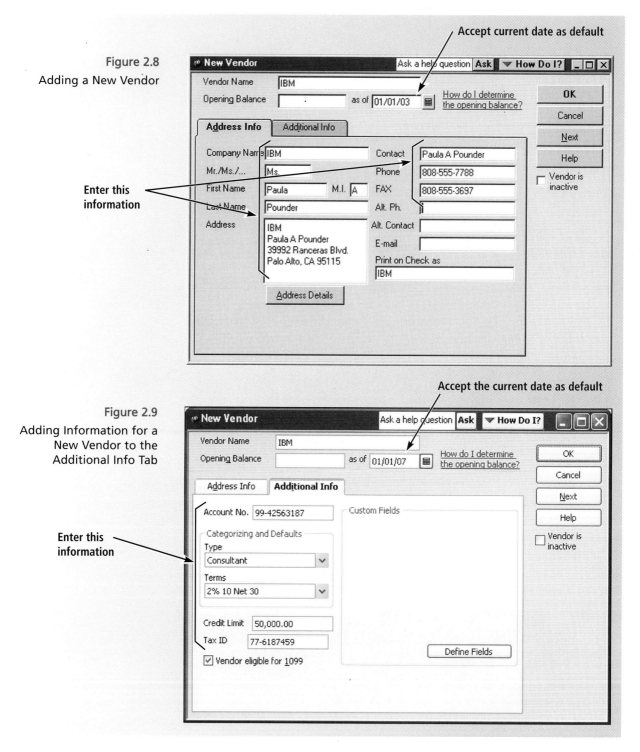

Figure 2.8

Adding a New Vendor

Accept current date as default

Enter this information

Accept the current date as default

Figure 2.9

Adding Information for a New Vendor to the Additional Info Tab

Enter this information

Employee List

QuickBooks can accommodate a lot of information about employees in an **employee list**. You know that for the time being Casey plans to have only three employees—himself and two people he worked with at his last job. For now, you decide to enter minimal employee information that will allow Casey to print each employee's name and address on payroll checks, track payroll expenses and withholdings, and track sales revenue generated by each employee.

To add a new employee:

1 Click **Lists**, then click **Employee List**. Click **No** when asked if you would like help in setting up payroll in QuickBooks. (We'll address this issue in the next chapter.) A blank Employee List window appears.

2 Click **Employee**, then click **New**. A New Employee window appears.

3 Be certain that the Personal tab is selected. Then fill in the blank spaces on this tab using the information in Figure 2.10.

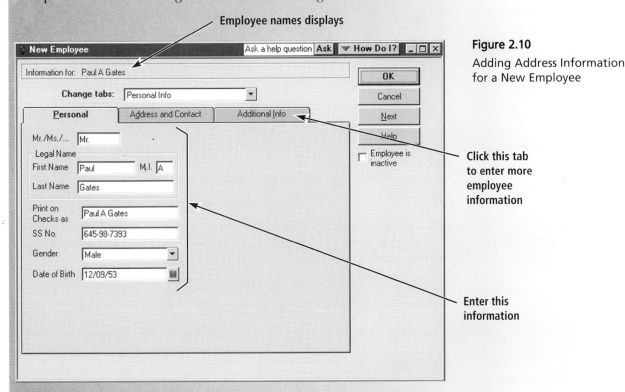

Employee names displays

Click this tab to enter more employee information

Enter this information

Figure 2.10
Adding Address Information for a New Employee

4 Click the **Address and Contact** tab, then enter Mr. Gates's address as **12 Ridgeway Lane, Los Gatos, CA, 95004** and phone **805-555-6874**.

5 Select **Payroll and Compensation Info** from the drop-down edit box labeled Change tabs:

6 Type **Salary** in the Earnings Item Name section, then press **Tab**.

7 Click **Set Up** in the Payroll Item Not Found window.

8 Be sure the Annual Salary option button is selected, then click **Next** in the Add new payroll item window.

9 Be sure the Regular Pay option button is selected, then click **Next** in the Add new payroll item window.

10 Click **Next**, and then click **Finish** to complete the payroll item set up process.

11 Type **50000** as the Annual Rate of earnings.

12 Select **Monthly** as the Pay Period. Your screen should look like Figure 2.11

Figure 2.11

Payroll and Compensation
Information for Paul Gates

Enter this
information

Click to view the taxes
for Paul A. Gates window
in Figure 2.12

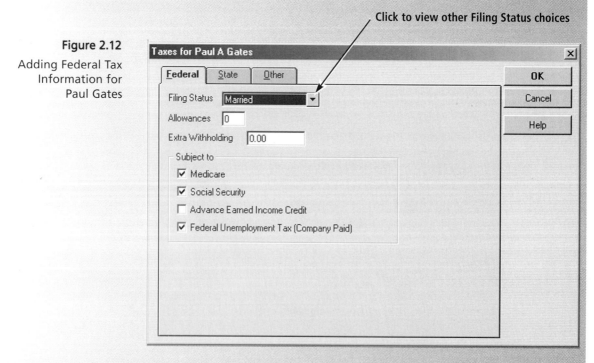

13 Click **Taxes**. The Taxes window appears.

14 Complete the federal taxes for the Paul Gates window using the information in Figure 2.12. Then click **OK** to accept this information and return to the Payroll Info tab.

   trouble? Be sure all tax checkboxes are checked and set the filing status to Married.

Click to view other Filing Status choices

Figure 2.12

Adding Federal Tax
Information for
Paul Gates

15 Select the Taxes button again and then click the State tab.

16 The State Taxes window appears as shown in Figure 2.13. Select **CA** as the State Worked. QuickBooks then provides two checkbox options. Click the **SUI (Company Paid)** box.

17 A Payroll Item Not Found window appears. Click **Set Up**.

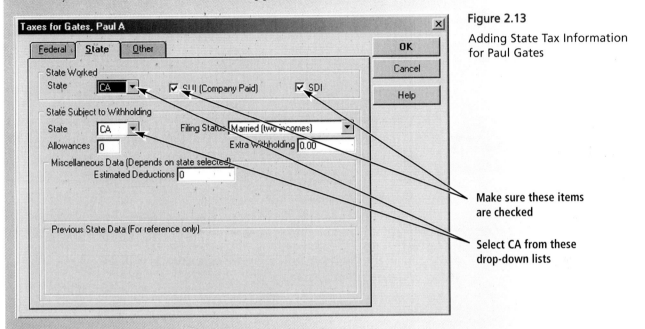

Figure 2.13

Adding State Tax Information for Paul Gates

18 The Add new payroll item (CA–State Unemployment Tax) window appears. Accept the given name as used in paychecks and payroll reports by clicking **Next**.

19 Enter **EDD** (Employment Development Department) as the name of the agency to which liability is paid by clicking **Next**.

20 The EDD is not currently a vendor, thus a Vendor Not Found window appears. Click **Quick Add** to enter this new vendor.

21 Enter **77-9999999** as the number that identifies you to the agency. Then click **Next**.

22 Click **Finish**.

23 A Payroll Item Not Found window appears. Click **Set Up**.

24 The Add new payroll item window appears. Accept the given name used in paychecks and payroll reports by clicking **Next**.

25 Enter **EDD** (Employment Development Department) as the name of the agency to which the liability is paid.

26 Enter **77-9999999** as the number that identifies you to the agency. Then click **Next**.

27 Click **Next** to accept the Employee tax rate provided by the table and to view the Taxable compensation section.

28 Click **Finish**.

29 Now, select **CA** as the State Subject to Withholding.

30 A Payroll Item Not Found window appears. Click **Set Up**.

31 The Add new payroll item window appears. Accept the given name used in paychecks and payroll reports by clicking **Next**.

32 Enter **EDD** (Employment Development Department) as the name of the agency to which the liability is paid. Then click the **Edit** box below.

33 Enter **77-9999999** as the number that identifies you to the agency. Then click **Next**.

34 Click **Finish**.

35 Enter **Married (two incomes)** as the filing status, then click **OK** to enter tax information for Paul Gates.

36 A QuickBooks Information Window appears indicating that QuickBooks added CA–Employment Training Tax to the employee. Click **OK** three times to accept the new payroll information for Paul Gates.

37 Click **Leave As Is** in the New Employee: Payroll Info (other) window which appears next.

38 Close the Employee List window.

The next list you want to show Casey is the chart of accounts.

Chart of Accounts

You know from your accounting course that a chart of accounts provides the structure of a financial reporting system. QuickBooks provides several preset charts of accounts.

"But we already created a chart of accounts when we set up the company," Casey protests. "We selected the 'Consulting' preset chart of accounts."

"Yes," you agree, "but that chart of accounts does not contain cash, accounts receivable, inventory, or accounts payable accounts."

Casey looks puzzled. "I'm sure I'll need those accounts for Phoenix Systems," he says, "so why did we pick 'Consulting'?"

"We picked 'Consulting' because it included most of the accounts we need for our company," you explain. "Now we need to customize the chart of accounts."

To customize a chart of accounts:

1 Click **Chart of Accounts** from the Lists menu. See Figure 2.14. The account titles in the preset Consulting chart of accounts appears. Look down this list to familiarize yourself with the titles.

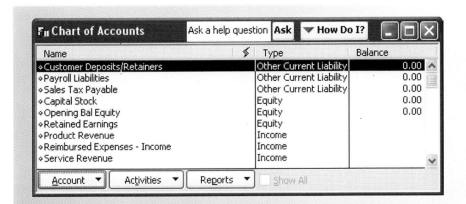

Figure 2.14

Phoenix Systems'
Chart of Accounts

2 Click **Account**, then click **New**. A New Account window appears.

3 Fill in the New Account window using the information in Figure 2.15.

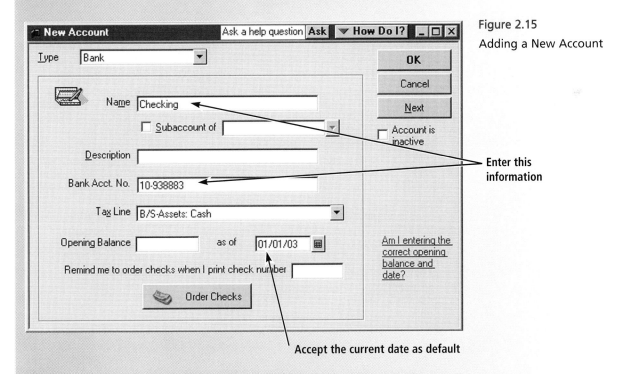

Figure 2.15

Adding a New Account

4 Click **OK** to add the account. The Chart of Accounts window appears. Note that it now includes the new account you just added. (If you had wanted to enter additional accounts, you would have clicked Next instead.)

5 Close the Chart of Accounts window.

Item List

Item lists expedite the recording and reporting of sales activities. An item can be a service performed, such as computer installation or maintenance; or it can be an inventory part, such as a hard disk or monitor. You tell Casey that he can use the information in item lists to help generate purchase orders and customer invoices as well as to manage inventory receipts. He suggests that you enter two new items—one is a service and one is an item of inventory.

To add a new item:

1 Click **Lists**, and then click **Item List**. An item list appears.

2 Click the **Item** button, then click **New**. A New Item window appears.

3 Fill in the New Item window using the information in Figure 2.16. Type **Maintenance & Repairs Revenue** in the Account box. When you click **OK**, an Account Not Found error message will appear, as shown in Figure 2.17. Click **Set Up**. A New Account window appears recognizing this new account as an Income type account. Click **OK** to create this new account.

trouble? Note that QuickBooks uses the word "income" to describe what most accountants refer to as "revenue." Unfortunately, there is no way to alter this word whenever QuickBooks uses it. But you can, if you wish, change the titles of the accounts themselves to "consulting revenues," "parts revenues," and so on.

Figure 2.16

Entering a New Service Item

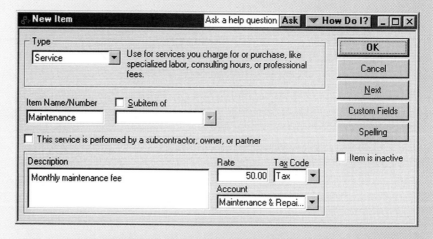

Figure 2.17

Error Message for an Account that Does Not Exist

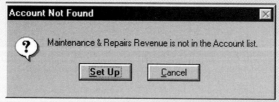

4 Click **Next** to enter this new account and reveal a New Item window.

5 Fill in the New Item window using the information in Figure 2.18. When you type **Computer Sales** in the Income Account box and then click **OK**, an Account Not Found error message will appear. Click **Set Up**. A New Account window appears recognizing this new account as an Income (that is, a revenue) type account.

Click to view other item types

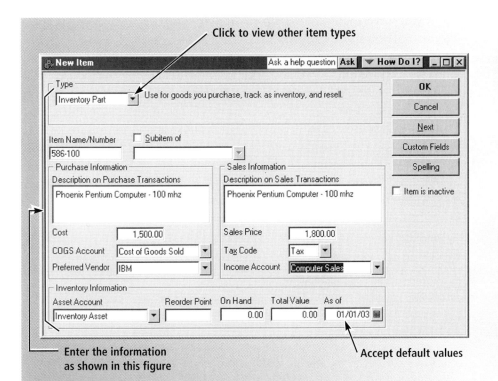

Figure 2.18

Adding a New
Inventory Item

**Enter the information
as shown in this figure**

Accept default values

trouble? You might think that this New Item window would be identical to the previous window. But when you change the type from Service to Inventory Part, the New Item window changes its format. If you haven't done so already, click the **Down Arrow** in the Type box and click **Inventory Part** in the New Item window.

6 Click **OK** to enter this new account.

7 Click **OK** to close this window. If you had wanted to enter additional items at this time, you would have clicked Next instead. A Check Spelling on Form window should appear. Click **Add** to include the words Pentium and mhz.

8 The Item List window appears, now including the two items you just added.

9 Click the **Item** button, then click **Print List**. Click **OK** in the List Reports window if it appears.

10 Click **Preview** in the Print Lists window to view the list without printing.

11 Zoom in on the list, then click **Close**.

12 Click **Cancel** to halt the printing of this list.

13 Close all remaining windows.

A WORD ABOUT THE
EASYSTEP INTERVIEW

At the beginning of this session, you skipped the EasyStep Interview to create Phoenix Systems. This was because the purpose of this text is to acquaint you with QuickBooks in the simplest and most efficient way.

But if you were really setting up your own company, Intuit Inc. recommends that you use EasyStep.

This is because the EasyStep Interview walks you through a complete setup procedure and eliminates the need to deal with your accounting information system "on the fly." Also, EasyStep helps you determine the best way to use all of QuickBooks's features for your type of business, and it automatically creates some of the QuickBooks accounts and items that you need. You can exit the interview at any time, and QuickBooks will save what you have entered.

Figure 2.19 presents a brief overview of how EasyStep is organized into five sections and four tabs.

Figure 2.19 An Overview of the EasyStep Interview

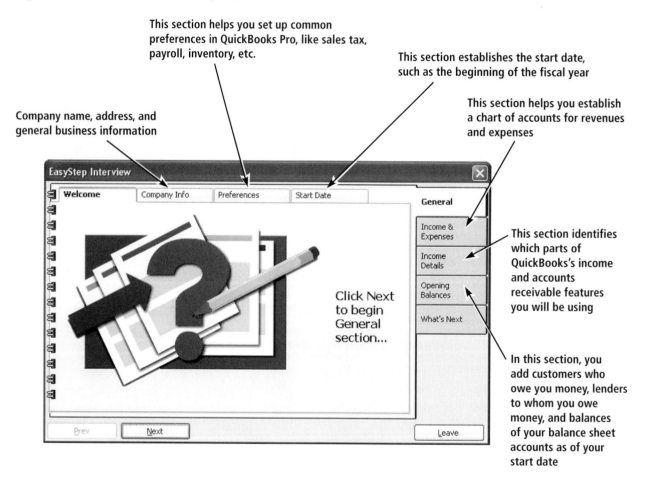

END NOTE

You've helped Casey begin the accounting information system for Phoenix Systems by setting up a new company, and by adding to this new company a new customer, a new vendor, a new employee, a new account, and two new items. You tell Casey that he can now begin recording Phoenix System's first business transactions. Casey is delighted with how easy QuickBooks has been to use, and he says he'll come back tomorrow with the details of Phoenix's first transactions.

practice

Chapter 2 Questions

1 Describe the two setup approaches that you can use to create a new QuickBooks company file.

2 How do you know when to use the EasyStep Interview and when to skip the Interview?

3 In your own words, explain what each of the following terms means in QuickBooks:

a. Customer
b. Vendor
c. Employee
d. Chart of accounts
e. Item

4 What payment terms are available to customers on the New Customer Additional Info tab?

5 What is the difference between a service item and an inventory part item? How is the window for adding new items different depending on whether you are adding a service item or inventory part item?

6 What are the types of accounts in the chart of accounts list?

7 What federal taxes might an employee be subject to?

8 What filing status options are available in the tax set-up for new employees?

9 What pay period options are available in the payroll set-up window?

10 Describe how accounts can be set up while entering information into a list.

Chapter 2 Assignments

1 *Adding More Information to Phoenix Systems Consulting, Inc.*

Use Phnx02cp.qbw. (Remember, you will need to restore this file from your Data Files CD first.)

a. Add the following new customers:

Customer: Los Gatos School District
Contact: Mr. Francis L Cahn
Address: 1000 Apple Farm Rd., Los Gatos, CA 95110
Phone: 408-555-9788
Type: Corporate
Terms: Net 30
Rep: PAG
Credit limit: 10,000
Customer is taxable: Yes
Tax item: Sales tax

Customer: Jdesign
Contact: Mr. John F Gomez
Address: 235 Ridgefield Place, Fremont, CA 95110
Phone: 408-555-3483
Type: Corporate
Terms: 2% 10 net 30
Rep: PAG
Credit limit: 5,000
Customer is taxable: Yes
Tax item: Sales tax

b. Add the following new vendors:

Vendor: Apple Computer, Inc.
Contact: Mr. Barry G Franks
Address: One Corporate Way, Cupertino, CA 95110
Phone: 408-555-9787
Account: 94-6856-0122
Type: Manufacturer
Terms: Due on receipt
Credit limit: 3,000
Tax ID: 77-6841257
Vendor eligible for 1099: Yes

Vendor: Bengal Drives, Inc.
Contact: Ms. Kelly Sweenie
Address: 4500 Rucker Rd., Santa Barbara, CA 93103
Phone: 805-555-8777
Account: 16-11123
Type: Manufacturer
Terms: 2% 10 net 30
Credit limit: 8,000
Tax ID: 77-1487125
Vendor eligible for 1099: No

c. Add the following new employees. Select the Leave As Is option when prompted for Local/Taxes and Sick/Vacation.

Employee: Mr. Casey K Nicks
Address: 345 Ocean View Dr., Santa Cruz, CA 95888
Phone: 408-555-1287
SS No: 566-79-3511
Hired: 1/1/03
Pay period: Monthly
Yearly salary: 60,000
Filing status: Married with one income, filing jointly
Taxes: Subject to federal taxes (Social Security, FUTA, and Medicare) and state taxes (SUI and SDI)
Filing state: CA

Employee: Ms. Kylie W Patrick
Address: 10101 Wildway, San Jose, CA 95822
Phone: 408-555-3050
SS No: 426-85-6974
Hired: 1/1/03
Pay period: Monthly
Clerical hourly rate: $7.50
Filing status: Head of household
Taxes: Subject to federal taxes (Social Security, FUTA, and Medicare) and state taxes (SUI and SDI)
Filing state: CA

d. Add the following new accounts:

Type: Income
Name: Computer Add-ons

Type: Long-Term Liability
Name: Long-Term Debt

e. Add the following new items:

Type: Inventory Part
Item name: 800mb HD
Description: 800mb Bengal Hard Disk
Cost: 250.00
COGS account: Cost of Goods Sold
Preferred Vendor: Bengal Drives
Asset Account: Inventory Asset
Sales Price: 300.00
Income Account: Computer Add-ons

Type: Inventory Part
Item name: 1 gig HD
Description: 1,000mb Bengal Hard Disk
Cost: 450.00
COGS account: Cost of Goods Sold
Preferred Vendor: Bengal Drives
Asset Account: Inventory Asset
Sales Price: 550.00
Income Account: Computer Add-ons

Type: Service
Item name: Installation
Description: Installation of computer add-ons
Rate: 45.00
Account: Maintenance & Repairs

f. Print an updated copy of each list modified above.

2 *Creating a new company: Central Coast Cellular*

a. Van Morrison would like to use QuickBooks for his new company, Central Coast Cellular, skipping the EasyStep Interview, like you did in the chapter example on page 87. Use the following information:

The company resides at 950 Higuera St., San Luis Obispo, CA 93401. The company's phone number is 805-555-9874 and its fiscal and tax year begins in January 2003. The company's main business is cellular phone sales and rentals, but it also earns revenue by consulting with customers on alternative cellular phone plans. The company's federal tax ID is 77-9418745.

b. Change the preferences in QuickBooks as follows:

- Set QuickBooks to move between fields after pressing the Enter key.
- Set dates to a two-digit year format.
- Set up sales tax at 8% payable to the State Board of Equalization.
- Make inventory and purchase orders active.
- Enable full payroll features.
- Enable reports and graphs to refresh automatically.

c. Set up the following customers:

- Tribune, 3825 S. Higuera St., San Luis Obispo, CA 93401, 805-781-7800, Terms: Net 30, Contact: Sara Miles
- City of San Luis Obispo, 990 Palm Street, San Luis Obispo, CA 93401, 805-781-7100, Terms: Net 30, Contact Robert Preston
- Sterling Hotels Corporation, 4115 Broad Street, Suite B-1, San Luis Obispo, CA 93401, 805-546-9388,Terms: Net 30, Contact: Monica Flowers.

d. Set up the following vendors:

- Verizon Communications, 1255 Corporate Drive, Irving, TX 75038, 972-507-5000, Terms: Net 30, Contact: Francisco Rojas
- Nokia Mobile Phones, 23621 Park Sorrento Road Suite 101, Calabasas, CA 91302, 818-876-6000, Terms: Net 30, Contact: Brandy Parker
- Ericsson, Inc., 740 East Campbell Road, Richardson, TX 75081, 972-583-0000, Terms: Net 30, Contact: Monty Python.

e. Set up the following employees using the company's federal tax ID # 77-9418745. All employees are paid semi-monthly and subject to social security, FUTA (at 3%), Medicare, SUI, SDI, and California's Employment Training Taxes payable to the Employment Development Department (EDD).

- Name: Mr. Jay Bruner, Address: 552 Olive St., San Luis Obispo, CA 93401, Phone: 805-555-7894, SS#: 578-94-3154, Start date: 1/1/03, Salary: $3,000 per month, Filing Status: Single.

- Name: Mr. Alex Rodriguez, Address: 1480 Monterey St., San Luis Obispo, CA 93401, Phone: 805-555-1579, SS#: 487-98-1374, Start date: 1/1/03, Salary: $4,000 per month, Filing Status: Married with one income.
- Name: Ms. Megan Paulson, Address: 400 Beach St., San Luis Obispo, CA 93401, Phone: 805-555-4489, SS#: 547-31-5974, Start date: 1/1/03, Hourly: $12 per hour, Filing Status: Married with two incomes.

f. Modify the existing chart of accounts to include the following:

- Checking, Type: Bank.
- Accounts Receivable, Type: Accounts Receivable
- Phone Sales, Type: Income
- Phone Rentals, Type: Income
- Consulting, Type: Income

g. Set up the following items:

- Consulting Services: Type: Service, Rate: $95, Taxable, and using income account: Consulting.
- Inventory Part: Item name/description: Nokia 8290, Cost: $150, Preferred vendor: Nokia, Sales price: $225, Taxable, and using income account: Phone Sales.
- Inventory Part: Item name/description: Nokia 8890, Cost: $175, Preferred vendor: Nokia, Sales price: $250, Taxable, and using income account: Phone Sales.
- Inventory Part: Item name/description: Nokia 3285, Cost: $200, Preferred vendor: Nokia, Sales price: $300, Taxable, and using income account: Phone Sales.
- Inventory Part: Item name/description: Ericsson LX588, Cost: $50, Preferred vendor: Ericsson, Sales price: $85, Taxable, and using income account: Phone Sales.
- Inventory Part: Item name/description: Ericsson T19LX, Cost: $75, Preferred vendor: Ericsson, Sales price: $100, Taxable, and using income account: Phone Sales.

h. Print the following:

- Customer list
- Vendor list
- Employee list
- Chart of accounts
- Item list

3   *Creating a New Company: Nashua AutoMarket*

a. Create a new company by skipping the EasyStep Interview. Use the following information:

Name: Nashua AutoMarket
Address: 555 Liberty Lane, Reno, NV 89557

Fiscal year begins: January
No sales tax:
Federal ID: 77-1233220
State: NV
State Employer ID: 77-3325099
Select a retail chart of accounts and create your own answers to any other questions asked in the setup process. Save this file with the default file name provided by QuickBooks on a separate disk.

b. Add a new customer to the Nashua AutoMarket file:

Name: Diaz-Cruz Automotive
Billing and Shipping address: 9396 Maryland Lane,
                                Pensacola, FL 99999
Create your own phone numbers, contacts, credit limit, and terms.

c. Add a new vendor to the Nashua AutoMarket file:

Name: Missoula Auto Supply
Address: 2231 Hawk Rd., Billings, MT 99999
Create your own phone numbers, contacts, credit limit, and terms.

d. Add a new employee to the Nashua AutoMarket file:

Name: William P Biaggi
Address: 2023 Lane, Reno, NV 99999
Create your own phone numbers, Social Security number, and hired date.
Pay period: Monthly
Yearly salary: $22,000
Taxes: Subject to all federal and state taxes including SUI
Filing status: Single

e. Add a new account to the Nashua AutoMarket file:

Type: Income
Name: Product Sales

f. Add a new item to the Nashua AutoMarket file:

Name: Bumper 100
Description: Blazer Bumper 1996
Type: Inventory part
Income Account: Product sales
On hand: 0
Cost: $300.00
Sales price: $400.00

g. Print a copy of each list created above.

4 *Using the South-Western Home Page for More Assignments or Cases*

If you have Internet access, go to the home page for this textbook at **http://owen.swlearning.com**.

Select the Chapter 2 section from the Additional Problem Sets, and complete the problem(s) your instructor assigns.

Go to
**http://owen.swlearning.
com**

Chapter 2 Case Problem 1: OCEAN VIEW FLOWERS

Ocean View Flowers, a wholesale flower distributor, is located at 100 Ocean Ave. in Lompoc, California, 93436. Ocean View started business January 1, 2004, and the owners would like you to use QuickBooks to keep track of their business transactions. Ocean View is a calendar year company (for both fiscal and tax purposes), and will need to use the inventory, purchase order, and full payroll features of QuickBooks. The company established a bank account, titled Union Checking, at the beginning of the year.

In addition, the company filed for federal (91–3492370) and state (23–432) tax ID numbers. All employees are paid semi-monthly but do not earn sick or vacation pay. All state taxes are paid to the Employment Development Department. The state unemployment tax (SUTA) rate is 1%. Tables 2.1 and 2.2 identify the company's expected customers and vendors.

Table 2.3 shows Ocean View Flowers Employees (all of whom are considered regular-type employees) were hired on 1/4/04 and are subject to federal and state taxes and withholdings, state unemployment, state disability, and state employee training taxes. The list of these employees is on the following page.

Customer	Address	Terms	Contact
Valley Florists	101 Main St. Los Angeles, CA 90113	2/10 net 30	Sam Davies
FTD	2033 Lakewood Dr. Chicago, IL 60601	net 30	Beverly Rose
California Beauties	239 Hyde Street San Francisco, CA 95114	2/10 net 30	Farrah Faucet
Eastern Scents	938 42nd Street New York, NY 10054	2/10 net 30	Nick Giovanni
Latin Ladies	209 Zona Rosa Mexico City, Mexico	2/10 net 30	Juan Valdez

Table 2.1

Ocean View Flowers Customers

Table 2.2

Ocean View Flowers Vendors

Vendor	Address	Terms	Contact
Hawaiian Farms	2893 1st Street Honolulu, HI 05412	Net 30	Mahalo Baise
Brophy Bros. Farms	90 East Hwy 246 Santa Barbara, CA 93101	Net 30	Tim Beach
Princess Flowers	92 West Way Medford, OR 39282	Net 30	Bonnie Sobieski
Keenan's Pride	10 East Betteravia Santa Maria, CA 93454	2/10 net 30	Kelly Keenan
Vordale Farms	62383 Lido Isle Newport, CA 90247	Net 30	Donna Vordale

Table 2.3 Ocean View Flowers Employees

Employee	Address	Social Security #	Compensation	Filing Status
Margie Coe	2322 Courtney Buellton, CA 93246	654-85-1254	$12/hour	Head of Household
Kelly Gusland	203 B St. Lompoc, CA 93436	567-78-1334	$15/hour	Single
Stan Comstock	383 Lemon St. Lompoc, CA 93436	126-85-7843	Annual Salary of $50,000	Married, one income (Married for Federal)
Marie McAninch	1299 College Ave. Santa Maria, CA 93454	668-41-9578	Annual Salary of $60,000	Married, two incomes (Married for Federal)
Edward Thomas	1234 St. Andrews Way Lompoc, CA 93436	556-98-4125	Annual Salary of $70,000	Single

Assignment:

Create a new company file for Ocean View Flowers without using the EasyStep Interview. Name this file Ocean.qbw, then print the following:

Customer list
Vendor list
Employee list
Chart of accounts

Chapter 2 Case Problem 2:
JENNINGS & ASSOCIATES—The EasyStep Interview

You saw in Chapter 1 that Kelly Jennings produced a balance sheet, an income statement, and supporting reports (as of January 31, 2004) for her banker. Unfortunately, the QuickBooks file that Kelly used to store these financial reports was destroyed by a nasty virus, and Kelly failed to make backup files to avoid loss of data! So she must now recreate her file.

Use the following information to create a new file for Kelly Jennings. Name it Mykelly1.qbw.

1 *General*

The company name is Jennings & Associates. It is located at 1200 Constellation Rd. Suite E, San Martin, CA 93107. Its federal tax ID is 77-9999999. Kelly began using QuickBooks on January 1, 2004; the fiscal year-end is December 31. The company is an advertising/public relations corporation and files a Form 1120 for federal taxes. Jennings & Associates inventories photograph film and wants to use QuickBooks's inventory capabilities. The company collects sales taxes at the rate of 7.75% from retail customers; however, all of their current customers are resellers and as such are nontaxable. Sales taxes collected from retail customers are then remitted to the State Board of Equalization. It has three employees. Kelly wants to use a service-oriented invoice form and QuickBooks's payroll feature. Kelly chooses to calculate payroll taxes manually.

Kelly has decided, for the time being, not to give customers written estimates, but she does want to track employee time on each job. She's decided to track and record reimbursable expenses as both income and expense. She does not want to use QuickBooks's classification feature, but she does want bills entered upon their receipt, even though she will not pay them until a later due date. She prefers to view the reminder list only by request. Finally, she's told you to start using QuickBooks as of January 1, 2004.

Although Kelly wants you to start using QuickBooks for 2004 transactions as of 1/1/04, it's essential that you specify a start date of 12/31/03. This is because of how the QuickBooks software treats net income.

2 *Income and Expenses*

Jennings & Associates never receives payment at the time a service is provided. They invoice each client as they provide services. The service items provided by QuickBooks for an advertising/public relations firm will be adequate for their current needs. There is no need for non-inventory items or other charges at this point.

The firm does charge for film costs incurred, and they use the inventory tools provided in QuickBooks to manage film purchases. Two types of film are inventoried. The first, regular grade film, costs $4.45 per roll and is normally purchased from Rex's Film Supply located at 800 North Central, Suite F, San Martin, CA 93017. The cost of the film is included in an inventory asset account until it is sold. When sold, the film cost is charged to an expense account (film expenses) and a revenue account (fee income:film) is recorded at the price of $7.50 per roll. A second grade of film (high quality) is also purchased from Rex's and costs $15.00 per roll. The same accounting rules as used for regular film are followed except the sales price of the film is $25.00 per roll. (***Note:*** All film is taxable.)

3 *Opening Balances*

Although Jennings & Associates will begin using QuickBooks 1/1/04, customer, vendor, and other account balances existed as of 12/31/03. Table 2.4 shows which customers owe Jennings & Associates as of 12/31/03.

Table 2.5 shows vendors with whom Jennings & Associates did business during 2003.

Jennings & Associates had two checking accounts, one at Union Bank with a balance of $2,590 on December 31, 2003 and one at First Valley Savings and Loan with a balance of $1,000 as of December 31, 2003. The firm owned computer equipment with an original cost of $4,000 and accumulated depreciation of $1,000, and furniture with an original cost of $2,500 and accumulated depreciation of $500 on December 31, 2003. Lastly, they owed $5,000 to the Bank of San Martin due and payable on December 31, 2005.

4 *Payroll*

Jennings & Associates' state employer ID is 77-1234567. Kelly pays her employees semi-monthly. The state (CA) unemployment tax rate is 3% payable to the EDD, and the company pays the full FUTA rate of 6.2% payable to the IRS. Kelly is salaried and her employees are paid hourly. All are subject to federal and state taxes. Currently, Kelly does not use QuickBooks to track and document sick and vacation time.

Table 2.6 shows Jennings & Associates employees of 1/1/04. As of January 1, 2004 Jennings & Associates has paid all salaries and taxes owed. Thus, it does not have any payroll tax liabilities carried over from prior years. For QuickBooks purposes you indicate a hired date of 1/1/04 for all employees.

5 *Assignment*

Print the following as of January 1, 2004:

Standard balance sheet
Customer list
Vendor list
Item list
Employee list
Chart of accounts

Customer	Address	Amount
AAA Appliance	Attn: Jane E. Seymor 1034 Sycamore San Martin, CA 93110	$350
Big 10 Sporting Goods	Attn: Sammy A. Goodwin 1003 A Street San Martin, CA 93100	$250
Bob and Mary Schultz	Bob and Mary Schultz 122 Garden Street San Martin, CA 93107	$500
Ray's Chevron	Attn: Fanny J. May 1990 Broadway San Martin, CA 93110	$150
Sally's Fabrics	Attn: Ray E. Farray 900 West Laurel San Martin, CA 93115	$200
Fancy Yogurt	Attn: Paul F. Montoya 3299 Bonita Lane San Martin, CA 93107	$500
Paulsons Nursery	Attn: Robert J. Paulson 100 Central San Martin, CA 93110	$600
Evelyn Walker Real Estate	Attn: Nancy P. Revlon 3233 Central San Martin, CA 93107	$700

Table 2.4

Jennings & Associates Customers and Balances as of 12/31/03

Vendor	Address	Terms	Amount Owed
Frank Mendez Properties	Attn: Frank Mendez 12400 Calle Real San Martin, CA 93110	Net 15	$700
Banks Office Supply	Attn: Pamela Reese 1209 Oak Lane San Martin, CA 93110	Net 30	$0
On-Time Copy Shop	Attn: Jennifer Jacobs 3402 A Street San Martin, CA 93110	Net 30	$125
So. Cal Gas	Attn: Kyle N. Schultz 200 South Main San Martin, CA 93110	Net 30	$65
Pacific Electric Company	12000 North Main San Martin, CA 93110	Net 30	$35
General Telephone	12100 North Main San Martin, CA 93110	Net 30	$75

Table 2.5

Jennings & Associates Vendors and Balances as of 12/31/03

Table 2.6 Jennings & Associates Employees as of 1/1/04

Name	Address	SS#	Hired	Salary	Status
Kelly Jennings	2333 Dire Straits Rd. San Martin, CA 93107	854-60-7882	1/1/04	$48,000	Head of household
Diane Murphy	455 Galaxy Rd. San Martin, CA 93107	556-89-9999	1/1/04	$15/hr	Married (two incomes)
Cheryl A. Boudreau	19090 Mockingbird Ln. San Martin, CA 93107	545-99-5512	1/15/04	$15/hr	Single

Cash-Oriented Business Activities

In this chapter you will:

- Record cash-oriented transactions classified as financing activities, such as owner contributions

- Record cash-oriented transactions classified as investing activities, such as equipment purchases

- Record cash-oriented transactions classified as operating activities, such as inventory purchases and sales

CASE: PHOENIX SYSTEMS CONSULTING, INC.

Three months have passed since Casey first appeared at your door asking for help, and Phoenix Systems has been growing quickly—so quickly, in fact, that Casey has decided to hire a full-time accountant. With your help, Casey has entered all of Phoenix's business transactions to date into QuickBooks. Now Casey has asked you to train his new accountant—Karen Yamamoto—who recently graduated from college with a degree in accounting. You agree to begin training Karen next week.

When you meet Karen, she confesses that this is her first full-time job, and she's a little nervous.

"Relax!" you say, trying to reassure her. "QuickBooks is very easy for first-time users to learn, and you'll be delighted with how much it will help you do your job."

"The best way to learn QuickBooks is to jump right in," you add. "As Casey probably told you, Phoenix's first quarter—January 1 through March 31—has just ended. I know he's already entered all of the transactions for the first quarter into the company's QuickBooks file. So I thought we should begin by reviewing some of Phoenix's first quarter transactions. Then you can practice entering transactions into a temporary file to see what it's like to use QuickBooks."

Karen suggests that you can give her a complete overview of QuickBooks's capabilities if you show her Phoenix's transactions organized by the three fundamental business activities—financing, investing, and operating. She explains that **financing activities** are initiated when money or other resources are obtained from short-term non-trade creditors, long-term creditors, and owners. Financing activities are completed when amounts owed are repaid to or otherwise settled with these same creditors and owners. She explains further that **investing activities** are initiated when the money obtained from financing activities is applied to non-operating uses, such as buying investment securities and productive equipment. Investing activities are completed when the investment securities or productive equipment are sold. Finally, **operating activities** occur when the money obtained from financing activities and the long-term assets obtained from investing activities are applied either to purchase or to produce goods and services for sale. Operating activities are substantially completed when goods are delivered or sold and when services are performed.

"Wow, they taught you well in college!" you exclaim. "Let's get started with a few of Phoenix's cash-oriented financing activities."

RECORDING CASH-ORIENTED FINANCING ACTIVITIES

You begin with two financing activities. The first occurred on January 2, 2003, when Casey contributed $25,000 to start the business.

To record Casey's deposit:

1 Restore the Phnx03.qbb file from your Data Files CD. See "Data Files CD" in Chapter 1 if you need more information.

2 Open Phnx03.qbw.

3 Click **Make Deposits** from the Banking menu. The Make Deposits window appears. Note that QuickBooks has automatically inserted today's date.

4 Enter the information for Casey's contribution as shown in Figure 3.1. Be sure to enter the correct date. Notice that QuickBooks speeds up data entry by providing drop-down lists and by recognizing and filling in names that Casey has already entered into the Phoenix file.

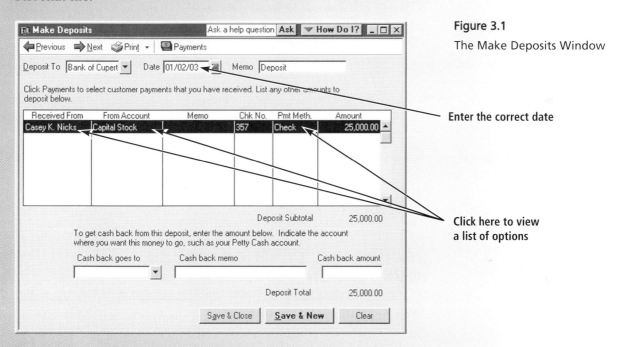

Figure 3.1
The Make Deposits Window

5 Click **Save & New** to record the deposit.

The second deposit was made on January 10, 2003, when New Endeavors—the venture capital company that invested in Phoenix Systems—contributed $50,000.

To record New Endeavors' deposit:

1 Type **New Endeavors** in the Received From edit box of the Make Deposits window.

2 Click in the **From Account** edit box.

3 Click **Set Up** in the Name Not Found window.

4 Click **Other** in the Select Name Type window, then click **OK.**

5 Enter the information for New Endeavors in the New Name window as shown in Figure 3.2, then click **OK.**

Figure 3.2

The New Name Window

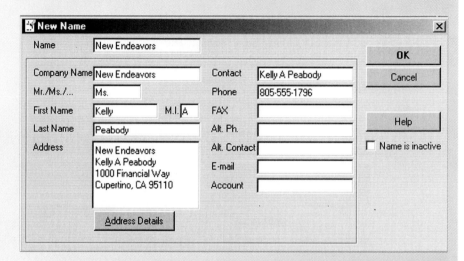

6 Enter the date of the deposit, **January 10, 2003**, and amount, **50,000**, and the account, **Capital Stock**, in the Make Deposits window. Then click **Save & Close** to close the Make Deposits window.

You decide to look next at investing activities.

RECORDING CASH-ORIENTED INVESTING ACTIVITIES

After depositing the contributions from Casey and New Endeavors, Phoenix Systems temporarily invested $8,000 in an investment opportunity offered by its bank, the Bank of Cupertino. By transferring funds from its checking account to a new investment account, Phoenix expected to earn a very attractive interest rate.

"But that wouldn't be a deposit," Karen says.

"You're right," you agree. "A new account is created and a transfer is initiated. I'll show you."

To create a new account and record a transfer of funds:

1 Click **Chart of Accounts** from the Company menu. (Alternatively, you could click Chart of Accounts from the Company Navigators or the Lists menu.)

2 Click the **Account** button then click **New**. A new Account window appears.

3 Enter **Bank** in the Type box, if it is not already there, and **Short-term Investments** in the Name box, then click **OK**.

4 With the Short-term Investments account name selected, click **Activities**, then click **Use Register**. After you enter the register, be sure the 1-line checkbox is unchecked.

5 Enter the information shown in Figure 3.3 to record the deposit. Begin by entering the deposit amount of **8,000.00** on the first line. Next, select **Bank of Cupertino** on the second line and type **Transfer** in Memo. Then click **Record**.

TRANSFR automatically appears when you enter a deposit amount and Bank of Cupertino

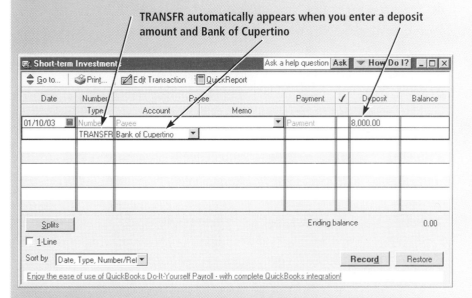

Figure 3.3

The Short-Term Investments Register

6 Close the Short-term Investments register.

7 Close the Chart of Accounts window.

Phoenix also had other investment activity over the last few months, and you want to walk Karen through two more transactions. Both transactions represent checks that were written from the Bank of Cupertino checking account. The first check represents the purchase of a computer used in the business.

To write a check to purchase equipment:

1 Click **Write Checks** from the banking menu. (Alternatively, you could click Check from the icon bar, or click Checks from the Banking Navigator.)

2 Click **Bank of Cupertino** as the Bank Account from the drop-down list, if it is not already there.

trouble? Be sure to select Bank of Cupertino as the bank account from which this check is written. The default account is the last one used, which in this case might be the Short-term Investments account.

3 Press the **Tab** key, enter check number **1013**, then press **Tab** again.

trouble? The check number specified on your check is dependent on what order you entered the information in this and other chapters. Do not worry if your check number is different from the check number shown in Figure 3.4 on the following page.

4 Type **2/3/03** as the date, then press the **Tab** key.

5 Type **Office Mart** as the payee, then press the **Tab** key. Note that since Office Mart is a new name, QuickBooks requires more information for this new vendor.

6 Click **Set up** in the Name Not Found window.

7 Click **Vendor**, if necessary, in the Select Name Type window, then click **OK**.

8 Type **Office Mart** as the Company Name in the New Vendor window, then type **2900 Fair Ct. [Enter] Cupertino, CA 95110** as the address for Office Mart in the Address edit box, then click **OK**.

9 Type **6750** as the amount, then press the **Tab** key five times to move the cursor to the Account field.

trouble? Near the bottom of the Write Checks window are two tabs—one labeled Expenses and one labeled Items. The Expenses label is somewhat misleading because you can type or select any account to appear here, including assets. On the other hand, you use the Items tab to enter inventory acquisitions only. Click on either the Expenses tab or the Items tab accordingly.

10 Type **Computer Equipment** in the Account field.

11 Press the **Tab** key, then click the **Set Up** button in the Account Not Found window that appears.

12 Change the Type to **Fixed Asset**, then click **OK**. QuickBooks recommends that all fixed asset accounts have a separate cost and accumulated depreciation account as subaccounts to the main classification. When a Tracking Fixed Asset window appears, click **No**.

13 To set up individual cost and accumulated depreciation accounts, click **Chart of Accounts** from the Company menu.

14 Click the **Account** button, then click **New**.

15 Change the Type to **Fixed Asset**, and the Name to **Cost**.

16 Click the checkbox next to Subaccount of, select **Computer Equipment** from the drop-down list, then click **Next**.

17 Follow the same steps to create an accumulated depreciation account as a subaccount of computer equipment. Click **OK**, then close the Chart of Accounts window.

18 Change the name of the account for this check from "Computer Equipment" to "Computer Equipment:Cost." When a Tracking Fixed Asset window appears, click **No**.

19 If necessary, click the **To be printed** checkbox to make sure it is *not* checked. Your screen should look like Figure 3.4.

Be sure to enter the correct date

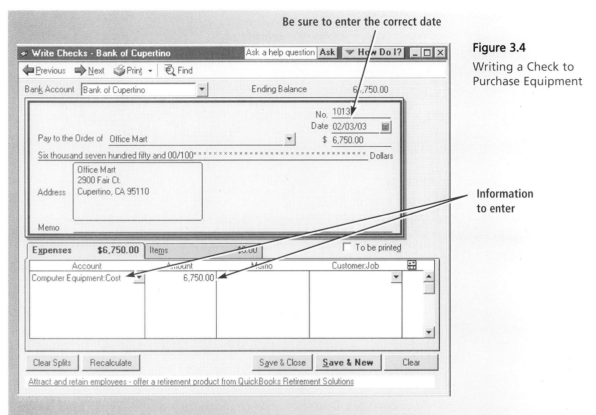

Figure 3.4

Writing a Check to
Purchase Equipment

Information
to enter

20 Click **Save & New** to record this check.

The second check you want to show Karen is for the purchase of a short-term investment—Casey has decided to use some of Phoenix's funds to invest in mutual funds.

To write a check to purchase mutual funds as a short-term investment:

1 Be certain that Bank of Cupertino is still selected as the Bank Account.

2 Type **Sky Investments** as the payee.

3 Press the **Tab** key once. Note that since Sky Investments is a new name, QuickBooks requires more information.

4 Click **Set up** in the Name Not Found window.

5 Click **Other** in the Select Name Type window, then click **OK**.

6 Type **Sky Investments** as the Company Name in the New Vendor window, then type **Paul R Getty [Enter] 9347 Piedmont [Enter] Cupertino, CA 95110.** Then type **408-555-9741** as Phone in the New Name window, then click **OK**.

7 Enter the additional information for the check to Sky Investments as shown in Figure 3.5. Note that the account type—Investments, an Other Current Asset Account—needs to be set up at this time as well.

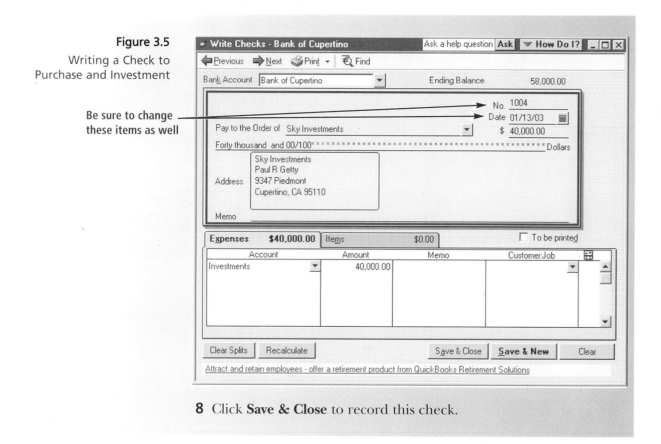

Figure 3.5

Writing a Check to Purchase and Investment

Be sure to change these items as well

8 Click **Save & Close** to record this check.

You're now ready to record the last type of fundamental business activity—operating activities.

RECORDING CASH-ORIENTED OPERATING ACTIVITIES

You tell Karen that Phoenix uses purchase orders to help manage its business activities. She remarks that, typically, purchase orders have no impact on financial statements. But you quickly point out that purchase orders are an important control feature in QuickBooks and so she should practice using them.

You decide to pull Purchase Order (PO) 3001 from the company's files and have Karen use it as a sample to practice creating a purchase order.

To create a purchase order:

1 Click **Create Purchase Orders** from the Vendors menu, or click **Purchase Orders** from the Vendors Navigator.

2 Enter the information shown in Figure 3.6 up to the Item column.

Enter this date   **Start with 3001**

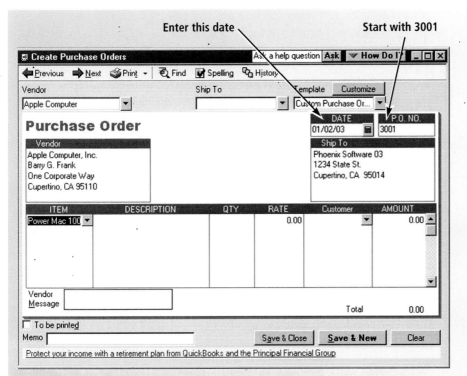

Figure 3.6
Creating a Purchase Order

3 Type **Power Mac 100** as the item to be purchased. This is a new item, and so additional information is required.

4 Click **Set Up** to create a new item. The New Item window appears.

5 Enter the information shown in Figure 3.7, then click **OK**. The Create Purchase Orders window reappears.

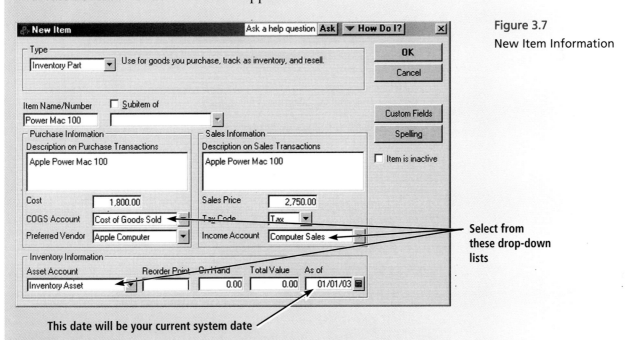

Figure 3.7
New Item Information

Select from these drop-down lists

This date will be your current system date

6 Type **5** in the Qty (Quantity) space, then click **Save & Close** in the Create Purchase Orders window.

Phoenix uses purchase orders for ordering products, as well as for receiving products. For example, Purchase Order 3001 was actually filled a few days after it was sent. As soon as Phoenix received this inventory, a check was generated to pay the bill. Phoenix is a relatively young company, so many vendors require payment on delivery. You show Karen how QuickBooks records this receipt of inventory and vendor payment.

To record the receipt and payment of inventory ordered:

1 Click **Write Checks** from the Banking menu.

2 Enter the Check number, **1003**, date, **1/09/03**, and payee, **Apple Computer**. Then press the **Tab** key.

3 The Open PO's Exist window appears because when you entered Apple Computer as the payee, QuickBooks searched its open purchase orders list to see if any already existed for this vendor. Click **Yes** to reveal the Open Purchase Orders window.

4 Click once near the **01/02/03** date in the Open Purchase Orders window to place a check on the PO No. 3001 line, then click **OK**.

5 The completed check appears with all the appropriate information to record the payment for the inventory. See Figure 3.8. Click **Save & New** to record the check.

Enter this information first

Figure 3.8
Completed Check
Number 1003

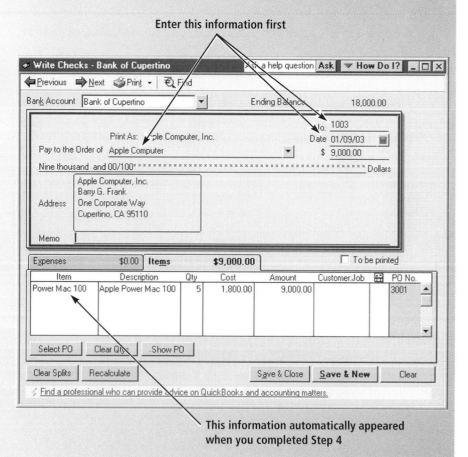

This information automatically appeared when you completed Step 4

Liability insurance is a must for today's businesses, and Phoenix is no exception. Often premiums are paid in advance, and this is what Casey had to do at Phoenix—he wrote a check for an insurance prepayment. Karen watches as you demonstrate how QuickBooks records this type of transaction.

To write a check for liability insurance:

1 Enter the Check number, **1001**, date, **1/07/03**, and payee, **Walker Insurance**, then press the **Tab** key. Note that since Walker Insurance is a new name, QuickBooks requires more information.

2 Click **Set up** in the Name Not Found window, click **Vendor**, and then click **OK**.

3 In the New Vendor window, create a new vendor: **Walker Insurance, Ms. Pamela Walker, 10778 Edgewood Way, Cupertino, CA 95110.** Click **OK** after you enter this information.

4 Enter **1,384.67** as the amount, and record this transaction by increasing a Prepaid Insurance account under Account in the Expenses tab. This is a new account; set it up as an Other Current Asset Type as shown in Figure 3.9, and click **OK**.

trouble? If you enter Prepaid Insurance in the Items tab you will be prompted to enter an Inventory Part. Instead, delete your entry on the Items tab and click the Expenses tab to properly continue.

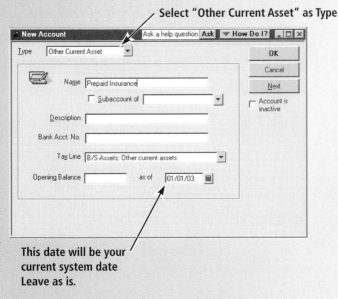

Figure 3.9

Entering a New Account

5 Click **Save & Close** to record this check.

You now want to show Karen how QuickBooks accounts for two recent cash sales.

To record two cash sales:

1 Click **Enter Sales Receipts** from the Customers menu or click the **Sales Receipt** icon from the Customer Navigator. You may get a Merchant Account Service Message box. Click **No**.

2 Enter the information shown in Figure 3.10 up to the Item box.

Click here to select customer   Start with 501

Figure 3.10
Sales Receipt 501

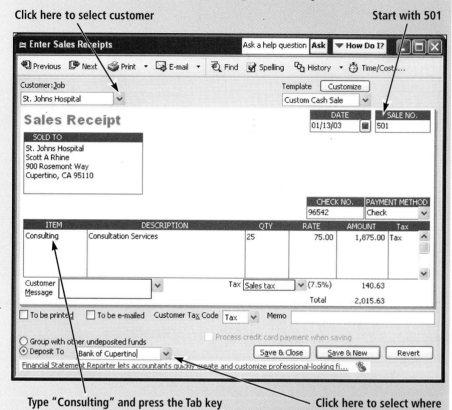

Type "Consulting" and press the Tab key   Click here to select where funds are deposited

3 Type **Consulting** in the Item column, then press the **Tab** key.

4 This is a new account, and therefore it requires setup. Enter the information specified in Figure 3.11 in the New Item window, including the account information, then click **OK**.

Click here to specify that this item is taxable

Figure 3.11
A New Item Window

QuickBooks requires an account to record this revenue (income)

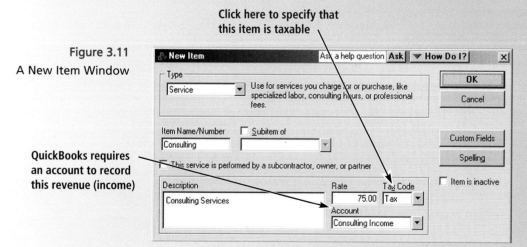

5 Type **25** in the Qty column, then click the **Deposit To** button.

6 Click **Bank of Cupertino** as the bank into which funds are deposited. Be sure the box labeled "Customer Tax Code" indicates Tax.

7 Click **Save & New** to enter this sales receipt and prepare to record another. A new Enter Sales Receipts window appears.

8 Enter the information shown in Figure 3.12.

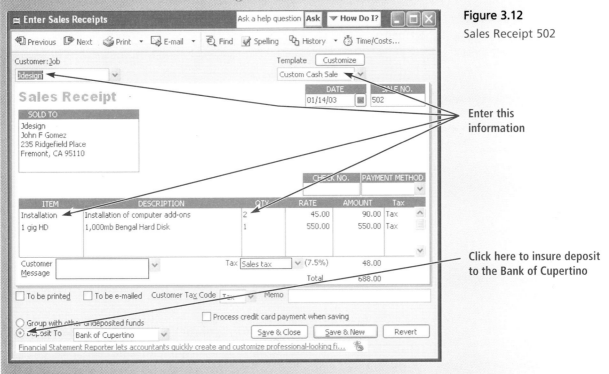

Figure 3.12
Sales Receipt 502

9 Click **Save & Close** to record this sales receipt.

Karen wants to know if Phoenix ever collects cash in advance of performing services. "Yes, Phoenix does," you reply. "I'll show you how QuickBooks records that type of transaction."

To record receipt of advance payment:

1 Click **Receive Payments** from the Customers menu or click **Receive Payments** from the Customer Navigator.

2 Enter the information provided in Figure 3.13 on the following page, then click **Save & Close**.

3 Note that since this payment occurs before a sale is recorded, this payment cannot yet be matched to an invoice. Thus, a QuickBooks for Windows message appears. Click **OK** to record this payment and generate a credit for this customer.

When Karen saw how Casey had recorded this transaction, she was perplexed. She knew that, strictly speaking, this transaction should have resulted in increases both to Cash and to a special liability account called

Figure 3.13

Receive Payments Window

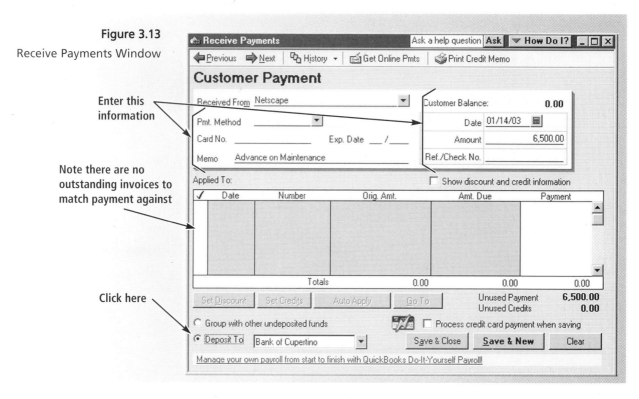

"Advances to Customers," rather than in an increase to Cash and a decrease to Accounts Receivable. It became clear to her, however, that this approach would ultimately work when the sale was made and the invoice was generated.

Karen has one last question about QuickBooks transactions at Phoenix. "Does QuickBooks handle your payroll too?" she asks.

"Absolutely," you reply. "Let me show you our January payroll. Besides you, two of Phoenix's employees are on salary, and one employee is hourly."

"Entering information about payroll is a little tricky since Phoenix has decided not to participate in Intuit's payroll tax service. To participate would have required a monthly fee, and we have so few employees at Phoenix, we decided to manually enter tax deductions."

"Wouldn't it be faster to use the tax service?" Karen asks.

"Well, yes" you respond, "but as you'll soon see, entering payroll withholding and tax information manually isn't that bad."

To initialize payroll setup:

1 Click **Pay Employees** from the Employees menu or from the Employee Navigator.

2 Click **OK** in the Intuit Payroll Services window to choose a payroll option.

3 Click **Next** in the Set Up CA—Employment Training Tax window.

4 Click the option **Yes, it includes the rate for CA-Employment Training Tax**. Then click **Next**.

5 Click the **Yes** button in the next window then click **Next**.

6 Click the option **No, I prefer to do all setup and adjustments myself**, then click **Next**.

7 Click **Leave** to end this process and begin to set up payroll.

8 Click **Choose a payroll option** in the Payroll Setup window as shown in Figure 3.14.

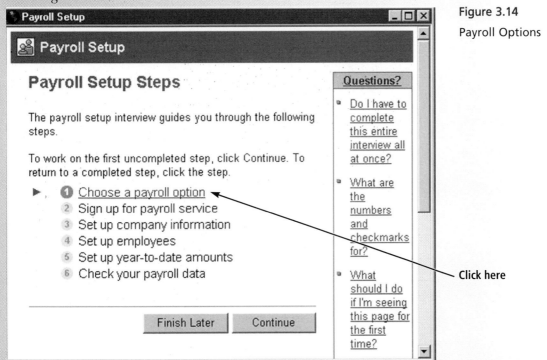

Figure 3.14
Payroll Options

9 In the Payroll Setup window, scroll to the bottom of the page presented and click the prompt **Learn more** after the sentence "If you don't want to use an Intuit Payroll Service, you can still use QuickBooks to prepare your payroll."

10 In the Payroll Setup window, click **To calculate payroll taxes manually**.

11 Scroll down the page and then click the button **I choose to manually calculate payroll taxes** as shown in Figure 3.15.

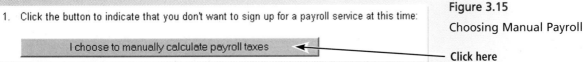

Figure 3.15
Choosing Manual Payroll

12 Click **Finish Later**. Since you have previously entered payroll tax information when you set up employees, you will not have to return to finish payroll setup. The Payroll Setup window will now close.

"What a pain!" exclaims Karen.

"No kidding" you respond. "But at least now we're good to go and ready to pay employees."

To record and pay employees:

1 Click **Pay Employees** from the Employees menu or from the Employee Navigator once again.

2 Click **No** when QuickBooks asks you if you would like more information.

3 Click **No** when asked if you would like to learn more.

4 Click **OK** in the Pay Employees window, since this is the first payroll for Phoenix.

5 Change the dates as shown in Figure 3.16. Click the **Mark All** button then click **Create**.

trouble? If a Payroll Subscription window appears, click **Continue**. Intuit is attempting to encourage your use of their payroll service, which is not required for this text.

Figure 3.16

Select Employees to Pay

Click this button if you need to unmark employees for payment—this button toggles between Mark All and Unmark All

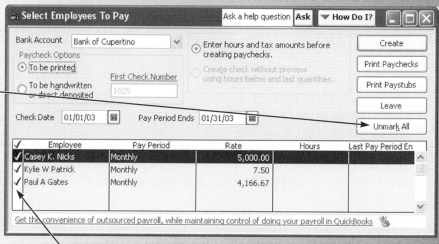

These checks appear after you click the Mark All button

6 Enter information into the Preview Paycheck window as shown in Figure 3.17. Then click **Create**.

Figure 3.17

Payroll Information for Casey Nicks

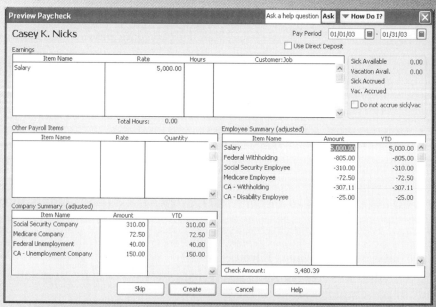

7 Enter information into the Preview Paycheck window as shown in Figure 3.18. Then click **Create**.

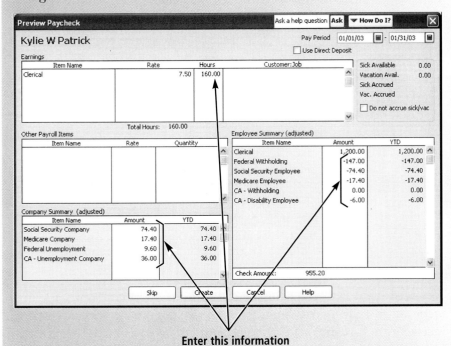

Enter this information

Figure 3.18

Entering Payroll Information for Kylie Patrick

8 Enter information into the Preview Paycheck window as shown in Figure 3.19. Then click **Create**.

trouble? Your instructor or college may have opted to purchase the tax table updates. In those instances, payroll taxes will be calculated for you. However, the amounts in your Preview Paycheck window will most likely be different from those shown in this text.

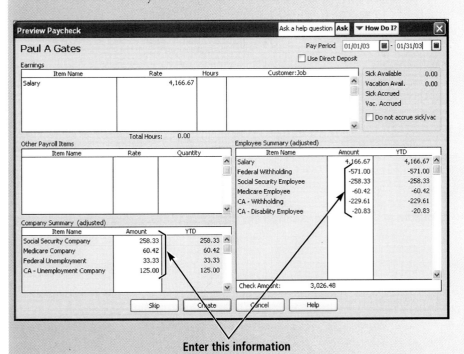

Enter this information

Figure 3.19

Entering Payroll Information for Paul Gates

9 Click **Leave** in the Select Employees To Pay window.

10 Close all open Windows and exit QuickBooks.

trouble? QuickBooks often prompts you to back up your data to avoid accidental data loss. If this message appears you may choose to accept or cancel this action. If you are storing your data on a disk, do not use the QuickBooks backup feature unless you intend to back up to a disk drive other than the one on which your data is currently stored. In Windows you would:

a In My Computer, click the icon for the disk you want to copy.

b On the File menu, click **Copy Disk**.

c Click the drive you want to copy from and the drive you want to copy to, and then click **Start**.

END NOTE

You've helped Karen understand some basic QuickBooks features, including how to make deposits, write checks, create purchase orders, receive inventory, record cash sales, and create payroll.

Karen tells you that she is very impressed with QuickBooks's capabilities. Even after this brief overview of cash-oriented activities—whether they are financing, investing, or operating—she can see how QuickBooks will help her be a very effective and productive Phoenix employee.

practice

Chapter 3 Questions

1 Compare and contrast operating, investing, and financing activities.

2 Which menu in QuickBooks contains the option for making deposits?

3 How do you create a new account in QuickBooks, and what information is required?

4 How do you write checks in QuickBooks, and what information is required?

5 How do you create a purchase order in QuickBooks, and what information is required?

6 How do you record the receipt and payment of inventory in QuickBooks, and what information is required?

7 How do you record cash sales in QuickBooks, and what information is required?

8 How do you record the receipt of cash payments in QuickBooks, and what information is required?

9 How do you record payroll in QuickBooks, and what information is required?

10 Where does the payroll information used in recording payroll originate?

Chapter 3 Assignment

1 *Adding More Information to Phoenix Systems, Inc.*

For this assignment use Phnx03cp.qbw. (Remember, you will need to restore this file from your Data Files CD first.) Add the following financing, investing, and operating activities, and then create and print a standard balance sheet as of March 31, 2003 and a standard income statement for the period January 1, 2003 to March 31, 2003.

Add the following financing activities:

a. Phoenix enters into a long-term loan agreement with New Endeavors for $25,000 on February 24, 2003. The loan is repayable at $500 per month. ***Hint:*** Use the Make Deposits activity to record this transaction. Enter "Long-Term Debt" in the From Account.

b. On March 11, 2003, Phoenix borrows $3,000 from the Bank of Cupertino on a short-term basis. ***Hint:*** Use the Make Deposits activity to record this transaction, use Quick Add to set up the Bank of Cupertino as an Other type, and create a new Short-term Debt account as an other current liability.

Add the following investing activities:

c. On January 17, 2003, Phoenix writes Check 1006 to purchase furniture from Office Mart for $3,756.44. ***Hint:*** Create a new Furniture account as a fixed asset account and two subaccounts —cost and accumulated depreciation.

d. Phoenix makes an additional $10,000 investment with Sky Investments using Check 1014 on February 4, 2003.

Add the following Phoenix operating activities:

e. Purchase Order 3008 is created on February 1, 2003, to Computer Wholesale for the purchase of ten 1 MB memory modules.

f. Purchase Order 3006 is created on February 5, 2003, to Bengal Drives for the purchase of five 800 MB hard drives and three 1 gigabyte hard drives.

g. Check 1015 is written on February 25, 2003, for $2,600 to Bengal Drives for receipt and payment of products requested on Purchase Order 3006.

h. Check 1002 is written to E-Max Realty on January 8, 2003, for $1,600 as payment of first and last months' rent. The check is properly recorded as Prepaid Rent, a current asset account. ***Hint:*** Set up E-Max Realty as a new vendor, contact Sonny Q. Bono, 93778 Texas Ave., Cupertino, CA 95110, 408-555-1130.

i. A $2,500 check (number 4930) is received from Boston Stores on March 6, 2003, and deposited to the Bank of Cupertino as an advance on maintenance services. ***Hint:*** Set up Boston Stores as a new customer, contact Zack H. Haselmo, 10032 West 5th Street, Cupertino, CA 95110, 408-555-9874, terms net 15, customer is taxable. Record this payment, using QuickBooks's Receive Payments Activity and leave it as a credit for this customer, because no invoice has been created.

j. Payroll for the month ended February 28, 2003 is recorded and paid on February 26, 2003. Kylie Patrick worked 150 hours during this month. Paul Gates and Casey Nicks worked the entire month. Payroll taxes and withholding for employees in January 2003 are shown in Table 3.1.

k. A cash sale, SR 503, is recorded to Penny's Pet Parlor on February 7, 2003. The contact is Penny Purdue at 8499 Central Ave., Cupertino, CA 95110, 408-555-1975. The type is corporate and taxable (use the Additional Info tab in the New Customer window to set these parameters). The sale is for three hours of installation, a 1 gigabyte hard drive, and three 1 MB memory modules—all taxable. Penny pays with her Check 1564 in the amount of $897.46. The check is held for deposit at a later time. ***Hint:*** Be sure to indicate on the sales receipt that this receipt is to be grouped with other undeposited funds.

l. A cash sale, SR 504, is recorded on February 21, 2003, to TRW. TRW's contact is Sally Q. Fairfield at 1000 Park Ave., Cupertino,

Tax or Withholding/Employee	Nicks	Patrick	Gates
Social Security Company	310.00	69.75	258.34
Medicare Company	72.50	16.31	60.41
Federal Unemployment	16.00	9.00	22.67
CA—Unemployment	60.00	33.75	85.00
Federal Withholding	–805.00	–136.00	–571.00
Social Security Employee	–310.00	–69.75	–258.34
Medicare Employee	–72.50	–16.31	–60.41
CA—Withholding	–307.11	0	–229.61
CA—Disability Employee	–25.00	–5.63	–20.84
Check Amount	3,480.39	897.31	3,026.47

Table 3.1

Payroll Taxes and Withholding for Employees in January 2003

CA 95110. The customer is taxable. The sale is for six 586-100 computers, 25 hours of consultation, and 5 hours of installation. TRW's Check 504 is deposited directly into the Bank of Cupertino.

2   *Adding More Information: Central Coast Cellular*

In Chapter 2, you created a new QuickBooks file for Central Coast Cellular (CCC), a cellular phone sales, phone rental, and consulting company. Make a copy of that file in Windows Explorer, name the file CCC3, and use that file to enter the following transactions.

a.   On January 3, 2003, Mr. Van Morrison deposited $200,000 of his personal funds into the company checking account and received 25,000 shares of stock in CCC. ***Hint:*** You will need to create a new *equity* account named Common Stock.

b.   On the same date he signed a lease with Central Coast Leasing (2830 Mcmillan Ave #7, San Luis Obispo, CA 93401, 805-544-2875) to rent retail space at $3,000 a month for five years. Payment is due on the 13th of the month.

c.   On January 6, 2003, the company temporarily invested $75,000 by writing check 3001 to Schwab Investments (1194 Pacific Street, San Luis Obispo, CA 93401, 805-788-0502). ***Hint:*** You will need to create another current assets account named Short-term Investment.

d.   On January 7, 2003, the company borrowed and then deposited $125,000 from Wells Fargo Bank (665 Marsh St., San Luis Obispo, CA 93401, 805-541-0143) due in five years with annual interest of 8 percent and payments made monthly. ***Hint:*** You will need to create a long-term liability account named Notes Payable.

e.   On January 8, 2003, the company purchased office furniture by writing check 3002 for $20,000 to Russco (3046 S. Higuera St. #A, San Luis Obispo, CA 93401, 805-547-8440). ***Hint:*** You will need to create a fixed assets account for office furniture with related subaccounts cost and accumulated depreciation.

f. On January 9, 2003, the company ordered inventory from the following vendors:

Purchase Order #	Vendor	Product	Quantity
101	Ericsson	LX588	40
		T19LX	60
102	Nokia	3285	25
		8290	50
		8890	15

g. On January 10, 2003, the company purchased supplies from Russco for $3,000 using check 3003. These supplies are expected to last over the next year. ***Hint:*** You will need to create another current asset account named Store Supplies.

h. On January 13, 2003, the company wrote check 3004 to Central Coast Leasing for $6,000 ($3,000 for January's rent, and $3,000 as a security deposit). ***Hint:*** You will need to create another asset account named Security Deposit.

i. On January 14, 2003, the company received and deposited an advance payment of $10,000 from the City of San Luis Obispo (a customer) as part of a consulting contract to be started in February.

j. On January 15, 2003, the company received a shipment of phones from Ericsson on purchase order 101. Items were received and a bill recorded due in 30 days.

k. On January 16, 2003, the company created sales receipt 501 to record 50 hours of consulting services and the sale of 25 Ericsson LX588 phones to Sterling Hotels Corporation. A check was received and deposited for $7,425.

l. On January 17, 2003, the company paid semi-monthly payroll starting with check 3005 for the period January 1 to January 15, 2003. Megan Paulson worked 80 hours during the period. Payroll tax information is shown in Table 3.2.

Table 3.2
Payroll Information for
Central Coast Cellular

Tax or Withholding/Employee	Rodriguez	Bruner	Paulson
Gross Pay	$ 2,000.00	$ 1,500.00	$ 960.00
California Employee Training Tax	$ 2.00	$ 1.50	$ 0.96
Social Security Company	$ 124.00	$ 93.00	$ 59.52
Medicare Company	$ 29.00	$ 21.75	$ 13.92
Federal Unemployment	$ 6.40	$ 4.80	$ 3.07
CA—Unemployment	$ 24.00	$ 18.00	$ 11.52
Federal Withholding	$ -300.00	$ -225.00	$ -144.00
Social Security Employee	$ -124.00	$ -93.00	$ -59.52
Medicare Employee	$ -29.00	$ -21.75	$ -13.92
CA—Withholding	$ -100.00	$ -75.00	$ -48.00
CA—Disability Employee	$ -10.00	$ -7.50	$ -4.80
Check Amount	$ 1,437.00	$ 1,077.75	$ 689.76

m. Print the following:
- Profit & Loss Standard report for the month of January 2003
- Balance Sheet Standard as of January 17, 2003
- Custom Transaction Detail Report for the period January 1 through January 17, 2003

3   *Using the South-Western Home Page for More Assignments or Cases*

If you have Internet access, go to the home page for this textbook at **http://owen.swlearning.com**.

Select the **Chapter 3** section from the Additional Problem Sets, and complete the problems(s) that your instructor assigns.

> Go to
> http://owen.swlearning.
> com

Chapter 3 Case Problem 1: OCEAN VIEW FLOWERS

In Chapter 2, you created a new QuickBooks file for Ocean View Flowers, a wholesale flower distributor. Make a copy of that file and use that copy to enter the following transactions. Then print a standard balance sheet report as of January 31, 2004, a standard profit and loss report for the month of January and a transactions by date report for the month of January. (Make sure this report is printed in landscape orientation and with the "fit report to one page wide" check box checked.)

1   On January 4, 2004, the company sold common stock to Scott Coe, an investor, for $100,000 cash. The company deposited the check into the Union checking account.

2   On January 6, 2004, the company borrowed $50,000 from Santa Barbara Bank & Trust. The long-term note payable is due in three years with interest due annually at 10%. The company deposited the check into the Union checking account.

3   On January 8, 2004, the company temporarily invested $25,000 in a certificate of deposit due in 3 months, which will earn 7% per annum. Check 101, drawn on the Union checking account, was made payable to Prudent Investments, 100 Main Street, San Francisco, CA 95154. (***Hint:*** Create a short-term investments account to record this transaction.)

4   On January 11, 2004, the company purchased office equipment from Stateside Office Supplies, 324 G St., Lompoc, CA 93436, for $20,000 with Check 102. (***Hint:*** Be sure to create a main office equipment account as well as separate fixed asset cost and accumulated depreciation subaccounts.)

5   On January 12, 2004, the company purchased computer equipment from Gateway Computers, 100 Cowabunga Blvd., Sioux City, IA 23442, for $15,000 with Check 103. (***Hint:*** Be sure to create a main computer equipment account as well as separate fixed asset cost and accumulated depreciation subaccounts.)

6 On January 13, 2004, the company ordered the following new items from Brophy Bros. Farms, who specializes in daylilies. All daylilies are recorded as sales in a subaccount of Sales called Daylilies, which you will have to create.

Daylily	Quantity Ordered	Cost	Sales Price
Almond Puff	1,000	$12.00	$24.00
Calistoga Sun	2,000	$8.00	$16.00
Caribbean Pink Sands	500	$13.00	$26.00

7 On January 15, 2004, the company paid payroll. All employees worked the entire period. Kelly Gusland worked 60 hours, Margie Coe 75 hours. Checks were written using the Union Bank account starting with Check 104. (Do not print these checks.) Payroll taxes and withholding for employees during the period 1/1/04 through 1/15/04 are shown in Table 3.3.

8 On January 18, 2004, the company received its order in full from Brophy Bros. Farms and paid the bill with a Union Bank Check 109 in the amount of $34,500.

9 On January 20, 2004, the company paid Stateside Office Supplies for supplies expected to last over the next six months using Union Bank Check 110 for $1,500.

10 On January 22, 2004 the company recorded its first cash sale to Valley Florists in which they sold 100 Almond Puffs, 100 Calistoga

Table 3.3 Payroll Taxes and Withholding for Employees from January 1, 2004 through January 15, 2004

Tax or Withholding/Employee	Thomas	Gusland	Coe	McAninch	Comstock
California Employee Training Tax	2.92	.90	.90	2.50	2.08
Social Security Company	180.83	55.80	55.80	155.00	129.17
Medicare Company	42.29	13.05	13.05	36.25	30.21
Federal Unemployment	23.33	7.20	7.20	20.00	16.67
CA—Unemployment	1.46	.45	.45	1.25	1.04
Federal Withholding	−667.00	−118.00	−118.00	−402.00	−286.00
Social Security Employee	−180.83	−55.80	−55.80	−155.00	−129.17
Medicare Employee	−42.29	−13.05	−13.05	−36.25	−30.21
CA—Withholding	−192.30	−19.32	−9.32	−153.55	−61.86
CA—Disability Employee	−14.58	−4.50	−4.50	−12.50	−10.42
Check Amount	1,819.67	689.33	699.33	1,740.70	1,565.67

Suns, and 100 Caribbean Pink Sands. The $6,600 sale was deposited directly to Union Bank.

11 On January 25, 2004, the company recorded its second cash sale to Eastern Scents in which they sold 600 Almond Puffs and 300 Caribbean Pink Sands. The $22,200 sale was deposited directly to Union Bank.

12 On January 28, 2004, the company received an advance payment on account from FTD in the amount of $5,000, which was deposited directly to Union Bank account.

13 On January 29, 2004, the company wrote the three following checks:

Check #	Payee	Amount	Category
111	Hawaiian Farms	$3,000	Rent Expense
112	Edison Inc.	$500	Utilities Expense
113	GTE	$400	Telephone Expense

14 On January 29, 2004, the company paid payroll for the period ended January 31, 2004. All employees worked the entire period. Kelly Gusland worked 65 hours, Margie Coe worked 70 hours. Checks were written using the Union Bank account starting with Check 114. (Do not print these checks.) Payroll taxes and withholding for employees during the period 1/16/04 through 1/31/04 are shown in Table 3.4.

Table 3.4 Payroll Taxes and Withholding for Employees from January 16, 2004 through January 31, 2004

Tax or Withholding/Employee	Thomas	Gusland	Coe	McAninch	Comstock
California Employee Training Tax	2.91	.98	.84	2.50	2.09
Social Security Company	180.84	60.45	52.08	155.00	129.16
Medicare Company	42.29	14.14	12.18	36.25	30.21
Federal Unemployment	23.34	7.80	6.72	20.00	16.66
CA—Unemployment	1.46	.49	.42	1.25	1.04
Federal Withholding	−667.00	−130.00	−109.00	−402.00	−286.00
Social Security Employee	−180.84	−60.45	−52.08	−155.00	−129.16
Medicare Employee	−42.29	−14.14	−12.18	−36.25	−30.21
CA—Withholding	−192.30	−23.63	−8.12	−153.55	−61.86
CA—Disability Employee	−14.59	−4.88	−4.20	−12.50	−10.41
Check Amount	1,819.65	741.90	654.42	1,740.70	1,565.69

Chapter 3 Case Problem 2: JENNINGS & ASSOCIATES—Cash-Oriented Activities

In Chapter 2 you recreated Kelly Jennings' QuickBooks file as of January 1, 2004 because a virus had infected and corrupted her file. Later, an associate reentered all the transactions for January 2004. Now Kelly wants you to record the cash-oriented activities that occurred in February 2004.

Assignment:

Use the file named Kj03cp.qbw to record the following activities. (Remember, you will need to restore this file from your Data Files CD first.) Then, print a standard balance sheet as of February 29, 2004 and a standard income statement for the month of February 2004.

Financing Activities

1 On February 1, 2004, the company deposited cash contributions to First Valley Savings and Loan of $20,000 from Kelly Jennings (employee) and recorded them as capital stock.

2 On February 15, 2004, the company deposited cash contributions to First Valley Savings and Loan of $50,000 from a local investor (Frugal Investments) and recorded them as capital stock. (This is a new name and must be set up. Use the Quick Add feature.)

Investing Activities

3 On February 2, 2004, the company purchased $3,000 of computer equipment from Phoenix Computers, issuing Check 1001 out of a First Valley Savings and Loan checking account.

4 On February 4, 2004, the company invested $5,000 with Dean Witter, acquiring short-term investments (another current asset) and paying with Check 1002 out of a First Valley Savings and Loan checking account. (Use the Quick Add and Set Up features of QuickBooks to add a new name and new account.)

Operating Activities

5 On February 7, 2004, the company ordered ten rolls of high quality film from Rex's Film Supply with Purchase Order 4. Delivery is expected February 10, 2004.

6 On February 10, 2004, the company received the film ordered on Purchase Order 4 and paid the bill with Check 1003 from a First Valley Savings and Loan checking account. *Hint:* Use the Write Checks Activity to record this transaction and receive inventory on Purchase Order 4.

7 On February 12, 2004, the company issued Check 1004 for $75 to Bruno's Stationers to pay for office supplies purchased during the month. (Use Quick Add for this vendor.)

Tax or Withholding/Employee	Boudreau	Murphy	Jennings
Social Security Company	73.47	74.40	124.00
Medicare Company	17.18	17.40	29.00
Federal Unemployment	9.48	9.60	16.00
CA—Unemployment	35.55	36.00	60.00
Federal Withholding	−167.00	−140.00	−396.00
Social Security Employee	−73.47	−74.40	−124.00
Medicare Employee	−17.18	−17.40	−29.00
CA—Withholding	−36.23	−37.13	−59.38
CA—Disability Employee	−5.93	−6.00	−10.00
Check Amount	885.19	925.07	1,381.62

Table 3.5

Payroll Taxes and Withholding for Employees from February 1, 2004 through February 15, 2004

8 On February 10, 2004, the company completed a cash sale to Yaskar Farms (Sale No. 50001), for 35 hours of promotional campaign work, 5 rolls of high quality film, and 2 rolls of regular film. Yaskar wrote their Check 5677 to pay for this sale. The payment was deposited directly to the Union Bank checking account.

9 On February 22, 2004, the company completed a cash sale to AAA Appliance Co. (Sale No. 50002), who paid for this sale with their Check 1344. AAA was invoiced for 75 hours for a magazine layout and 40 rolls of regular film. The payment was deposited directly to the Union Bank checking account.

10 On February 26, 2004, the company received a $2,000 check (#2999) from Bob and Mary Schultz as an advance payment for services to be rendered next month. The amount is recorded as a credit to their receivable account. Deposit this check in the Union Bank checking account.

11 On February 15, 2004, and February 29, 2004, the company paid its employees. Kelly Jennings collected her salary based on an annual salary of $48,000. Diane Murphy worked 80 hours and 76 hours for the two pay periods, while Cheryl Boudreau worked 79 and 73 hours for the two pay periods. Payroll checks are paid from the Union Bank checking account. (*Hint:* Hourly employees use staff as their payroll item name.)

Tax or Withholding/Employee	Boudreau	Murphy	Jennings
Social Security Company	67.89	70.68	124.00
Medicare Company	15.88	16.53	29.00
Federal Unemployment	8.76	9.12	8.00
CA—Unemployment	32.85	34.20	30.00
Federal Withholding	−148.00	−131.00	−396.00
Social Security Employee	−67.89	−70.68	−124.00
Medicare Employee	−15.88	−16.53	−29.00
CA—Withholding	−30.83	−33.53	−59.38
CA—Disability Employee	−5.47	−5.70	−10.00
Check Amount	826.93	882.56	1,381.62

Table 3.6

Payroll Taxes and Withholding for Employees from February 16, 2004 through February 29, 2004

Comprehensive Problem 1

Use the following information to create a new company in QuickBooks. Then create and print the reports as requested below.

Sarah Duncan, CPA is starting her new practice at One Constellation Road, Vandenberg Village, CA 93436. She'll start effective 9/1/04 and use a calendar year for fiscal and tax purposes. She'll be using QuickBooks full payroll, inventory, and purchase order features. She does not collect sales tax for her services. She will perform both audit and individual income tax services for $150 per hour (**Hint:** Create two new items). Employees are paid monthly. Add the following transactions (**Note:** Be sure to enter these transactions in the proper date period):

1 On 9/1/04 she opened a business checking account at Union Bank with a $50,000 deposit as her investment in the business in exchange for common stock.

2 On 9/4/04 she purchased furniture and fixtures from Sam Snead, a prior tenant in her rented office space, for $4,000 using check #1001 from Union Bank. (Be sure to create a Furniture & Fixtures account and the related sub accounts of cost and accumulated depreciation).

3 On 9/5/04 she wrote check 1002 for $15,000 to Dean Witter for a short-term investment.

4 On 9/6/04 she wrote check 1003 to Wiser Realty as payment for the first and last months' rent and security deposit for $3,000 (one third for rent, one third for last month's rent recorded as prepaid rent, and one third for the security deposit.) (**Note:** Both the prepaid rent and security deposit are considered other non-current assets.)

5 On 9/7/04 she created purchase order #500 to purchase 50 tax guides from the AICPA for $250. She sells these to clients for $10 each and categorizes them as an inventory item. Income from the sale of this tax guide is reported in a Tax Guide income account. The cost of the guide when sold is reported in a Tax Guide Cost expense account.

6 On 9/8/04 Sarah completed 30 hours of tax consulting to Valley Medical Group, received payment by check, and deposited it to Union Bank.

7 On 9/11/04 she completed audit services for Pactuco, Inc. She received payment by check for 40 hours of work, and deposited it to Union Bank.

8 On 9/13/04 she received a payment in the amount of $5,000 from a new client, Celite Corporation, as an advance. She anticipates completing services for this client by the end of the year. She deposited the check into the Union Checking account.

9 On 9/15/04 she created purchase order #501 to purchase 100 audit guides from the AICPA for $5,000 ($50 each). She sells these to clients for $100 each and categorizes them as an inventory item. Income from the sale of this audit guide is reported in a Audit Guide

income account. The cost of the guide when sold is reported in a Audit Guide Cost expense account.

10 On 9/20/04 she borrowed $3,000 from Wells Fargo bank and then used the proceeds to purchase a copier from Xerox Corporation. She deposited the proceeds from the loan into Union Bank and then wrote check #1007 to record the equipment purchase. (Remember the subaccounts.)

11 On 9/25/04 the tax guides were delivered and paid for with check 1004.

12 On 9/28/04 Sarah completed 50 hours of audit consulting to Lompoc Hospital, received payment by check, and deposited it to Union Bank.

13 On 9/30/04, Sarah paid herself her $3,000 monthly salary and her secretary Bob Humphrey for 80 hours of work at $12 per hour. Sarah's SS# is 556-84-7464. She is single and subject to social security, FUTA, Medicare, SUI, and SDI taxes. Bob is married with one income and subject to social security, FUTA, Medicare, SUI, and SDI taxes. His SS# is 546-48-7897. Sarah's company deposits her state withholding and taxes to the Employment Development Department using her state taxpayer ID 01-90988. Sarah and Bob are subject to the state's employment training tax.

	Sarah Duncan	Bob Humphrey
Federal withholding	$200.00	$0.00
Social security employee	$186.00	$59.52
Social security employer	$186.00	$59.52
Medicare employee	$43.50	$13.92
Medicare employer	$43.50	$13.92
CA—withholding	$0.00	$0.00
CA—disability employee	$27.00	$8.64
CA—training tax	$3.00	$0.96
Federal unemployment	$24.00	$7.68
CA—unemployment	$30.00	$9.60

Create and print the following reports for September 2004.

1 Custom Transaction Detail Report by date (in landscape orientation)

2 Standard balance sheet as of 9/30/04, with a % of column, and a right page layout alignment

3 Standard profit and loss statement for the month ended 9/30/04, with a % of Income column, and a right page layout alignment

4 Statement of cash flows for the month ended 9/30/04 and a right page layout alignment

Comprehensive Problem 2

Pacific Brew Inc. was incorporated January 1, 2006 upon the issuance of 50,000 shares of $1 par value common stock for $50,000. Located at 500 West Ocean, Arcata, California, 95521, Michael Patrick, president, oversees this beer distributor's operations. The company will have a calendar fiscal year and has a federal employer id number of 77-1357465 and plans to use QuickBooks inventory, purchase orders, and payroll features. The items the company intends to carry in inventory, the suppliers it purchases from, and the customers lined up whose billing and shipping addresses are the same are listed below.

In addition to distributing beer, Pacific Brew also provides consulting services to customers on bar operations, menu plans, and beverage selection. These services are billed out to customers at the rate of $85 per hour and recorded in an income account called consulting revenue. (*Hint*: You'll need to create a service type item called consulting as item 100 and a consulting revenue account.)

Pacific has two other employees, as shown below. The company's unemployment rate is 3% and it uses only two payroll items for wages: salary—regular, and wages—regular. Federal withholding, unemployment, social security, and medicare are paid to the U.S. Treasury while California withholding, unemployment, employee disability, and employee training tax are paid to the EDD (Employment Development Department). Payroll is paid semi-monthly.

Vendors

Name	Mad River	Lost Coast	JD Salinger	Humboldt
Address	195 Taylor Way	123 West Third St.	101 Market St.	865 10th St.
City	Blue Lake	Eureka	San Francisco	Arcata
State	CA	CA	CA	CA
Zip	95525	95501	94102	95521
Phone	707-555-4151	707-555-4484	707-555-6141	707-555-2739

Inventory Items

Name/#	Description	Cost	Price
302	Mad River Pale Ale	5.00	6.00
303	Mad River Stout	6.00	7.00
304	Mad River Amber Ale	4.00	5.00
305	Mad River Porter	5.50	6.50
402	Lost Coast Pale Ale	5.25	6.25
403	Lost Coast Stout	6.25	7.25
404	Lost Coast Amber Ale	4.25	5.25
502	Humboldt Pale Ale	5.50	6.50
506	Humboldt IPA	6.50	7.50
507	Humboldt Red Nectar	7.00	8.00

Customers

Name	Avalon Bistro	Hole in the Wall	Ocean Grove
Address	1080 3rd St	590 G St.	570 Ewing St.
City	Arcata	Arcata	Trinidad
State	CA	CA	CA
Zip	95521	95521	95570
Phone	707-555-0500	707-555-7407	707-555-5431

Name	River House	Michael's Brew House	Bon Jovi's
Address	222 Weller St.	2198 Union St.	4257 Petaluma Hill
City	Petaluma	San Francisco	Santa Rosa
State	CA	CA	CA
Zip	95404	94123	95404
Phone	707-555-0123	707-555-9874	707-555-5634

Employees

Name	Michael Patrick	Shawn Lopez	Emilio Duarte
Address	333 Spring Rd.	234 University Dr.	23 Palm Dr. #23
City	Arcata	Arcata	Arcata
State	CA	CA	CA
Zip	95521	95521	95521
Phone	707-555-9847	707-555-1297	707-555-6655
SS#	655-85-1253	702-54-8746	012-58-4654
Earnings	Salary—$50,000	Wages—$12/hour	Wages—$11/hour
Filing Status	Married	Single	Single

Chronological List of Business Transactions

Date	Transaction
1/03/06	Sold 50,000 shares of $1 par value common stock for $50,000 cash to various shareholders. Deposited these funds into a Wells Fargo checking account.
1/04/06	Using purchase order 1001, ordered 500 each of item 302, 303, 304, and 305 for immediate delivery, terms: due on receipt, from Mad River. (Note: Use QuickBooks Help to customize the purchase order so that the terms of the sale are specified on both the screen and print versions of the purchase order. Always save the terms for the vendor.)
1/04/06	Using purchase order 1002, ordered 400 each of item 502, 506, and 507 for immediate delivery, terms: due on receipt, from Humboldt.
1/05/06	Using purchase order 1003, ordered 300 each of item 402, 403, and 404 for immediate delivery on 30-day terms, from Lost Coast.

1/05/06 Rented a warehouse from JD Salinger, landlord, for $2,500 per month by paying first and last month's rent with Wells Fargo check 101 for $5,000.

1/06/06 Purchased shelving, desks, and office equipment from JD Salinger for $8,000 with Wells Fargo check 102. (Shelving and desks of $5,000 should be classified as Furniture/Fixtures:Cost while the office equipment of $3,000 should be classified as Equipment:Cost.)

1/09/06 Invested $30,000 in a short-term investment with Schwab Investments with Wells Fargo check 103.

1/10/06 Borrowed $40,000 from Wells Fargo Bank as a long-term note payable due in 3 years. The money was deposited into the company's Wells Fargo account.

1/10/06 Purchased several computer systems and printers (classified as Equipment:Cost). Check 104 was written for $10,200 to West Coast Computer Supply to purchase the systems.

1/11/06 Received and paid for items on purchase order 1001 to Mad River with check 105 for $10,250.

1/11/06 Provided 50 hours of consulting services on order (5001) to Michael's Brew House. Payment of $4,250 was deposited into Wells Fargo Bank that same day.

1/12/06 Received and paid for items on purchase order 1002 to Humboldt with check 106 for $7,600.

1/13/06 Received and shipped an order (5002) to Bon Jovi's for 25 units of item 305, 30 units of item 506, and 50 units of item 507. Payment of $787.50 was deposited into Wells Fargo Bank that same day.

1/13/06 Provided 60 hours of consulting services on order (5003) to River House Payment of $5,100 was deposited into Wells Fargo Bank that same day.

1/16/06 Received and shipped an order (5004) to Ocean Grove for 30 units of item 304, 40 units of item 302, and 50 units of item 502. Payment of $715 was deposited into Wells Fargo Bank that same day.

1/16/06 Paid employees. Duarte worked 80 hours and Lopez worked 75 hours during the period. See tax information in the following table.

1/16/06 Received and shipped an order (5005) to Avalon Bistro for 40 units of item 302, 50 units of item 507, and 35 units of item 506. Payment of $902.50 was deposited into Wells Fargo Bank that same day.

1/16/06 Received and shipped an order (5006) to Michael's Brew House for 100 each of item 302, 305, and 506. Payment of $2,000 was deposited into Wells Fargo Bank that same day.

Pay/Tax/withholding	Duarte	Lopez	Partick
Gross Pay	$880.00	$900.00	$2,083.33
Federal Withholding	120.56	123.30	285.42
Social security employee	54.56	55.80	129.17
Medicare employee	12.76	13.05	30.21
CA—withholding	48.40	49.50	114.58
CA—disability	4.40	4.50	10.42
CA—employment training tax	0.88	0.90	2.08
Social security company	54.56	55.80	129.17
Medicare company	12.76	13.05	30.21
Federal unemployment	7.04	7.20	16.67
CA—unemployment company	26.40	27.00	62.50
Check amount	639.32	653.85	1,513.53

Requirements

1. Create a QuickBooks file for Pacific Brew without using the Interview and save the file as Brew.qbw.

2. Add vendors, inventory items, customers, and employees first.

3. Record business transactions in chronological order (remember dates are in the month of January 2006).

4. After recording the transactions in item 3, create and print the following lists:
   a. Chart of accounts
   b. Customer:Job list
   c. Employee list
   d. Item list
   e. Vendor list

5. Create and print the following reports:
   a. Custom transaction detail report by date for the period 1/1/06 through 1/16/06 (in landscape orientation). Memorize this report for later use.
   b. Standard balance sheet as of 1/16/06, with a left page layout alignment. Memorize this report for later use.
   c. Standard profit and loss statement for the period 1/6/06 through 1/16/06, with a % of Income column, and a left page alignment. Memorize this report for later use.
   d. Statement of cash flows for the period 1/1/06 through 1/16/06, with a left page layout alignment. Memorize this report for later use.

Additional Business Activities

In this chapter you will:

- Record transactions classified as financing activities, such as borrowing from banks and repaying previous loans

- Record transactions classified as investing activities, such as selling short-term investments

- Record transactions classified as operating activities, such as purchasing inventory on account and selling that inventory on account

- Record transactions classified as non-cash investing and financing activities, such as purchasing equipment with long-term debt

CASE: PHOENIX SYSTEMS CONSULTING, INC.

. . . .

At your next meeting with Karen, you explain to her that Phoenix Systems engaged in financing, investing, and operating activities during the first three months of 2003 in addition to those already discussed (in Chapter 3). Karen suggests that you look at these additional transactions in the same order as before—financing, investing, and operating.

RECORDING ADDITIONAL FINANCING ACTIVITIES

. . . .

You tell Karen that Phoenix often engages in financing activities such as borrowing funds and paying back previous loans. You suggest looking at some loan activity that took place during the quarter. For example, in January Phoenix borrowed $12,500 from the Bank of Cupertino. Then in March Phoenix repaid $10,500 of this loan by writing a check.

To record the deposit:

1 Open Phnx04.qbw. (Remember to restore this file from your Data Files CD first.)

2 Click **Banking** and then click **Make Deposits**.

3 Before the Make Deposits window appears, a Payments to Deposit window is shown. QuickBooks will prompt you to choose a payment if any payment had been recorded but not yet deposited. The payment shown in this window will be deposited later. For now click **Cancel**.

4 Select **Bank of Cupertino** in the Deposit To edit box.

5 Enter the Date, Received From, Amount, and From Account information as shown in Figure 4.1 to record the deposit.

Figure 4.1

The Make Deposits Window

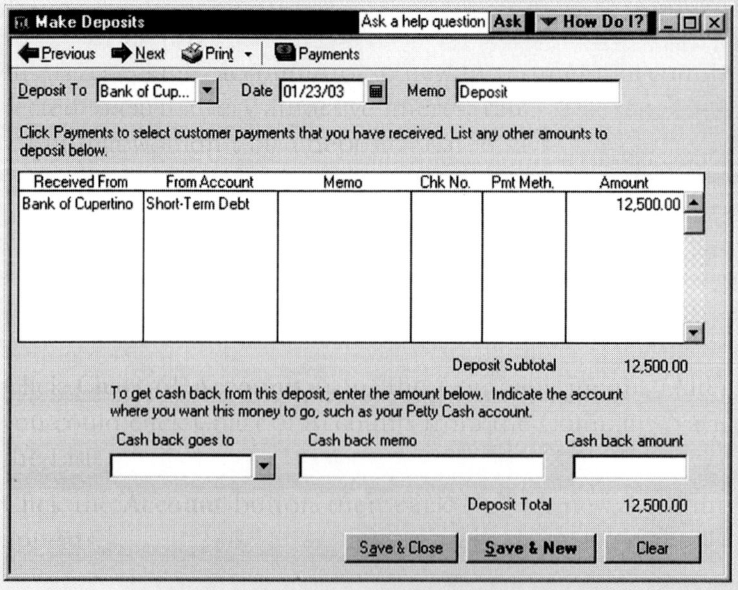

6 Click **Save & Close** to record the deposit.

A couple of months later, Phoenix repaid part of the loan. You show Karen how to record the repayment.

To record repayment:

1 Click **Banking** then click **Write Checks**.

2 Enter the check number, **1024**, date, **3/24/03**, payee, **Bank of Cupertino**, amount, **10,500**, and account, **Short-Term Debt**, as shown in Figure 4.2

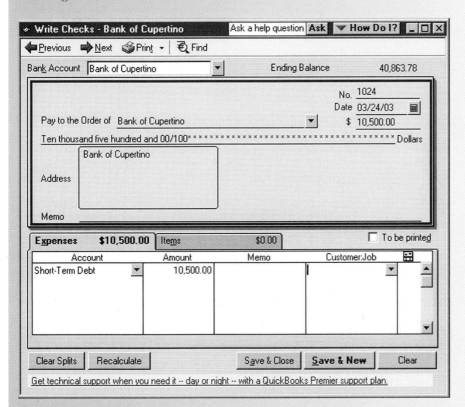

Figure 4.2
The Write Checks Window

3 Click **Save & Close** to record the check.

Karen asks how you'd record a loan in QuickBooks if you purchase new equipment by borrowing funds—in other words a non-cash financing and investing activity.

"We'll get to that in a minute," you reply. "First let's cover some additional cash-oriented activities."

RECORDING ADDITIONAL INVESTING ACTIVITIES

You know from your accounting course that investing activities generally result in the acquisition of non-current assets from buying or selling investment securities or productive equipment. During the first quarter of 2003, Phoenix Systems engaged in two particular investing activities that you want to show Karen—the company transferred additional funds from the Bank of Cupertino to its short-term investments account, and it sold previously purchased investment securities for a profit.

Recall from Chapter 3 that Phoenix transferred $8,000 from its checking account to its Short-term Investments account on January 10. On February 24, Phoenix transfers $7,000 more to this account.

To record this additional transfer:

1 Click **Company** then click **Chart of Accounts**.

2 Click **Short-term Investments** in the Chart of Accounts window, then click **Activities**, then click **Use Register** to reveal the Short-term Investments register. Alternately, you could double-click on the words "Short-term Investments."

3 Make sure the 1-Line checkbox is checked—found in the lower-left portion of the Register window. Your screen should look like Figure 4.3 below.

4 Enter the date, the account, and the deposit information as shown in Figure 4.3. Then click **Record** to record the $7,000 deposit.

Figure 4.3

The Short-Term Investment Register

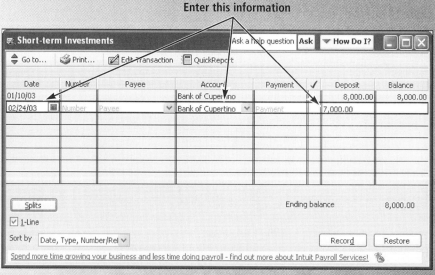

5 Close the Short-term Investments Register window.

6 Close the Chart of Accounts window.

The investment sold amounted to $32,000 of the $40,000 and was a portion of the investment that Phoenix invested in Sky Investments on January 13. The cash proceeds from the sale of this investment were $35,000, which, as you will see, means that Phoenix earned a $3,000 profit.

To record the sale of an investment and the resulting deposit of funds:

1 Click **Banking** and then **Make Deposits**.

2 Before the Make Deposits window appears, a Payments to Deposit window is shown. For now click **Cancel**.

3 Select **Bank of Cupertino** in the Deposit To edit box. Then enter the date and then the receipt of $35,000—$32,000 from the original investment and a profit of $3,000—as shown in Figure 4.4.

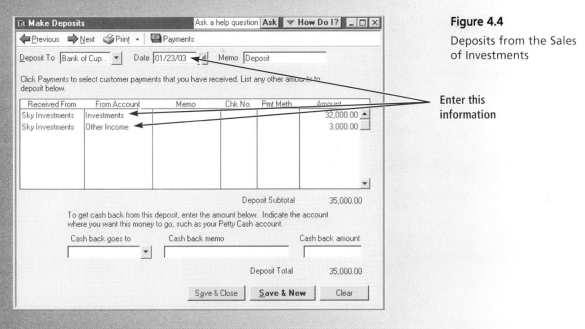

Figure 4.4

Deposits from the Sales of Investments

Enter this information

4 Click **Save & Close** to record this deposit.

RECORDING ADDITIONAL OPERATING ACTIVITIES

Now that you've seen how QuickBooks handles additional financing and investing activities, you want to show Karen how QuickBooks records invoices when sales are recorded before the receipt of cash; in other words—sales on account. You'll also show her inventory purchases on account.

As you've seen earlier, Phoenix uses purchase orders to help manage its inventory. These are used even if purchases are made on account.

To create a purchase order for merchandise purchased on account:

1 Click **Vendors**, then **Create Purchase Orders.**

2 Enter the Vendor, Date, PO Number, Item, and Quantity information as shown in Figure 4.5. QuickBooks will automatically fill in the Description, Rate, and Amount.

Figure 4.5
Purchase Order 3009

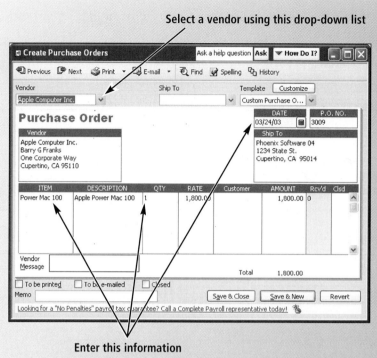

Select a vendor using this drop-down list

Enter this information

3 Click **Save & Close** to record the purchase.

You must also use a purchase order when inventory is received along with a bill requesting payment.

To record the receipt of inventory ordered and the related bill:

1 Click **Vendors**, then **Receive Items and Enter Bill**.

2 Select **Apple Computer** from the drop-down Vendor list in the Enter Bills window.

3 Since open purchase orders exist for this vendor, the Open PO's Exist window appears. See Figure 4.6. Click **Yes**.

Figure 4.6
Open PO Warning

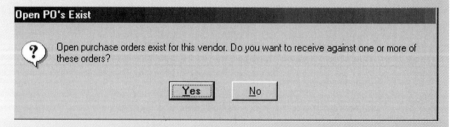

4 Click once near the **3/24/03** date in the Open Purchase Orders window to place a check on the PO No. 3009 line, then click **OK**.

5 The corresponding bill appears containing all the appropriate information already filled in. But the Terms line indicates that payment is due upon receipt. Change the Terms by selecting **Net 30** from the drop-down Terms list and, as you do, note that the Bill Due date changes accordingly. See Figure 4.7.

6 Click **Save & Close** to record the receipt of inventory and enter the bill.

7 Since you changed the terms for Apple Computer, QuickBooks displays a Name Information Changed window. Click **No** to maintain the old terms.

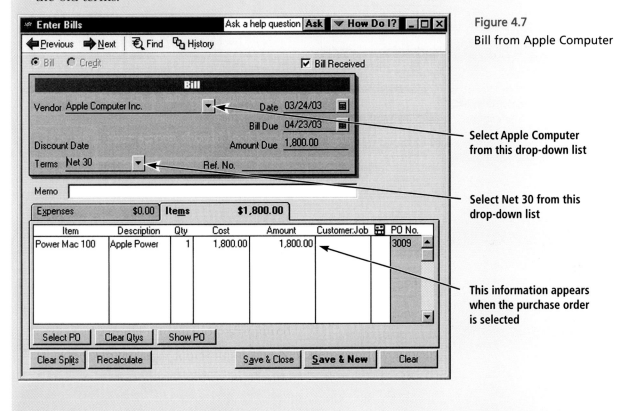

Figure 4.7
Bill from Apple Computer

Select Apple Computer from this drop-down list

Select Net 30 from this drop-down list

This information appears when the purchase order is selected

"Cash sales are the best!" Casey exclaims as he enters the room.

"Not necessarily," Karen responds. "Phoenix might be losing quality customers if you're not offering credit terms."

"Of course, you're right," Casey quickly agrees. "I was just kidding. We often sell on credit to customers who've demonstrated credit worthiness. As long as we keep good records and monitor tardy customers, we don't take too much of a risk extending credit. Show her some of our credit sales," Casey suggests.

To record credit sales:

1 Click **Customers**, then **Create Invoices**.

2 Change the custom template from Intuit Service Invoice to Intuit Professional Invoice.

3 Enter the Customer, Date, Invoice Number, the two Items sold, and their respective Quantities as shown in Figure 4.8. QuickBooks will automatically enter the other information and calculate the total.

Figure 4.8
Invoice Number 20001

Choose a customer from this drop-down list

Click here to change this to a Professional Invoice

Enter this information

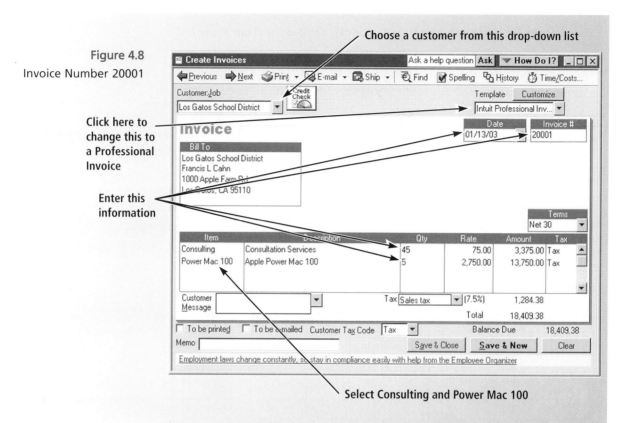

Select Consulting and Power Mac 100

4 Click **Save & New**.

5 The credit limit for Los Gatos is $10,000, and this invoice exceeds that amount. Since this is just a practice session for Karen, you decide to click **Yes** to allow the sale.

6 You decide to give Karen more practice. Enter the following two invoices:

Customer	Date	Invoice #	Terms	Item	Quantity
St. Johns	1/20/03	20002	Net 15	Maintenance	100
Netscape	3/31/03	20007	2% 10 Net 30	Maintenance	60

7 Click **Save & Close** to enter the last invoice and close the Create Invoices window.

"I'm not an accountant," Casey says, "but don't you have to wait until the customer pays before recording this sale?"

"No," replies Karen, "because on the accrual basis—which Phoenix uses—revenue is recognized when Phoenix delivers the product or performs the service."

"What happens when the customer pays us?" asks Casey.

"Then we use the Receive Payments activity," you explain. "I'll show you."

To record receipt of payment from previously recorded sales:

1 Click **Customers**, then **Receive Payments**. You might receive the Merchant Account Service message. Read and click on "Do not display this message in the future," or click either Yes or No.

2 On February 14, 2003, Phoenix received payments from two customers. The first was from the Los Gatos School District for $18,409.38 to pay Invoice 20001. Carefully enter the appropriate information for this customer payment as shown in Figure 4.9. Be sure to click the **"Group with other undeposited funds"** option button. Then click **Save & New** to record this receipt.

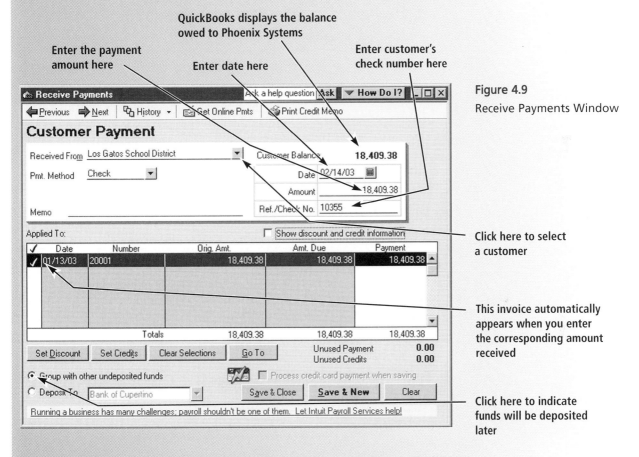

Figure 4.9
Receive Payments Window

3 The second payment received was $5,375 from St. Johns Hospital for Invoice 20002 with their Check 89544. This payment was also grouped with other undeposited funds. Carefully enter the appropriate information in the Receive Payments window. Then click **Save & Close**.

"When are these funds deposited?" asks Karen.

"In this case a deposit was made on February 16, 2003," you reply. "Casey deposited all receipts received that week. Let me show you how QuickBooks handles deposits of previously recorded receipts."

To record the deposit of previously recorded receipts:

1 Click **Banking**, then **Make Deposits**. The Payments to Deposit Window appears. See Figure 4.10.

When all payments are selected, check marks appear here

Figure 4.10
Receive Payments Window

Click here to select all payments

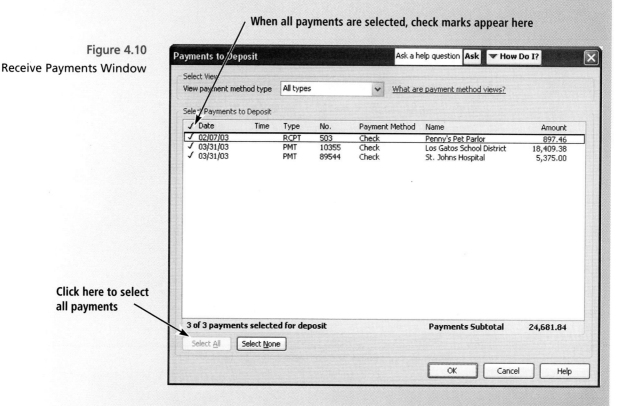

2 Three receipts are shown in the Payments to Deposit window. Click **Select All** to select all receipts for deposit, then click **OK**. The Make Deposits window appears. See Figure 4.11.

Change the date here

Figure 4.11

Deposits to Be Made on
February 16, 2003

These names appear automatically

The original payments were recorded to undeposited funds

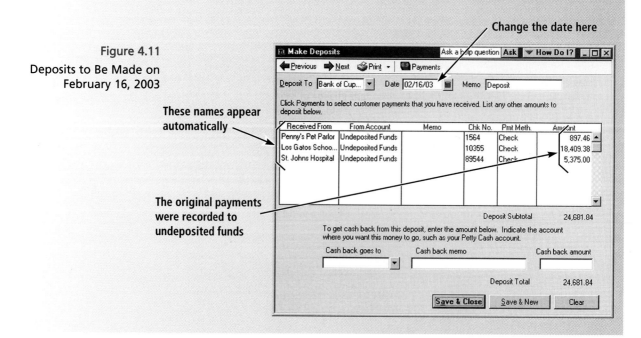

3 Change the date in the Make Deposits window to 02/16/03, then click Save & Close to record the deposit.

"Does Phoenix always immediately pay cash for expenses?" asks Karen.

"No, not since we've been able to establish credit with our vendors and they've extended us terms," you answer. "We record our bills during the month as they come in, and then we pay them at the end of each month. Let me show you how we recorded some bills in January."

To record some January bills:

1 Click **Vendors**, then **Enter Bills**. The Enter Bills window appears.

2 Enter **GTE** in the Vendor section of the Enter Bills window, then press the **Tab** key.

3 Since GTE is a new vendor, the Vendor Not Found window appears. Click **Set Up**.

4 Enter the Company Name, **GTE**, and the address, **3899 Stevens Creek #230, Cupertino, CA 95110**, in the Address Info tab section of the New Vendor window. Then click the **Additional Info** tab and enter the Terms, **Net 15**.

5 Click **OK** to enter this new vendor information.

6 Enter the additional GTE bill information as shown in Figure 4.12, then click **Save & New**.

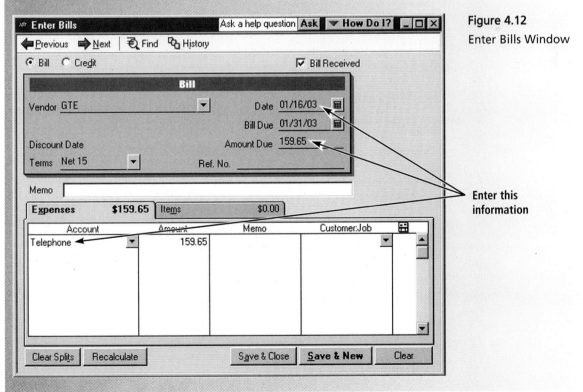

Figure 4.12
Enter Bills Window

7 You decide to show Karen two additional bills which were received on the same day. Enter the following bills.

Vendor	Date	Amount	Terms	Expense
PG&E *	1/16/03	$230.00	Net 15	Utilities: Gas and Electric
Office Mart	1/16/03	$560.00	Net 15	Office Supplies

*Company Name—Pacific Gas & Electric, Address—9100 Town Center Dr., Cupertino, CA 95110, Terms—Net 15

8 Click **Save & Close** after you enter both bills.

You then explain to Karen that, at the end of the month, all of these bills were paid. To pay bills using QuickBooks, you use the Pay Bills activity.

To pay the January bills and print checks:

1 Click **Vendors**, then **Pay Bills**.

2 Change the Show bills due on or before date to **1/31/03**.

3 In the Payment Method box, choose "**Check**" and "**To be printed**" and make sure the correct bank account is showing. See Figure 4.13. Then press the **Tab** key.

Click here to show all bills due on or before the specified date

Figure 4.13

Pay Bills Window

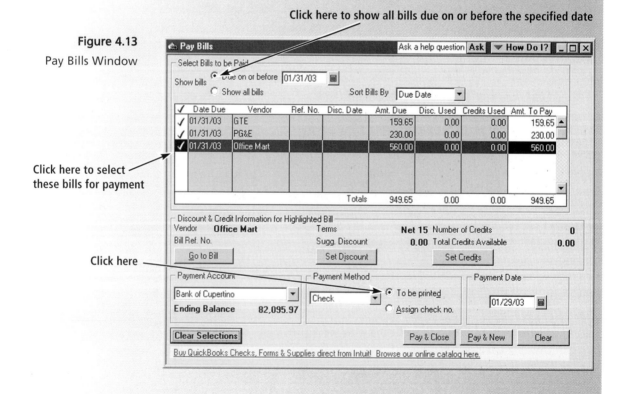

Click here to select these bills for payment

Click here

4 Select the GTE, PG&E, and Office Mart bills to pay by clicking once next to each vendor's date due in the Check column as shown. Enter payment date, 1/29/03. Then click Pay & Close.

5 Click File, click Print Forms, click Checks.

6 Change the First Check Number to 1007 as shown in Figure 4.14, then click OK.

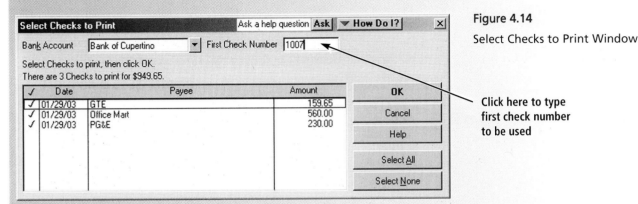

Figure 4.14

Select Checks to Print Window

Click here to type first check number to be used

7 Click on **Print company name and address** in the Print checks window. Note that all the checks that appear are selected for payment.

8 Don't print the checks at this time. Instead, close all open windows.

You've now explained and demonstrated to Karen the financing, investing, and operating activities that are typical at Phoenix Systems. But there remains one transaction that you haven't yet shown her—one that is classified as a non-cash investing and financing activity. This transaction, you both believe, is just as important as the cash transactions.

RECORDING NON-CASH INVESTING AND FINANCING ACTIVITIES

Although non-cash investing and financing activities do not affect the cash position of a company, they do have an impact on a firm's financial position. One example of such an activity was Phoenix's purchase of computer equipment in March of 2003 that was completely financed with long-term debt. You explain the nature of this transaction to Karen and now demonstrate how it was recorded.

To record the purchase of equipment with long-term debt:

1 Click **Company**, then **Chart of Accounts**.

2 Click to select the **Computer Equipment:Cost** account in the Chart of Accounts window, then click **Activities**, then click **Use Register**. Alternately, you could double-click on "Computer Equipment:Cost."

3 Click in the **1-Line** checkbox to make columns easier to input information.

4 Fill in the information for the second entry in this register as shown in Figure 4.15: the Date, **03/31/03**, the Payee, **IBM**, the Account, **Long-Term Debt**, and the Increase, **$15,000**. Then click **Record** to record the transaction.

5 Close all windows.

This is a previously recorded transaction

Figure 4.15

The Computer Equipment: Cost Register Window

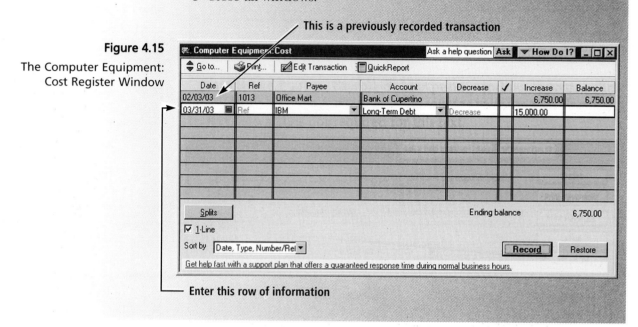

Enter this row of information

END NOTE

. . . .

You've now helped Karen understand even more of QuickBooks's features, including how to record the repayment of loans, sale of investments, receipt of inventory items and related bills, credit sales, and the receipt of payments on account.

practice

Chapter 4 Questions

1 Describe two ways you can create purchase orders in QuickBooks.

2 How do you record the receipt of inventory and bills in QuickBooks, and what information is required?

3 How do you access vendor names from the Enter Bills window?

4 What payment terms are available in QuickBooks when entering bills?

5 Consider this statement: "QuickBooks records revenue when an invoice is generated even though cash has not been received." Is this practice acceptable? Why or why not?

6 Identify the QuickBooks activity required to record payments received on account.

7 Should payments received on account be deposited immediately? If yes, why? If no, what account is increased to record these receipts?

8 How does the QuickBooks software respond if a bill is entered with a vendor name not included on the vendor list?

9 What are non-cash investing and financing activities, and how are they recorded in QuickBooks?

10 Describe the QuickBooks process for printing checks.

Chapter 4 Assignments

1 *Adding More Information to Phoenix Systems, Inc.*

For this assignment use Phnx04cp.qbw. (Remember to restore this file from your Data Files CD first.) Add the following financing, investing, and operating activities. Then create a standard balance sheet as of March 31, 2003 and a standard income statement for the period January 1, 2003 through March 31, 2003.

Add the following financing activities:

a. On March 31, 2003, Phoenix borrows $40,000 from the Bank of Sedona (because this is a new name, use Quick Add and add as name type: Other). The loan is due September 30, 2003, with interest at 10%. These funds are deposited into the Bank of Cupertino account.

b. On March 28, 2003, Phoenix pays New Endeavors $500 as partial repayment of long-term debt (no interest) with Check 1031.

Add the following investing activities:

c. On February 25, 2003, Phoenix sells $6,000 of their investment with Sky Investments for $5,000, depositing the funds in the

Bank of Cupertino account, thereby incurring a $1,000 investment loss. (Record as a reduction in Other Income similar to the text example where income was earned. In this case, however, the loss is entered as a negative number. An alternative approach is to record the loss as an increase in Other Expense.)

d.   On January 17, 2003, Phoenix transfers $2,000 from the Short-term Investments account to the Bank of Cupertino checking account.

Add the following operating activities:

e.   On January 24, 2003, Phoenix generates Purchase Order 3005 to IBM to purchase three IBM Pentium Plus computers at a cost of $7,500 each. (**Note:** This item has already been set up in your QuickBooks data file.)

f.   On February 6, 2003, the computers ordered under Purchase Order 3005 are received and a bill is recorded.

g.   Phoenix creates the following invoices. Notice how QuickBooks warns you that the Los Gatos School District has exceeded its credit limit. When this warning appears, click **Yes**. (If terms change for any customer, accept the change as permanent.)

Date	Invoice #	Customer	Customer PO #	Terms	Product	Qty
2/19/03	20003	Netscape	542215	2% 10 Net 30	586-160	5
					Consultation	4
					Installation	10
3/26/03	20006	Los Gatos School District	none	Net 30	IBM Pentium	3
					Consultation	5
3/31/03	20008	Boston Stores	none	Net 15	Monthly Maintenance	30

h.   On February 18, 2003, Phoenix receives the following bills: (If terms change for any vendor, accept the change as permanent.)

Vendor	Operating Expense	Terms	Amount
E-Max Realty	Rent	Net 15	800.00
GTE	Telephone	Net 15	92.56
Office Mart	Office supplies	Net 15	32.56
PG&E	Utilities: Gas and Electric	Net 15	179.00

i.   On February 27, 2003, Phoenix pays the following bills: (**Hint:** Use a two-step process; that is, pay the bills first, then print checks. Also be sure to click the Show All Bills box in the Pay Bills window.)

Vendor	Check #	Amount
Computer Wholesale	1016	15,199.75
E-Max Realty	1017	800.00
GTE	1018	92.56
Office Mart	1019	32.56
PG&E	1020	179.00

j. Phoenix receives payments (checks) from customers as follows: (*Note:* Deposits for each payment were made to the Bank of Cupertino on the day following the payment date.)

Date	Customer	Apply to Invoice #	Amount
3/19/03	Netscape	20003	10,250.00
3/19/03	St. Johns Hospital	20005	500.00
3/27/03	Los Gatos School Dist.	20006	5,000.00

k. Phoenix has one non-cash investing and financing activity on March 31, 2003 in which computer equipment is acquired from Apple Computer Inc. in exchange for a long-term note payable of $7,000 due in two years.

2   *Adding More Information: Central Coast Cellular*

In Chapter 3, you added some business transactions to your QuickBooks file for Central Coast Cellular (CCC), a cellular phone sales, rental, and consulting company. Make a copy of that file in Windows Explorer, name the file CCC4, and use that file to enter the following transactions.

a. On January 20, 2003 the company received a shipment of phones from Nokia on purchase order 102. Items were received and a bill recorded due in 30 days.

b. On January 21, 2003 the company invoiced the City of San Luis Obispo, using product invoice #10001 for 20 Nokia 8290 phones, 15 Nokia 8890 phones, 30 hours of consulting time, and 35 commissions earned on cell phone contacts (cell phone contracts are a new service item called Commissions, valued at $50 per contract, and recorded to a revenue account titled Commissions).

c. On January 22, 2003 the company purchased equipment in the amount of $95,000 cash from Kyle Equipment, Inc. using check #3008.

d. On January 24, 2003 the company paid the Ericsson bill of $6,500 with check #3009.

e. On January 31, 2003 the company paid semi-monthly payroll starting with check #3010 for the period January 16 to January 31, 2003. Megan Paulson worked 85 hours during the period. Payroll tax information is shown in Table 4.1.

f. Print the following:
    * Profit & Loss Standard report for the month of January 2003
    * Balance Sheet Standard as of January 31, 2003
    * Custom Transaction Detail Report for the period January 20 through January 31, 2003

3   *Using the South-Western Home Page for More Assignments or Cases*

If you have Internet access, go to the home page for this textbook at **http://owen.swlearning.com**.

Go to
http://owen.swlearning.com

http://

Table 4.1
Payroll Information for
Central Coast Cellular

Tax or Withholding/Employee	Rodriguez	Bruner	Paulson
Gross Pay	$ 2,000.00	$ 1,500.00	$1,020.00
California Employee Training Tax	$ 2.00	$ 1.50	$ 1.02
Social Security Company	$ 124.00	$ 93.00	$ 63.24
Medicare Company	$ 29.00	$ 21.75	$ 14.79
Federal Unemployment	$ 6.40	$ 4.80	$ 3.26
CA—Unemployment	$ 24.00	$ 18.00	$ 12.24
Federal Withholding	$ –300.00	$ –225.00	$ –153.00
Social Security Employee	$ –124.00	$ –93.00	$ –63.24
Medicare Employee	$ –29.00	$ –21.75	$ –14.79
CA—Withholding	$ –100.00	$ –75.00	$ –51.00
CA—Disability Employee	$ –10.00	$ –7.50	$ –5.10
Check Amount	$ 1,437.00	$ 1,077.75	$ 732.87

Select the **Chapter 4** section from the Additional Problem Sets and complete the problem(s) that your instructor assigns.

Chapter 4 Case Problem 1: OCEAN VIEW FLOWERS

In Chapter 3, you modified your QuickBooks file for Ocean View Flowers, a wholesale flower distributor. Make a copy of that file and use that copy to enter the following transactions. Then print a Standard Balance Sheet report as of February 29, 2004, a Standard Profit and Loss report for the month of February and a Transactions By Date report for the month of February. (Make sure this report is printed in landscape orientation and with the "fit report to one page wide" checkbox checked.)

1 On February 1, 2004, the company repaid a portion of the long-term debt it borrowed from Santa Barbara Bank & Trust with Union Bank Check 119 in the amount of $1,000. (All of this payment was principal, none was interest.)

2 On February 3, 2004, the company prepaid a one year liability insurance policy to State Farm Insurance with Union Bank Check 120 in the amount of $2,500. (The transaction was properly recorded to Prepaid Insurance, another current asset account.)

3 On February 5, 2004, the company created Purchase Order 2 to Vordale Flowers for the following items to be purchased on terms Net 30. All anthuriums are recorded as sales in a subaccount of Sales called Anthuriums, which you will have to create.

Anthuriums	Quantity Ordered	Cost	Sales Price
Bright Red	700	$20.00	$35.00
Peach	800	$22.00	$40.00
White	600	$27.00	$50.00

4 On February 9, 2004, the company cashed in $5,000 of their $25,000 short-term investment early and received $5,200, which was deposited into the Union Bank account. The $200 difference represents interest revenue. (Be sure to change the company's interest income account title to interest revenue before entering this transaction.)

5 On February 12, 2004, the company received the following bills. (Accept any terms changes and add any new vendors necessary.)

Vendor	Amount	Terms	Expense
GTE	$250	Net 15	Telephone
Edison	$300	Net 15	Utilities
FlowerMart	$60	Net 30	Subscriptions

6 On February 15, 2004, the company paid payroll. All employees worked the entire period. Kelly Gusland worked 62 hours, Margie Coe worked 72 hours. Checks were written using the Union Bank account starting with Check 121. (Do not print these checks.) Payroll taxes and withholding for employees is shown in Table 4.2.

7 On February 18, 2004, the company received items and entered the bill from Purchase Order 2 to Vordale Flowers on terms Net 30.

8 On February 22, 2004, the company created invoices to customers as follows: (If terms change, accept them as permanent.)

Customer	Invoice #	Item Sold	Total Quantity	Terms	Invoice
Latin Ladies	10001	Calistoga Sun Daylilies	400	Net 15	$9,000
		Caribbean Pink Sands	100		
California Beauties	10002	Anthuriums–White	500	2/10 Net 30	$25,000
FTD	10003	Anthuriums–Bright Red	300	Net 30	$10,500

Table 4.2 Payroll Taxes and Withholding for Employees from February 1, 2004 through February 15, 2004

Tax or Withholding/Employee	Thomas	Gusland	Coe	McAninch	Comstock
California Employee Training Tax	1.17	.93	.86	2.00	2.08
Social Security Company	180.83	57.66	53.57	155.00	129.17
Medicare Company	42.30	13.48	12.53	36.25	30.20
Federal Unemployment	9.33	7.44	6.91	16.00	16.67
CA—Unemployment	.58	.46	.43	1.00	1.05
Federal Withholding	–667.00	–123.00	–113.00	–402.00	–286.00
Social Security Employee	–180.83	–57.66	–53.57	–155.00	–129.17
Medicare Employee	–42.30	–13.48	–12.53	–36.25	–30.20
CA—Withholding	–192.30	–20.93	–8.60	–153.55	–61.86
CA—Disability Employee	–14.58	–4.65	–4.32	–12.50	–10.42
Check Amount	1,819.66	710.28	671.98	1,740.70	1,565.68

9 On February 24, 2004, the company paid the GTE and Edison bills using Union Bank Checks 126 and 127.

10 On February 25, 2004, the company received $9,000 as payment on account from Latin Ladies. The amount was held for deposit at a later time.

11 On February 26, 2004, the company purchased a warehouse and land for $300,000 ($50,000 of the purchase price is attributable to the land). A cash payment using Check 128 for $30,000 was made to Hawaiian Farms. The remaining balance of $270,000 was satisfied by signing a long-term note payable to the Bank of California. (Be sure to create a land and building fixed asset account along with a related subaccount of cost and accumulated depreciation for the building. Also make sure the land account appears in the chart of accounts before all other fixed assets and that cost precedes accumulated depreciation under the building account.)

12 On February 26, 2004, the company paid payroll for the period ended February 29, 2004. All employees worked the entire period. Kelly Gusland worked 50 hours, Margie Coe worked 45 hours. Checks were written using the Union Bank account starting with Check 129. (Do not print these checks.) Payroll taxes and withholding for employees is shown in Table 4.3.

Chapter 4 Case Problem 2: JENNINGS & ASSOCIATES—Cash-Oriented Activities

In Chapter 2 you recreated Kelly Jennings' QuickBooks file as of January 1, 2004, because a virus had infected and corrupted her file. Later, an associate reentered all the transactions for January 2004. You entered the transactions that took place in February 2004 in Chapter 3. Now Kelly wants you to enter additional transactions that occurred in March 2004.

Table 4.3 Payroll Taxes and Withholding for Employees from February 16, 2004 through February 29, 2004

Tax or Withholding/Employee	Thomas	Gusland	Coe	McAninch	Comstock
California Employee Training Tax	0.00	.75	.54	0.00	.75
Social Security Company	180.83	46.50	33.48	155.00	129.17
Medicare Company	42.29	10.88	7.83	36.25	30.21
Federal Unemployment	0.00	6.00	4.32	0.00	6.00
CA—Unemployment	0.00	.38	.27	0.00	.37
Federal Withholding	−667.00	−96.00	−64.00	−402.00	−286.00
Social Security Employee	−180.83	−46.50	−33.48	−155.00	−129.17
Medicare Employee	−42.29	−10.88	−7.83	−36.25	−30.21
CA—Withholding	−192.30	−13.32	0.00	−153.55	−61.86
CA—Disability Employee	−14.58	−3.75	−2.70	−12.50	−10.42
Check Amount	1,819.67	579.55	431.99	1,740.70	1,565.67

Assignment:

Use the file named Kj04cp.qbw to record the following transactions. Remember to restore this file from your Student Disk first. (*Note:* Additional transactions have already been entered into this file for you that were not included in Chapter 3, so do not use your completed Kj03cp.qbw file.) After entering the transactions, print a standard balance sheet as of 3/31/04 and a standard income statement (profit & loss) for the month ended 3/31/04.

Financing Activities

1 On March 1, 2004, the company deposits $8,000 into the First Valley Savings & Loan account as the proceeds from a short-term note payable agreement between First Valley Savings & Loan and Jennings & Associates.

2 On March 2, 2004, the company issues Check 1005 from First Valley Savings & Loan to pay off a $5,000 loan from the Bank of San Martin.

Investing Activities

3 On March 3, 2004, the company sells some short-term investments, which had cost $3,000, for a $500 profit. The proceeds of the sale from Dean Witter are deposited immediately to First Valley Savings & Loan.

4 On March 4, 2004 the company purchases computer equipment from Phoenix Computers for $7,000 using Check 1006 written from the First Valley Savings & Loan account.

Operating Activities

5 On March 6, 2004, the company orders 50 rolls of regular film from Rex's Film Supply that are expected by March 10, 2004. Use Purchase Order 5.

6 On March 10 the company receives the film ordered under Purchase Order 5 and records a bill.

7 The company records the following invoices: (Accept all changes in terms as permanent.)

Date	Invoice #	Customer	Customer PO #	Terms	Product	Qty
3/15/04	13	Bob and Mary Schultz	5611	Net 30	Magazine Layout	5
					HQ Film	3
3/18/04	14	Yaskar Farms	B23	Net 30	Press Release	5
3/25/04	15	Fancy Yogurt	9988	Net 15	TV Commercial	75

8 The company receives the following bills on March 18, 2004: (Accept all changes in terms as permanent.)

Vendor	Operating Expense	Terms	Amount
Frank Mendez Properties	Rent	Net 15	700.00
Pacific Electric	Utilities: Gas and Electric	Net 15	65.00
KCOY TV	TV Commercial Spots	Net 15	7,500.00
Owen & Owen	Professional Fees: Legal Fees	Net 15	375.00

9 On March 29, 2004, the company pays all bills due as of March 31. Bills are paid out of the First Valley Savings & Loan account starting with Check 1007. Do not print checks. (**Hint:** Total payments should total $7,156.50. Remember, pay only bills due as of 3/31/04. If your total payments are different, check to make sure you entered the correct dates and payment terms for all bills.)

10 The company receives the following payments (checks) from customers: (**Note:** Deposits for each payment were made to the First Valley Savings & Loan on the same day.)

Date	Customer	Apply to Invoice #	Amount
3/26/04	Big 10	5	325.00
3/28/04	Evelyn Walker Real Estate	4	200.00
3/29/04	Ray's Chevron	8	650.00

Non-Cash Investing and Financing Activities

11 On March 15 the company purchased a small sport utility vehicle for $18,500. The purchase was 100% financed with a loan from First Valley Savings & Loan and bears monthly payments that will pay off the loan with interest at 10% in five years. (**Hint:** Create a Vehicles Fixed Asset account and two subaccounts—Cost and Accumulated Depreciation. Also create a Vehicle Loan: long-term liability account.)

Adjusting Entries

In this chapter you will:

- Accrue expenses incurred but not yet recorded
- Accrue revenue earned but not yet recorded
- Record the expiration of assets and their related expenses
- Record the reduction of unearned revenues and their related revenues
- Prepare a bank reconciliation and record related adjustments

CASE: PHOENIX SYSTEMS CONSULTING, INC.

Casey has recorded the majority of Phoenix's financing, investing, and operating activities for January through March 2003. To help him prepare financial statements for the first quarter, he asks Karen and you to prepare any necessary adjusting entries for the period January 1 through March 31, 2003.

"Some people have trouble with adjusting entries" Karen remarks, "but I'm not one of them. I was always helping my classmates understand these types of journal entries. Why don't I give them a try?"

"Okay with me," you respond. "Traditional journal entries are available in QuickBooks, but you don't have to use them." You explain that in QuickBooks the most common adjusting entries—accruing expenses, accruing revenue, recording asset expirations, and recording liability reductions—can be made by using the Make Journal Entry menu item in the Company menu or by using account registers. You decide to show Karen the journal entry process.

ACCRUING EXPENSES

Phoenix borrowed $12,500 on a short-term basis from the Bank of Cupertino on January 23 and another $3,000 on March 11. On March 24, Phoenix repaid $10,500 of that $15,500 balance. The $5,000 ending balance on March 31 represents the principal owed on that date but does not include interest on the loan. The bank has just informed Phoenix that $250 of interest was charged to their loan balance due.

To accrue interest expense:

1 Open Phnx05.qbw

2 Click **Company**, and then click **Make General Journal Entries.**

3 An Assigning Numbers to Journal Entries window should appear explaining that QuickBooks automatically assigns numbers to journal entries. Accept this process by clicking in the Do not display this message in the future check box and then clicking **OK** as shown in Figure 5.1.

Figure 5.1

Assigning Numbers to Journal Entries Window

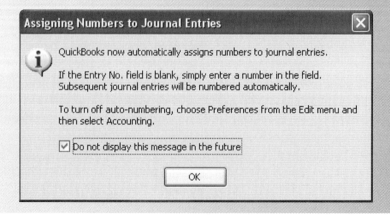

4 Type 3/31/03 as the journal entry date.

5 Type **AJE1** in the Entry No. box (AJE is Adjusting Journal Entry.)

6 Select **Interest Expense: Loan Interest** as the first account.

7 Type **250** as the amount in the Debit column. (This will increase interest expense (an expense account).

8 Select **Short-Term Debt** as the second account.

9 Accept **250** as the amount in the Credit column. This will increase short-term debt (a liability account). The resulting journal entry should look like Figure 5.2

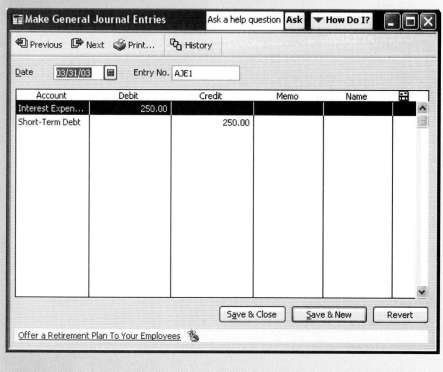

Figure 5.2

Adjusting Journal Entry 1 (AJE1)

10 Click **Save and New**.

Most financial accounting textbooks illustrate the accrual of interest expenses by using an Interest Payable account rather than a Short-Term Debt account. Although either approach is acceptable, using a Short-term Debt account allows you to more quickly reconcile your records with the Bank of Cupertino's loan statement.

ACCRUING REVENUE

You tell Karen that she can also use journal entries to record revenue earned on investments. She recalls that during the quarter the company had some bond investments with Sky Investments that earned interest. The interest is paid semi-annually. Since no interest was paid during the quarter, no interest revenue has been recorded. After checking with their investment advisor, Karen learns that $500 interest revenue was earned but unpaid as of March 31, 2003. QuickBooks has a pre-established account for interest revenue although it is labeled interest income. Karen decides to change the account title first before accruing the interest.

To edit the Interest Income account:

1 Open the Chart of Accounts window.

2 Click the **Interest Income** account button, located near the bottom of the Chart of Accounts.

3 Click the **Account** button, and then click **Edit** to edit the Interest Income account and change its name and description to Interest Revenue.

4 Click **OK** to close the Edit Account window.

5 Close the Chart of Accounts window.

To accrue interest revenue:

1 Type **3/31/03** as the journal entry date (if the Make General Journal Entries window has been closed, click **Company**, and then click **Make General Journal Entries**).

2 Accept **AJE2** in the Entry No. box. (AJE is Adjusting Journal Entry.)

3 Select **Investments** as the first account. (*Note*: If you are continuing from the previous section both the date and journal entry number are already entered for you.)

4 Type **500** as the amount in the Debit column. This will increase Investments (an asset account).

5 Select **Interest Revenue** as the second account.

6 Accept **500** as the amount in the Credit column. (This will increase Interest Revenue, an income account). The resulting journal entry should look like Figure 5.3 on the following page.

7 Click **Save and New**.

Although either approach is acceptable, some accountants prefer to separate the principal of the loan from the interest on the loan by using an Interest Receivable account rather than an Investments Other Current Asset account.

RECORDING THE EXPIRATION OF ASSETS AND THEIR RELATED EXPENSES

The two adjustments you've shown Karen accounted for previously unrecorded transactions. Next you want to show her how to record adjustments that affect previously recorded business activity, such as the

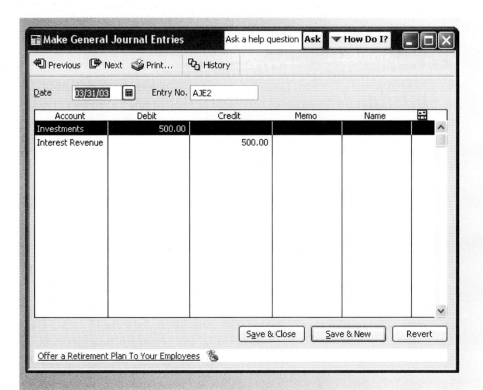

Figure 5.3
Adjusting Journal Entry 2 (AJE2)

prepayment of costs, the purchase of fixed assets, and the receipt of unearned revenue.

On January 7, 2003, Phoenix paid a premium of $1,384.67 to Walker Insurance for a one year liability insurance policy. Since this payment represented an expenditure that benefited more than the accounting period January 1 to March 31, it was correctly recorded to Prepaid Insurance, an asset account.

On March 31, 2003, one-fourth of the time period covered by the insurance had expired. Thus one-fourth of the cost ($346.17) should be recorded as liability insurance expense, and the prepaid insurance account reduced accordingly.

To adjust prepaid insurance:

1 Type **3/31/03** as the journal entry date.

2 Type **AJE3** in the Entry No. box.

3 Select **Insurance: Liability Insurance** as the first account.

4 Type **346.17** as the amount in the Debit column. This will increase the liability insurance subaccount (an expense account.)

5 Select **Prepaid Insurance** as the second account.

6 Accept 346.17 as the amount in the Credit column. This will decrease Prepaid Insurance (an asset account). The resulting journal entry should look like Figure 5.4 on the following page.

7 Click **Save and New**.

Figure 5.4
Adjusting Journal Entry 3 (AJE3)

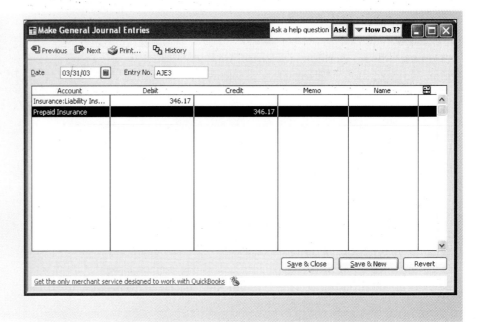

A similar adjustment called **depreciation** is needed to document the use or expiration of a previously recorded depreciable asset. Phoenix had purchased some computer equipment early in 2003 and had calculated depreciation expense of $375 for the period ending March 31, 2003. Depreciation on fixed assets is usually accumulated in a separate contra-asset account on the balance sheet for control purposes.

To record depreciation expense:

1 Type **3/31/03** as the journal entry date.

2 Type **AJE 4** in the Entry No. box. (**Note:** Once again, if you are continuing from the previous section both the date and journal entry number are already entered for you.)

3 Select **Depreciation Expense** as the first account.

4 Type **375** as the amount in the Debit column. This will increase the depreciation expense.

5 Select **Computer Equipment:Accumulated Depreciation** as the second account.

6 Accept **375** as the amount in the Credit column. This will increase accumulated depreciation (a contra-asset account.) The resulting journal entry should look like Figure 5.5

7 Click **Save and New**.

8 If a Tracking Fixed Assets on Journal Entries window appears ignore it for now and click **OK**. (Coverage of this process is included in the appendix.)

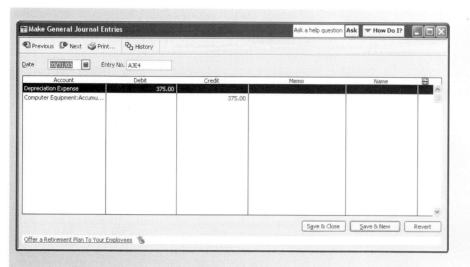

Figure 5.5

Adjusting Journal Entry 4 (AJE4)

Karen asks about the order of subaccounts shown in the Chart of Accounts window. In particular, she wonders why Accumulated Depreciation is listed before the asset's cost. You explain that QuickBooks automatically lists subaccounts in alphabetical order as shown in Figure 5.6. Karen is correct in questioning this order as standard presentation for these assets should reflect cost before accumulated depreciation. Before moving on, you suggest a change in the order of these accounts using the Chart of Accounts.

To change the order of fixed asset subaccounts:

1 Scroll down the Chart of Accounts window to the fixed asset section shown in Figure 5.6.

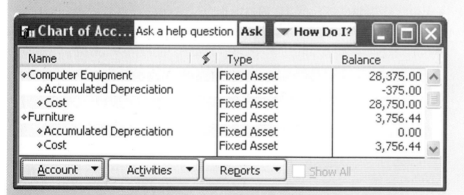

Figure 5.6

Fixed Assets Accounts

2 Click and hold the cursor over the far left side of the Computer Equipment Accumulated Depreciation account. Note that the cursor changes to a four-arrow shape.

3 Drag the Accumulated Depreciation account to a place between Cost and the next account, then release the mouse button. (The Accumulated Depreciation account should now be shown below Cost.)

4 Repeat Steps 2 and 3 to move the Accumulated Depreciation account for furniture to below the Cost subaccount. The revised chart of accounts should look like Figure 5.7.

Figure 5.7
Revised Fixed Assets

5 Close the Chart of Accounts window.

Karen finds the above procedures very straightforward, but she is curious about the financial statement impact of these depreciation entries. She wonders if QuickBooks provides a way to view financial statements so she can see what effect this adjustment had. You tell her that QuickBooks does have such a feature—you can view financial statements at any time without having to post entries. You suggest that she look at the balance sheet as of March 31, 2003, to see the effect of this adjustment on the fixed assets.

To view the fixed assets portion of the balance sheet as of March 31, 2003:

1 Click **Reports, Company & Financial**, and then click **Balance Sheet Standard**.

2 Enter the dates **From 01/01/03 to 03/31/03** in the Modify Report window, then click **OK**.

3 Scroll down the balance sheet to the fixed assets section as shown in Figure 5.8.

Note the changed order of accounts

Figure 5.8
A Partial View of the Balance
Sheet on March 31, 2003

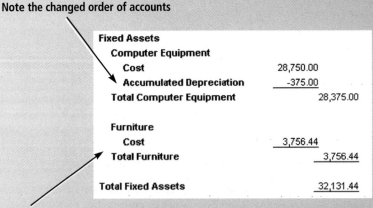

Accumulated depreciation is not shown here because
the account currently has a zero balance

4 Close all windows.

Having tackled prepaid asset and depreciable asset adjustments, you and Karen are now ready to move to the last adjustment category— adjusting unearned revenue.

ADJUSTING UNEARNED REVENUE

On March 6, 2003, Phoenix received $2,500 from its customer, Boston Stores. On this date, Boston Stores had no existing balance outstanding. As described in Chapter 3, Casey recorded this transaction by increasing Cash and decreasing Accounts Receivable. Casey later learned that $1,612.50 had subsequently been billed to Boston Stores on invoice 20008. Since the remaining $887.50 was an advance to future maintenance service, Casey correctly decided to reclassify it as unearned revenue, a liability, on March 31, 2003. Here's why. Cash has been received, but the maintenance service has not yet been fully provided. Thus, on March 31, you need to apply $1,612.50 to invoice 20008 and reclassify the balance of $887.50 to an unearned revenue account (a liability). When Phoenix performs the maintenance in a future period, Phoenix will create an invoice, decrease the liability, and increase sales revenue, all in the amount of $887.50.

To apply the advance to invoice 20008 at March 31, 2003:

1 Click **Customers** and then click **Receive Payments**. (You might get a Merchant's Account Service Message. Click on **do not display this message in the future** or click **No**.)

2 Click **Previous** six times or until you come across the Boston Stores receipt of March 6, 2003.

3 Click **Auto Apply** as shown in Figure 5.9.

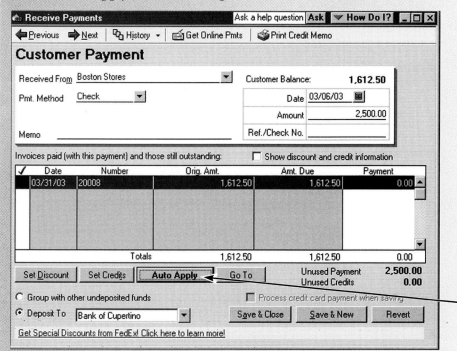

Figure 5.9

The Boston Stores Receive Payments Window Before Application

Click here to automatically apply $1,612.50 of the $2,500.00 in invoice 20008

4 Click **Save & Close** and then click **Yes** to accept the application of $1,612.50 to invoice 20008. This leaves an unused payment amount of $887.50.

You now have to reclassify the unused payment amount as unearned revenue. To do so you first have to create an unearned revenue account. Then you have to remove the credit balance in the Boston Stores receivable account and move it to a liability account.

To create an unearned revenue account:

1 Open the Chart of Accounts window.

2 Click **Account** then **New**

3 Select **Other Current Liability** as the account type.

4 Type **Unearned Revenue** in the Name edit box.

5 Click **OK** to close the New Account window.

6 Close the Chart of Accounts window.

To reclassify the unused payment amount as unearned revenue:

1 Type **3/31/03** as the journal entry date

2 Type **AJE5** in the Entry No. box (*Note*: Once again, if you are continuing from the previous section both the date and journal entry number are already entered for you.)

3 Select **Accounts Receivable** as the first account.

4 Accept **887.50** as the amount in the Debit column. This will increase accounts receivable. The resulting journal entry will now look like Figure 5.10.

Figure 5.10
Adjusting Journal Entry 5

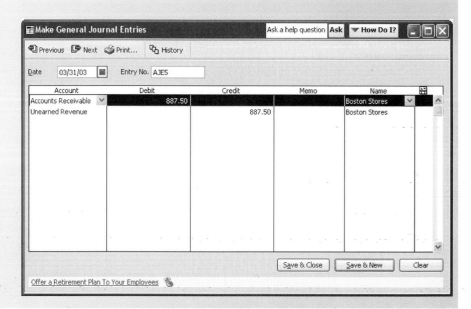

Together, you and Karen have now made all adjustments necessary except for those necessitated by the preparation of the bank reconciliation.

BANK RECONCILIATION

Every month the Bank of Cupertino sends Phoenix a checking account statement that lists all deposits received by the bank and all checks and payments that have cleared the bank as of the date of the statement. You and Karen examine the current bank statement, which indicates an ending balance of $85,206.87 as of February 28, 2003. You now turn your attention toward reconciling that balance with the balance reported by QuickBooks. You note that QuickBooks indicates an ending checking account balance of $77,988.06 at that same date and that most of the difference between these two amounts is probably attributable to "outstanding checks" that Phoenix has written but that the bank hasn't yet paid.

To reconcile the bank statement as of 2/28/03:

1 Click **Banking** and then click **Reconcile**.

2 Click **Bank of Cupertino** from the Account drop-down list.

3 Accept the bank reconciliation date of **02/28/03** in the Statement Date box shown in Figure 5.11. (Note the opening balance shown of $67,667.52. This is the sum of all previously cleared items in the register, which would equal the opening balance on the bank statement.)

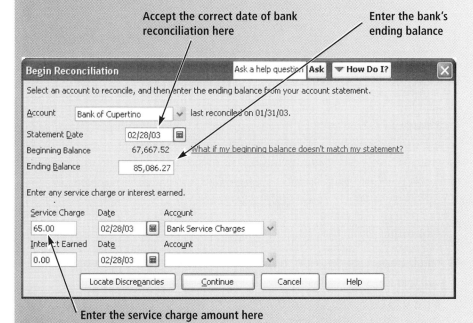

Accept the correct date of bank reconciliation here

Enter the bank's ending balance

Enter the service charge amount here

Figure 5.11

The Begin Reconciliation Window

4 Enter the ending balance, **$85,086.27**, and service charge, **65.00**.

5 Click **Bank Service Charges** from the Account drop-down list, then click **Continue**.

6 In the Deposits and Other Credits section, place a check next to all the deposits by clicking in the column to the left of every date except those deposits recorded in March. This check indicates that these deposits have been received by the bank.

7 In the Checks, Payments, and Service Charges section, place a check next to all checks and payments having a January or February date except checks 1021, 1022, and 1023. Each check mark you insert indicates that these checks have been paid by the bank.

The resulting difference between the Ending Balance (the ending balance per the bank statement) and the Cleared Balance (the total of the opening balance plus the transactions you've marked) should now be 0, as shown in Figure 5.12.

Figure 5.12
The Reconcile Window

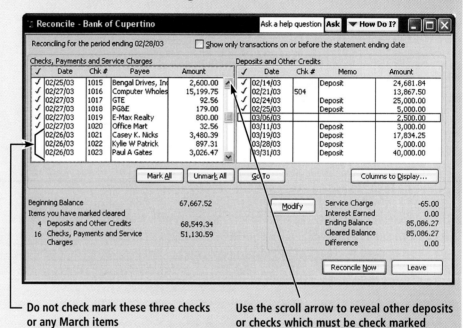

Do not check mark these three checks or any March items

Use the scroll arrow to reveal other deposits or checks which must be check marked

trouble? If the difference is not 0, your account is not balanced for the period. The problem could be errors in your account register or errors made by the bank. Alternatively, you may not have checked the correct number of deposits or checks. If you failed to enter the $65.00 Bank Service Charge, click on **Modify** in the Reconcile—Bank of Cupertino account now and enter. Click **Continue**.

8 Click **Reconcile Now** to complete the reconciliation. You may get an Information window. Close the window or click **OK**.

trouble? If the difference is not 0, and you've clicked Reconcile Now, you will see a Reconcile Adjustments window. Do not click OK to adjust the balance. Instead, look for an item you have checked which did not clear.

9 Click **Summary** in the Select Reconciliation Detail Report window to indicate you want a summary bank reconciliation report. Then click **Display**. Then change the Report Date Range to be from 02/01/03 to 02/28/03, then click **OK**. A Reconciliation Summary window appears showing your new Ending Balance as of 2/28/03 as shown in Figure 5.13.

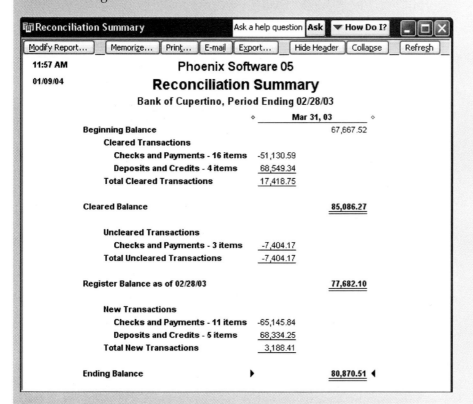

Figure 5.13
Reconciliation Summary

The only adjustment created in this bank reconciliation was the recognition of bank service fees. QuickBooks automatically records this reduction in the checking account and increases bank service charges, an expense account. Once reconciled, QuickBooks also inserts a check mark next to each transaction that has cleared the bank, as shown in Figure 5.14.

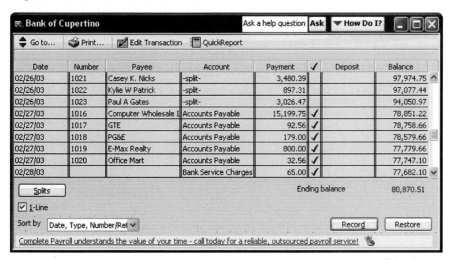

Figure 5.14
The Check Register After Reconciliation

END NOTE

You've now helped Karen record various adjustments to Phoenix Systems, including accrued expenses, accrued revenues, expiration of prepaid and depreciable assets, reduction of unearned revenue, and one which reflected a completed bank reconciliation. You're almost ready to create Phoenix's financial statements.

practice

chapter

5

Chapter 5 Questions

1 Explain the journal entry method of recording period end adjustments.

2 Give an example of an accrued revenue at Phoenix Systems other than the example given in this chapter. Explain how this example of accrued revenue would be adjusted using journal entries.

3 Give an example of an accrued expense at Phoenix Systems other than the example given in this chapter. Explain how this example of accrued expense would be adjusted using journal entries.

4 Give an example of an asset expiration at Phoenix Systems other than the example given in this chapter. Explain how this example would be adjusted using journal entries.

5 Give an example of unearned revenue at Phoenix Systems and explain the process for period-end adjustments involving unearned revenue.

6 Explain how to access general journal entries.

7 What menu item do you use to start a bank reconciliation?

8 What account is typically used to record service charges?

9 When you've finished reconciling a bank account, what should be the difference between the ending balance and the cleared balance?

10 What information is included in the reconciliation summary report?

Chapter 5 Assignments

1 *Adding More Information to Phoenix Systems Consulting, Inc.*

Use Phnx05cp.qbw. (Remember, you will need to restore this file from your Data Files CD first.)

a. Make the following adjustments as of March 31, 2003:

(1) Interest revenue of $225 on short-term investments was earned, but not received.

(2)   Loan interest expense of $275 on long-term borrowing was incurred, but not paid.

(3)   Depreciation on furniture for the period amounted to $313.04.

(4)   Prepaid rent of $800 expired during the period.

(5)   A payment of $6,500 was received from Netscape and recorded January 14, 2003. Of this, $3,225 should be applied to Invoice 20007. The balance ($3,275) represents advance payment for services to be performed at a later time.

b.   Prepare and print a summary bank reconciliation as of March 31, 2003, using the following information:

(1)   The bank statement balance as of March 31, 2003, was $48,297.80.

(2)   Bank service charges amounted to $75.00 during the month.

(3)   All deposits listed in the QuickBooks Reconciliation window were received by the bank in March, except for one deposit for $40,000 dated March 31.

(4)   All checks and payments listed in the QuickBooks Reconciliation window were paid by the bank, except for checks 1032, 1033, and 1034.

c.   Prepare and print a standard balance sheet as of March 31, 2003, and a standard income statement for the quarter ended March 31, 2003.

2   *Adding More Information: Central Coast Cellular*

In Chapter 4, you added some business transactions to your QuickBooks file for Central Coast Cellular (CCC), a cellular phone sales, phone rental, and consulting company. Make a copy of that file in Windows Explorer, name the file CCC5, and use that file to enter the following transactions and perform a bank reconciliation.

a.   On January 31, 2003, the company recorded depreciation expense of $1,000 for Equipment and $500 for Office Furniture with adjusting journal entry #1.

b.   On January 31, 2003, the company accrued interest on the note payable of $950 to an interest payable account via adjusting journal entry #2.

c.   On January 31, 2003, the company created an adjustment for unearned revenue via adjusting journal entry #3.

d.   The bank statement dated January 31, 2003 indicated a bank balance of $133,640.49, with all checks clearing except numbers 3010, 3011, and 3012. All deposits cleared. A bank service charge of $80 was reported.

e.   Print the following:
   • Profit & Loss Standard report for the month of January 2003
   • Balance Sheet Standard as of January 31, 2003
   • Custom Transaction Detail Report for January 31, 2003
   • Bank reconciliation summary as of January 31, 2003

http://

Go to
http://owen.swlearning.
com

3 *Using the South-Western Home Page for More Assignments or Cases*

If you have Internet access, go to the home page for this textbook at **http://owen.swlearning.com**.

Select the **Chapter 5** section from the Additional Problem Sets, and complete the problem(s) your instructor assigns.

Chapter 5 Case Problem 1: OCEAN VIEW FLOWERS

In Chapter 4, you modified your QuickBooks file for Ocean View Flowers, a wholesale flower distributor. Make a copy of that file and use that copy to enter the following transactions. Then print a Standard Balance Sheet report as of February 29, 2004, a Standard Profit and Loss report for the two months ended February 29, 2004, and a Transactions List by Date report for the period January 1 to February 29, 2004. (Make sure this report is printed in landscape orientation and with the "fit report to one page wide" checkbox checked.)

1 On February 29, 2004, the company received its bank statements from Union Bank for both January and February. Print a summary reconciliation for each month.

- The January statement reported an ending balance of $76,340.30, bank service charges of $45, and interest revenue of $100 as of January 31, 2004. Deposits for $100,000, $50,000, $6,600, and $22,200 were recorded. Checks 101–110 were paid.

- The February statement reported an ending balance of $65,579.64, bank service charges of $55, and interest revenue of $75 as of February 29, 2004. Deposits for $5,000 and $5,200 were recorded. Checks 111–127 were paid.

2 The company decided to prepare generally accepted accounting principle (GAAP) based financial statements as of February 29, 2004. As a result the following adjustments were required on that date:

- $800 of interest revenue had been earned as of February 29, 2004 on short-term investments and must be accrued.
- $200 of prepaid liability insurance expired as of February 29, 2004.
- $2,000, $600, and $500 of depreciation expense was incurred for the building, computer equipment, and office equipment, respectively.
- FTD's advance payment was applied to its open invoice.
- Legal fees incurred during the period had not been billed. This includes an estimated $2,500 in professional fees: legal fees need to be accrued as legal fees payable to Bear and Bull, Attorneys at Law.

Chapter 5 Case Problem 2: JENNINGS & ASSOCIATES—Adjustments

In Chapters 2, 3, and 4 you recreated Kelly Jennings' QuickBooks file as of March 31, 2004 before adjustments. Now it is time to enter those adjustments using the Kj05cp.qbw file. Note that additional transactions have been included in this file that were not included in Chapter 4, so do not use your completed Kj04cp.qbw file.

1 Add the following adjustments:

  a. Interest revenue on short-term investments was earned, but not received. In February, $300 was earned; in March, $159.

  b. Loan interest expense of $80 on a vehicle loan was incurred in March, but not paid.

  c. Depreciation on computer equipment for February and March amounted to $145 and $290, respectively.

  d. Depreciation on furniture for February and March amounted to $41.67 for each month.

  e. Depreciation on vehicles in March amounted to $300.00.

  f. Prepaid liability insurance of $200 expired during February and again in March.

  g. Of the $2,000 received from Bob and Mary Schultz, $575 was earned during the month of March and billed via invoice 13. Apply this amount to the invoice and reclassify the balance as unearned revenue.

2 Prepare and print a summary bank reconciliation for the First Valley Savings & Loan account as of March 31, 2004, given the following information:

  a. The bank statement balance as of March 31, 2004 was $56,945.50.

  b. Bank service charges amounted to $45.00 during the month.

  c. All deposits listed in the QuickBooks Reconciliation window were received by the bank.

  d. All checks and payments listed in the QuickBooks Reconciliation window were paid by the bank, except for Checks 1018 through 1020.

3 Prepare and print a standard balance sheet as of March 31, 2004, and a standard income statement for the quarter ended March 31, 2004.

Budgeting

In this chapter you will:

- Create budgets for specific revenue accounts

- Create budgets for specific expense accounts

- Create a budgeted income statement

- Create specific budgets for assets, liabilities, and owners' equity accounts

- Create a budgeted balance sheet

CASE: PHOENIX SYSTEMS CONSULTING, INC.

Today Casey asks you and Karen to prepare financial statements for the first quarter of the year. He reminds you that he has already recorded all of the transactions for January through March, so you're ready to prepare the statements.

"But just preparing the statements is half the job," Karen points out. "You have to interpret these statements. How will you know if the company is doing well?"

Casey is quick to respond. "At the beginning of the year I used a spreadsheet program to establish budgets for the year. I can compare the actual results shown in the statements you prepare with these budgets."

"Doesn't QuickBooks have a budgeting feature?" you ask.

"You're right!" exclaims Casey, "I didn't use that feature, but now that you mention it, I should have. Would the two of you mind entering my budget estimates into QuickBooks as well?"

"Not at all," you respond.

After Casey leaves, you explain to Karen that QuickBooks allows you to set up a budget for an account or for a customer within an account. To do this, you enter budget amounts for the income statement accounts or balance sheet accounts you wish to track.

"Are you able to track actual versus budgeted amounts?" Karen asks.

"Yes," you reply. "I'll show you how to use QuickBooks's budget reports to examine the budget by itself, as well as how to compare Phoenix's actual results to its budgeted amounts."

Karen has another question. "Can we create different budgets based on different assumptions in QuickBooks?"

"No," you answer. "QuickBooks allows you to have a different budget for different fiscal years, but you may have only one budget per fiscal year."

You explain that QuickBooks allows you to set up budgets for specific accounts within financial statements or for all specific financial statements. While it is easier to budget for specific accounts, it might be more useful to prepare a budgeted income statement or budgeted balance sheet.

To begin, you suggest that Karen print Casey's spreadsheet budget and then the two of you establish the monthly budget for revenues.

BUDGETS FOR SPECIFIC REVENUES

Quickbooks provides a set-up window to enter budget information. In this window you specify fiscal year, account, customer, and/or class and the corresponding amounts for each month. As you fill in this information, you are setting up a budget for a single account, such as a balance sheet or an income statement account. If you also choose a customer:job or a class, you can set up a budget for that account and for that customer:job or class.

"I remember entering customer:job information in QuickBooks, but what are classes?" asks Karen.

"Classes are categories QuickBooks provides to help you group data into departments, product lines, locations, and the like."

"Do we need to set up budgets for customers or classes?" asks Karen.

"Casey's budget isn't that detailed," you respond. "We'll enter information for accounts only."

Karen also asks about QuickBooks's use of the term *income* instead of *revenues* for products and services. You explain that although revenues is the traditional accounting term for these items, QuickBooks has chosen to classify them as "income" in the type section of the chart of accounts.

To create a budget for specific revenues:

1 Open Phnx06.qbw.

2 Click **Company**, then **Planning & Budgeting**, and then click **Set Up Budgets**.

3 Select **2003** as the budget year and **Profit and Loss** as the budget type in the Create New Budgets window, then click **Next** twice.

4 Select **Create budget from scratch** and click **Finish**.

5 The resulting Set Up Budgets window is shown in Figure 6.1.

trouble? Your screen may show the budget split into two 6-month periods based on your screen size. If that occurs, in order to enter information in the second 6-month period, you will need to press the Show Next 6 Months or Show Prev 6 Months button. Screen shots displayed in this chapter presume that your screen size will accommodate all 12 months.

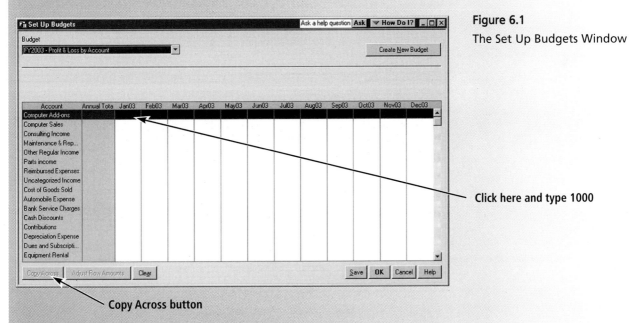

Figure 6.1
The Set Up Budgets Window

Click here and type 1000

Copy Across button

6 Click in the cell at the intersection of the Jan03 column and the Computer Add-ons row.

7 Type **1000**, then click the **Copy Across** button at the bottom of the window. The result should look like Figure 6.2.

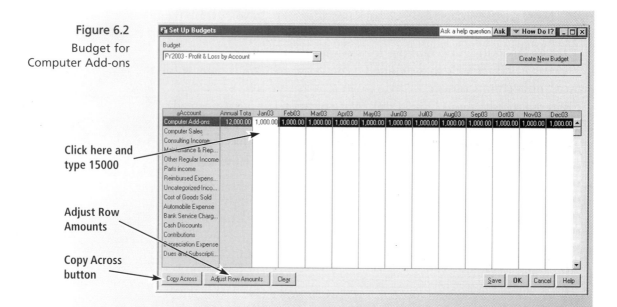

Figure 6.2

Budget for
Computer Add-ons

Click here and
type 15000

Adjust Row
Amounts

Copy Across
button

8 Click in the cell at the intersection of the Jan03 column and the Computer Sales row.

9 Type **15000**, then click the **Copy Across** button.

10 Click the **Adjust Row Amounts** button.

11 Then select **Currently selected month** from the drop-down menu for Start at. Type **5000** as the amount to increase each monthly amount, then check **Enable compounding** as shown in Figure 6.3.

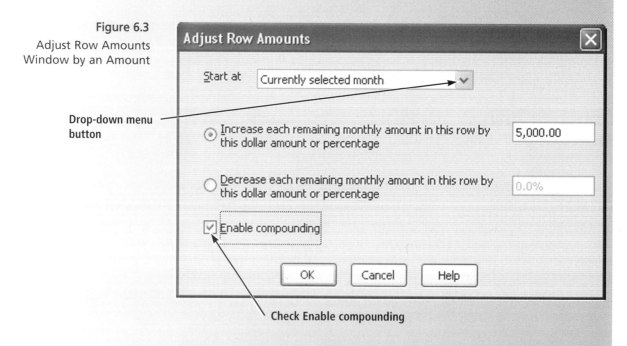

Figure 6.3

Adjust Row Amounts
Window by an Amount

Drop-down menu
button

Check Enable compounding

12 Click **OK** to accept this budget amount. The resulting total budgeted Computer Sales should be 510,000.

13 Click at the intersection of the Jan03 column and the Consulting Income row.

14 Type **3000**, then click the **Copy Across** button.

15 Click at the intersection of the Jan03 column and the Maintenance & Repair row.

16 Type **3000**, then click the **Copy Across** button.

17 Click the **Adjust Row Amounts** button.

18 Then select **Currently selected month** from the drop-down menu for Start at. Type **10.0%** as the percentage to increase each monthly amount, then check **Enable compounding** as shown in Figure 6.4.

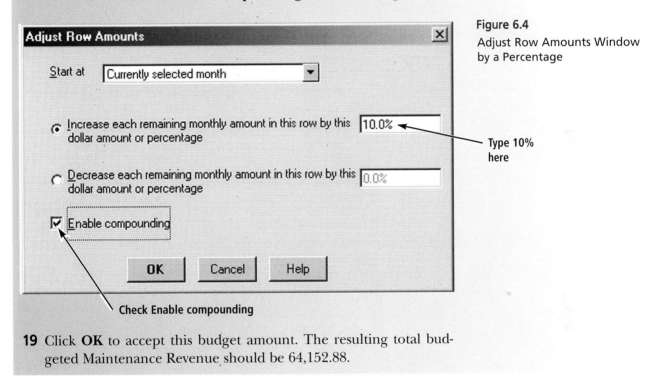

Figure 6.4
Adjust Row Amounts Window by a Percentage

19 Click **OK** to accept this budget amount. The resulting total budgeted Maintenance Revenue should be 64,152.88.

Now you're ready to set up budgets for specific expenses.

BUDGETS FOR SPECIFIC EXPENSES

The budget for Phoenix System's cost of goods sold or cost of sales depends on product sales. Casey estimated that product cost should amount to approximately 70% of sales. Thus, as budgeted sales increase, so should budgeted cost of sales. Karen recalls that in January you set up the budget to include $1,000 for Computer Add-ons and $15,000 for Computer Sales. Thus, expected cost of sales should be 70% of the total January sales of $16,000, or $11,200. Each month thereafter, Casey expects the combination of these two accounts to increase $5,000. Accordingly, the related costs of sales should increase monthly by 70%, or $3,500.

Casey expects payroll expenses, the largest budgeted expense item for Phoenix, to remain constant at $12,000 for six months and then increase to a constant $13,000 for the remaining six months. Depreciation expense, based on the fixed asset acquisitions, are recorded quarterly and are expected to be $700 in March, $800 in June, $1,000 in September, and $1,100 in December. Additional expenses may be budgeted at a later time.

To create a budget for specific expenses:

1 Click at the intersection of the Jan03 column and the Cost of Goods Sold row.

2 Type 16000 * 0.70, as shown in Figure 6.5, then click the Copy Across button. (Computer Sales 15,000 + Computer Add-ons 1,000 times 70%.)

Figure 6.5

Using the Calculator During Budget Set Up

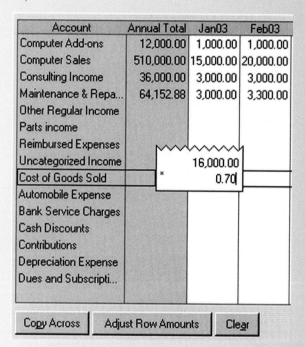

3 Click the **Adjust Row Amounts** button.

4 Then select **Currently selected month** from the drop-down menu for Start at. Type **3500** (the result of multiplying 5,000 by 0.70) as the amount to increase each monthly amount, then check **Enable compounding**, then click **OK.**

5 Scroll down the budget and click at the intersection of the Jan03 column and the Payroll Expenses row.

6 Type **12000**, then click the **Copy Across** button.

7 Click at the intersection of the Jul03 column and the Payroll Expenses row.

8 Type **13000**, then click the **Copy Across** button.

9 Click at the intersection of the Mar03 column and the Depreciation Expense row. Type **700**.

10 Click at the intersection of the Jun03 column and the Depreciation Expense row. Type **800**.

11 Click at the intersection of the Sep03 column and the Depreciation Expense row. Type **1000**.

12 Click at the intersection of the Dec03 column and the Depreciation Expense row. Type **1100**. You are skipping months since depreciation for this company is recorded only once a quarter.

13 Click **OK** to save your budget changes and close the Set Up Budgets window.

Now that Karen has entered budgetary information for several specific income statement accounts, she is curious to see a complete budget. Thus, she will enter and print a budgeted income statement for the first quarter of 2003.

To create and print a budgeted income statement:

1 Click **Edit**, then click **Preferences**, then click the **Reports & Graphs** icon.

2 Be sure that the checkbox labeled Display Modify Report window automatically, located at the bottom of the Preferences window, is checked. If it is, click **OK**; if it is not, click in the checkbox, then click **OK**.

3 Click **Reports**, then select **Budgets**, then select **Budget Overview**.

4 Select **FY2003—Profit & Loss by Account**, then click **Next**.

5 Select **Account by Month**, then click **Next**.

6 Click **Finish**.

7 Enter **1/1/03** and **3/31/03** as the from and to dates respectively in the Modify Report: Profit & Loss Budget Overview window. (Alternatively, you could use the calendar icons and choose specific dates.)

8 Click the **Header/Footer** tab and change the report title to Budgeted Income Statement, then click **OK**.

9 Click the **Print** button in the report window.

10 Click **Portrait,** click the **Fit Report to One Page Wide** checkbox, then click **Print** to print the report. Your report should look like Figure 6.6 on the next page.

11 Review the revised report, then close its window.

"Are we ready to compare our budget with actual results?" asks Karen.

"Not yet," you reply. "We still have to enter budgeted data for assets, liabilities, and owners' equity."

Figure 6.6
Budgeted Income Statement
for the First Quarter of 2003

Phoenix Software 06
Budgeted Income Statement
January through March 2003

	Jan '03	Feb '03	Mar '03	Total Jan-Mar '03
Ordinary Income/Expense				
Income				
Computer Add-ons	1,000.00	1,000.00	1,000.00	3,000.00
Computer Sales	15,000.00	20,000.00	25,000.00	60,000.00
Consulting Income	3,000.00	3,000.00	3,000.00	9,000.00
Maintenance & Repairs	3,000.00	3,300.00	3,630.00	9,930.00
Total Income	22,000.00	27,300.00	32,630.00	81,930.00
Cost of Goods Sold				
Cost of Goods Sold	11,200.00	14,700.00	18,200.00	44,100.00
Total COGS	11,200.00	14,700.00	18,200.00	44,100.00
Gross Profit	10,800.00	12,600.00	14,430.00	37,830.00
Expense				
Depreciation Expense			700.00	700.00
Payroll Expense	12,000.00	12,000.00	12,000.00	36,000.00
Total Expense	12,000.00	12,000.00	12,700.00	36,700.00
Net Ordinary Income	-1,200.00	600.00	1,730.00	1,130.00
Net Income	**-1,200.00**	**600.00**	**1,730.00**	**1,130.00**

BUDGET FOR ASSETS, LIABILITIES, AND OWNERS' EQUITY

You explain to Karen that creating specific budgets for assets, liabilities, and owners' equity accounts is not a simple task. First, you cannot complete this task until the budget for revenues and expenses has been established. This is due to the relationship that exists between net income and retained earnings. Budgeted retained earnings is dependent on net income/net loss. That is, budgeted retained earnings must be increased by monthly net income and decreased by monthly net losses, if any.

Second, budgets for accounts receivable are dependent on sales, while budgets for inventory and accounts payable are dependent on cost of sales and projected sales. Budgeted accumulated depreciation accounts are increased by monthly depreciation expenses. Fortunately for you and Karen, Casey has already created this budget in his spreadsheet program.

Karen suggests that you complete this task one step at a time—first entering the budget for assets, then the budget for liabilities, followed by the budget for owners' equity.

You agree with her suggestion and remind her that the budget amounts for these accounts are the ending balance expected for each month.

To create a budget for assets:

1 Click **Company**, then **Planning & Budgeting**, and then click **Set Up Budgets**.

2 The budget you created earlier appears. Click **Create New Budget** button.

3 Select **2003** as the budget year and **Balance Sheet** as the budget type, then click **Next**, and then click **Finish**.

4 Click at the intersection of the Jan03 column and the Bank of Cupertino row.

5 Enter the projected budget balances as shown in Figure 6.7.

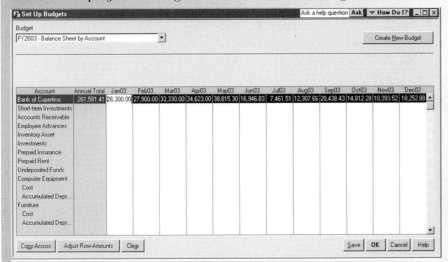

Figure 6.7

Budget Balances for the Bank of Cupertino Account

6 Click at the intersection of the Jan03 column and the Short-term Investments row.

7 Enter the projected budget balances as shown in Figure 6.8.

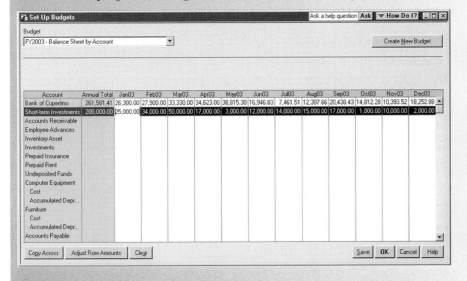

Figure 6.8

Budget Balances for the Short Term Investment Account

8 Click at the intersection of the Jan03 column and the Accounts Receivable row.

9 Type **15000**, then click **Copy Across**.

10 Click the **Adjust Row Amounts** button.

11 Then select **Currently selected month** from the drop-down menu for Start at.

12 Type **5000** as the amount to increase each monthly amount, then check **Enable compounding**, then click **OK**.

13 Click at the intersection of the Jan03 column and the Inventory Asset row.

14 Type **20000**, then click **Copy Across**.

15 Click the **Adjust Row Amounts** button.

16 Then select **Currently selected month** from the drop-down menu for Start at.

17 Type **10000** as the amount to increase each monthly amount, then check **Enable compounding**, then click **OK**.

18 Click at the intersection of the Feb03 column and the Computer Equipment: Cost row.

19 Type **7000**, then press **Tab**.

20 Type **30000**, then press **Tab**.

21 Type **35000**, for Apr03, May03, and Jun03, then press **Tab**.

22 Type **40000** for Jul03, then click **Copy Across**.

23 Click at the intersection of the Mar03 column and the Computer Equipment: Accumulated Depreciation row.

24 Type **−400**, then click **Copy Across**.

25 Click at the intersection of the Jun03 column and the Computer Equipment: Accumulated Depreciation row.

26 Change the amount in this box to **−800**, then click **Copy Across**.

27 Click at the intersection of the Sep03 column and the Computer Equipment: Accumulated Depreciation row.

28 Change the amount in this box to **−1300**, then click **Copy Across**.

29 Click at the intersection of the Dec03 column and the Computer Equipment: Accumulated Depreciation row.

30 Change the amount in this box to **−1800**.

31 Click at the intersection of the Jan03 column and the Furniture: Cost row.

32 Type **3500**, then click **Copy Across**.

33 Click at the intersection of the Mar03 column and the Furniture: Accumulated Depreciation row.

34 Type **−300**, then click **Copy Across**.

35 Click at the intersection of the Jun03 column and the Furniture: Accumulated Depreciation row.

36 Change the amount in this box to **–700**, then click **Copy Across**.

37 Click at the intersection of the Sep03 column and the Furniture: Accumulated Depreciation row.

38 Change the amount in this box to **–1200**, then click **Copy Across.**

39 Click at the intersection of the Dec03 column and the Furniture: Accumulated Depreciation row.

40 Change the amount in this box to **–1800**.

41 Your partially completed Budgeted Balance by Account should look like Figure 6.9

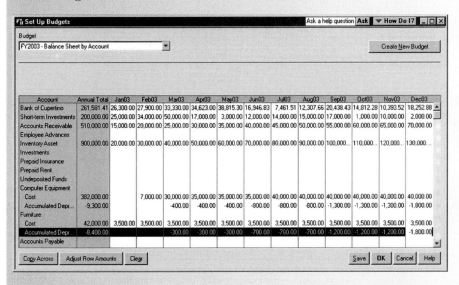

Figure 6.9
Partially Completed Budgeted Balance Sheet by Account

"Why would a budget for balance sheet accounts include an annual total?" asks Karen.

"Good question," you respond. "Perhaps it is used as a control total since it otherwise has no meaning."

Karen comments that budgeted liabilities are also related to operating activities. For example, accounts payable will vary with projected purchases for inventory, and payroll tax liabilities will vary with employment and the frequency of tax deposits. Likewise, sales tax liabilities will vary with sales of taxable items and the frequency of tax deposits.

Short-term and long-term debt will vary with financing requirements and cash flows. Slow cash flow from increasing accounts receivable and inventory will require more financing and must be planned early. Karen is happy to see that Casey has anticipated this need; he has arranged for future financing and has included it in his budget.

Casey's budget reveals a consistent pattern of increasing accounts payable to support planned inventory purchases. He plans to pay payroll and sales taxes quarterly. He believes that short-term debt will remain constant over the year, while he expects long-term financing to grow steadily.

With this background information, you are ready to create a budget for liabilities.

To create a budget for liabilities:

1 Enter the amounts shown in Figure 6.10 into your Balance Sheet by Account budget worksheet.

Account	Annual Total	Jan03	Feb03	Mar03	Apr03	May03	Jun03	Jul03	Aug03	Sep03	Oct03	Nov03	Dec03
Undeposited Funds													
Computer Equipment													
Cost	382,000.00		7,000.00	30,000.00	35,000.00	35,000.00	35,000.00	40,000.00	40,000.00	40,000.00	40,000.00	40,000.00	40,000.00
Accumulated Depr...	-9,300.00			-400.00	-400.00	-400.00	-800.00	-800.00	-800.00	-1,300.00	-1,300.00	-1,300.00	-1,800.00
Furniture													
Cost	42,000.00	3,500.00	3,500.00	3,500.00	3,500.00	3,500.00	3,500.00	3,500.00	3,500.00	3,500.00	3,500.00	3,500.00	3,500.00
Accumulated Depr...	-8,400.00			-300.00	-300.00	-300.00	-700.00	-700.00	-700.00	-1,200.00	-1,200.00	-1,200.00	-1,800.00
Accounts Payable	450,000.00	10,000.00	15,000.00	20,000.00	25,000.00	30,000.00	35,000.00	40,000.00	45,000.00	50,000.00	55,000.00	60,000.00	65,000.00
Payroll Liabilities	96,000.00	4,000.00	8,000.00	12,000.00	4,000.00	8,000.00	12,000.00	4,000.00	8,000.00	12,000.00	4,000.00	8,000.00	12,000.00
Sales Tax Payable	78,000.00	2,000.00	5,000.00	8,000.00	3,000.00	6,000.00	9,000.00	4,000.00	7,000.00	10,000.00	5,000.00	8,000.00	11,000.00
Short-Term Debt	110,000.00		10,000.00	10,000.00	10,000.00	10,000.00	10,000.00	10,000.00	10,000.00	10,000.00	10,000.00	10,000.00	10,000.00
Unearned Revenue													
Long-Term Debt	731,500.00		10,000.00	55,000.00	55,000.00	50,000.00	45,000.00	68,400.00	78,100.00	90,000.00	105,000...	90,000.00	85,000.00

Figure 6.10 Amounts to Be Entered for Budgeted Liabilities

You comment that this budgeting process is more complicated than you thought it would be. Karen agrees, but she assures you that creating the budget for owners' equity won't be as difficult, because owners' equity should increase or decrease by the amount of net income.

"That makes sense," you agree, "but what about other owners' equity transactions, such as additional investments and dividends?"

"I think we would budget them just like other accounts, but Casey's budget doesn't include these items," Karen replies.

"Good. Let's just figure the balance in Retained Earnings each month as being the prior month's balance plus net income or minus net losses. We can't forget Capital Stock either; although it didn't change during the year, it still has to be budgeted."

To create a budget for owners' equity:

1 Click at the intersection of the Jan03 column and the Capital Stock row.

2 Type **75000**, then click **Copy Across**.

3 Click at the intersection of the Jan03 column and the Retained Earnings row.

4 Type the following amounts (including the − sign) as balances for retained earnings each month for January through December 2003: **−1200.00, −600.00, 1130.00, −2577.00, −4384.70, −10353.14, −12939.49, −13792.34, −13561.67, −10187.72, −4606.48, −2152.88.**

5 Click **OK** to save and close this window.

Now that you have completed entering the budget information, you will want to see how a quarterly report will look. To keep it manageable, Karen suggests that you create and print only the budgeted balance sheet as of the end of the first three months of the year.

To create and print a budgeted balance sheet:

1 Click **Reports**, click **Budgets**, then click **Budget Overview**.

2 Select **FY2003—Balance Sheet by Account**, then click **Next**.

3 Click **Finish**.

4 Enter **1/1/03** and **3/31/03** as the from and to dates, respectively, in the Modify Report: Balance Sheet Budget Overview window, then click **OK**.

5 Click the **Print** button on the report toolbar.

6 Click the **Portrait** orientation option button, click the **Fit Report to One Page Wide** checkbox, and then click **Print** to print the report shown in Figure 6.11.

7 Review the revised report, then close its window.

END NOTE

You and Karen have now entered all budgetary information for the first quarter of 2003. Casey can make changes to the budget at any time if additional information becomes available, and QuickBooks will automatically update any related budget report. In Chapter 7 you will generate the financial statements Casey requested, so he can compare the budget with actual results.

Figure 6.15 Balance Sheet Budget Overview for the First Quarter of 2003

		Phoenix Software 06 **Balance Sheet Overview** As of March 31, 2003		
		Jan 31, '03	Feb 28, '03	Mar 31, '03
ASSETS				
Current Assets				
Checking/Savings				
Bank of Cupertino		26,300.00	27,900.00	33,330.00
Short-term Investments		25,000.00	34,000.00	50,000.00
Total Checking/Savings		51,300.00	61,900.00	83,330.00
Accounts Receivable				
Accounts Receivable		15,000.00	20,000.00	25,000.00
Total Accounts Receivable		15,000.00	20,000.00	25,000.00
Other Current Assets				
Inventory Asset		20,000.00	30,000.00	40,000.00
Total Other Current Assets		20,000.00	30,000.00	40,000.00
Total Current Assets		86,300.00	111,900.00	148,330.00
Fixed Assets				
Computer Equipment				
Cost			7,000.00	30,000.00
Accumulated Depreciation				-400.00
Total Computer Equipment			7,000.00	29,600.00
Furniture				
Cost		3,500.00	3,500.00	3,500.00
Accumulated Depreciation				-300.00
Total Furniture		3,500.00	3,500.00	3,200.00
Total Fixed Assets		3,500.00	10,500.00	32,800.00
TOTAL ASSETS		**89,800.00**	**122,400.00**	**181,130.00**
LIABILITIES & EQUITY				
Liabilities				
Current Liabilities				
Accounts Payable				
Accounts Payable		10,000.00	15,000.00	20,000.00
Total Accounts Payable		10,000.00	15,000.00	20,000.00
Other Current Liabilities				
Payroll Liabilities		4,000.00	8,000.00	12,000.00
Sales Tax Payable		2,000.00	5,000.00	8,000.00
Short-term Debt			10,000.00	10,000.00
Total Other Current Liabilities		6,000.00	23,000.00	30,000.00
Total Current Liabilities		16,000.00	38,000.00	50,000.00
Long-term Liabilities				
Long-term Debt			10,000.00	55,000.00
Total Long-term Liabilities			10,000.00	55,000.00
Total Liabilities		16,000.00	48,000.00	105,000.00
Equity				
Capital Stock		75,000.00	75,000.00	75,000.00
Retained Earnings		-1,200.00	-600.00	1,130.00
Total Equity		73,800.00	74,400.00	76,130.00
TOTAL LIABILITIES & EQUITY		**89,800.00**	**122,400.00**	**181,130.00**

practice

Chapter 6 Questions

1 Explain how the budgeting process is accomplished in QuickBooks.

2 Can multiple budgets be created in QuickBooks? Explain.

3 Explain how the Copy Across & Adjust Row Amounts feature helps in creating QuickBooks budgets.

4 Does the Fill Down feature allow you to increase or decrease by specific dollar amounts only? Explain.

5 Explain the typical relationship between cost of goods sold and sales in the budgeting process and how this information is included in the QuickBooks budgeting process.

6 Compare the process of budgeting revenues and expenses with the process of budgeting assets, liabilities, and owners' equity and how this information is included in the QuickBooks budgeting process.

7 Explain the typical relationship between accumulated depreciation and depreciation expense in the budgeting process and how this information is included in the QuickBooks budgeting process.

8 Which menus are used to create budget reports in QuickBooks?

9 Describe how you use the calculator feature that is built into QuickBooks for the budgeting process.

10 Explain the typical relationship between retained earnings and net income/loss in the budgeting process and how this information is included in the QuickBooks budgeting process.

Chapter 6 Assignments

1 *Modifying Budgets for Phoenix Systems, Inc.*

Casey has revised his original budget. He asks you to modify the QuickBooks file accordingly. Use the Phnx06cp.qbw data file to make the following changes. Then create a Profit & Loss Budget Overview report and Balance Sheet Budget Overview report for the first quarter ending March 31, 2003.

a. Computer sales are expected to be $13,000 in Jan 2003 and increase $6,000 each month thereafter.

b. The budget for cash (checking account Bank of Cupertino) will change as follows for Jan03–Dec03: 24,300.00; 22,900.00; 23,330.00; 20,623.00; 34,815.30; 20,946.83; 20,461.51; 35,307.66; 54,438.43; 60,812,28; 69,393.52; 91,252.88.

c. Accounts payable are expected to be $10,000 at the end of January 2003, increase 30% in February 2003, and then remain constant for 3 months. Thereafter Casey expects accounts payable to increase 100% in May 2003 and continue to increase by $10,000 per month throughout the remainder of the year.

d. Casey changed the budget for retained earnings as follows for Jan03–Dec03: –3.200.00; –3,600.00; –1,870.00; –4,577.00; –4,384.70; –7,053.17; –5,939.49; –1,792.34; 4,438.43; 14,812.28; 28,393.52.

e. Parts Income is expected to be $0 throughout the year.

2   *Adding More Information: Central Coast Cellular*

In Chapter 5, you added some business transactions to your QuickBooks file for Central Coast Cellular (CCC), a cellular phone sales, phone rental, and consulting company. Make a copy of that file in Windows Explorer, name the file CCC6, and use that file to enter the following budget information.

a. Enter your own estimate of revenues for the period January through March of 2003.

b. Enter your own estimate of expenses for the period January through March of 2003.

c. Enter your own estimate of assets for the period January through March of 2003.

d. Enter your own estimate of liabilities and equity for the period January through March 2003. (Remember that retained earnings for each period must be the previous period balance in retained earnings plus your budgeted net income or less net loss. Also remember that when you have entered assets, liabilities, and equities, your budgeted balance sheet must balance. Use the cash account to make this balance.)

e. Print the following:
   • Profit & Loss Budget Overview report for the months of January through March 2003.
   • Balance Sheet Budget Overview report as of March 31, 2003.

3   *Using the South-Western Home Page for More Assignments or Cases*

If you have Internet access, go to the home page for this textbook at **http://owen.swlearning.com**.

Select the **Chapter 6** section from the Additional Problem Sets, and complete the problem(s) your instructor assigns.

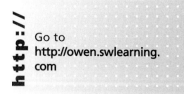

Go to http://owen.swlearning.com

Chapter 6 Case Problem 1: OCEAN VIEW FLOWERS

In Chapter 5, you modified your QuickBooks file for Ocean View Flowers, a wholesale flower distributor. Make a copy of that file and use that copy to enter the following transactions. Then print a Profit & Loss Budget Overview report as of March 31, 2004 listing each month separately and a Balance Sheet Budget Overview report as of March 31, 2004, again listing each month separately.

1 Budgeted revenues and expenses follow:

Account	January	February	March
Sales Anthuriums	$0	$30,000	$30,000
Sales Daylilies	35,000	10,000	35,000
Cost of sales	15,000	25,000	30,000
Payroll expenses	20,000	20,000	20,000
Legal fees	500	500	500
Rent	3,000	3,000	3,000
Telephone	400	400	400
Utilities	300	300	300

2 Budgeted ending balances for assets, liabilities, and equity accounts follow:

Account	January	February	March
Union Bank checking	$83,300	$46,300	$58,900
Short-term investments	25,000	25,000	25,000
Accounts receivable	10,000	15,000	20,000
Prepaid insurance	1,000	1,000	1,000
Office supplies	1,500	1,500	1,500
Inventory	25,000	30,000	35,000
Land		50,000	50,000
Building		250,000	250,000
Computer equipment	16,000	16,000	16,000
Office equipment	21,000	21,000	21,000
Accounts payable	30,000	35,000	40,000
Payroll liabilities	7,000	14,000	21,000
Long-term note payable	50,000	320,000	320,000
Common stock	100,000	100,000	100,000
Retained earnings	–4,200	–13,200	–2,600

Chapter 6 Case Problem 2: JENNINGS & ASSOCIATES—Budgets

Kelly Jennings is anxious to compare her operating, investing, and financing activities with corresponding budgeted amounts. To do this she must first enter her budget into QuickBooks.

Use Kj06cp.qbw. (*Note:* Transactions that were not included in Chapter 5 have been added to this file. Do not use your completed Kj05cp.qbw file.)

1 Create and print a Profit & Loss Budget Overview report for the first quarter of 2004 assuming the following information:

    a. Fee income of $14,000 is expected in the first month, increasing by 10% each month thereafter.

b. Depreciation expense of $200 per month is expected.
c. Payroll expenses of $10,000 are expected for January 2004, and then expected to remain at $14,000 for each month thereafter.
d. Rent expense is anticipated at $700 per month.

2 Create and print a Balance Sheet Budget Overview report for the first quarter of 2004 assuming the following information: (Remember that balance sheet accounts represent balances at the end of each month. Thus, amounts provided are not monthly increases but ending balances.)

a. Cash in the First Valley Savings & Loan account is budgeted at $2,000 at the end of January 2004 and $50,000 at the end of February 2004. Thereafter it is expected to decline $5,000 each month.
b. Cash in the Union Bank checking account is budgeted as follows for Jan04–Dec04: 3,840.00; 26,600.00; 29,227.20; 35,354.86; 45,129.16; 56,710.43; 70,474.51; 86,014.24; 104,141.10; 124,886.97; 148,506.12; 175,277.33.
c. Accounts Receivable is budgeted at $12,000 at the end of January 2004 and is expected to increase at the rate of 12% per month.
d. Inventory is expected to average $2,500 each month.
e. Computer Equipment:Cost is budgeted for $4,000 in January 2004, $8,000 in February 2004, and $14,000 per month for the remainder of the year.
f. Computer Equipment:Accumulated Depreciation is budgeted for –$1,000 in January 2004 and is expected to change by –$175 each subsequent month.
g. Furniture:Cost is budgeted to remain at $2,500 for the year.
h. Furniture:Accumulated Depreciation is budgeted for –$500 in January 2004, increasing –$25 each month for the rest of the year.
i. Accounts Payable is budgeted at $8,000 in January 2004, increasing $1,000 each month thereafter.
j. Payroll Liabilities are budgeted at $3,500 in January 2004, $8,000 in February 2004, $10,000 in March 2004, and are expected to remain at $8,000 each month throughout the rest of the year.
k. The Bank of San Martin long-term liability is budgeted at $5,000 per month for the year.
l. Capital Stock is budgeted for $3,590 in January 2004 and should remain at $73,590 for February through December 2004.
m. Retained Earnings began the year at $2,150 and is adjusted monthly by the amount of net income or loss. (***Hint:*** Examine the budgeted income statement you prepared in Item 1 above to identify the budgeted net income or loss each month. Add net income to [or subtract net loss from] the prior month's ending retained earnings to calculate each month's ending retained earnings.)

7

Reporting Business Activities

In this chapter you will:

- Create an end-of-period income statement and a budgeted vs. actual income statement

- Create an end-of-period balance sheet and a budgeted vs. actual balance sheet

- Create graphs to illustrate sales and income and expenses

- Create graphs to illustrate receivables and payables

- Create additional reports for sales, purchases, and inventory, and for accounts receivable and accounts payable aging

- Export a report to Microsoft Excel

CASE: PHOENIX SYSTEMS CONSULTING, INC.

Now that you have entered the budget information for Phoenix System's first fiscal year and have made all first quarter operating, investing, and financing transactions as well as adjustments, you are ready to prepare Phoenix's first quarter financial statements. Casey has asked you and Karen to prepare these statements and to provide any additional information that will help him better understand Phoenix's financial performance. So you decide that in addition to the financial statements, you will give Casey the related supporting schedules and graphs that QuickBooks can so easily create.

You decide to prepare an income statement, a balance sheet, an accounts receivable and accounts payable schedule, and an inventory status report. To further enhance Casey's financial analysis of the business, you also decide to prepare one graph showing revenues and expenses and another showing the aging of accounts receivable and payable.

"The report and graph features of QuickBooks are quite extensive," you explain to Karen. "You can customize each report by adding percentages, hiding cents, changing report titles, and modifying the page layout."

"Can we also compare the current quarter's results with the budget we just created?" asks Karen.

"Absolutely!" you confirm. "Now that we have created the budget in QuickBooks, we can easily generate a report comparing our budgeted activity with our actual results. We can also produce graphs to help Casey or other users of this information visually evaluate the financial results."

"Sounds like QuickBooks saves hours of work," Karen remarks. "Let's get started."

CREATING INCOME STATEMENTS

You decide to create one income statement for the period without examining each month separately, because adjustments were made only as of March 31.

You explain to Karen that QuickBooks enables you to create reports for any period you desire. It also lets you create separate columns for a time segment—such as a day, a week, four weeks, a month, a quarter, and so on—within each period. You decide that this income statement will report totals only, because adjustments were made only once in the quarter. Then at the end of the fiscal year, you'll create an income statement report for the year with separate columns for each quarter.

"Do we have to go through this customization effort every time?" Karen asks.

"No," you reply. "QuickBooks has a Memorize feature that can "memorize" or retain the customization—what columns we want, what period, what layout, and so on. That way the next time we want a similar report, it will be available from a memorized report list."

To create the first quarter income statement:

1 Open Phnx07.qbw.

2 Click **Reports**, **Company & Financial:**, then **Profit & Loss Standard**.

3 Change the report dates to read from **01/01/03** to **03/31/03** in the Modify Report window, then click the **% of Income** checkbox.

4 Click the **Fonts & Numbers** tab, then click the **Without Cents** checkbox.

5 Click the **Header/Footer** tab. Change the Report Title to **Income Statement**. Select **Left** from the Page Layout alignment drop-down edit box, and alter the Subtitle to **for the three months ended March 31, 2003**. Then click **OK**.

6 Click the **Print** button.

7 Click **Portrait** in the Orientation box. (If the Print Features window appears, click **OK**.) Then click **Print** in the Print Reports window to print the report shown in Figure 7.1 on the following page.

8 Click the **Memorize** button, click on the **Save in Memorized Report Group** checkbox, then choose **Company** in the Memorized Report Group drop-down edit box, then click **OK** to retain this customized report as Income Statement in the Company Memorized Report group.

9 Close all windows.

Notice in this report that 79% of the company's revenue comes from computer sales and 10% from maintenance and repairs. This percent column reports each item's percentage of total revenue (what QuickBooks calls total income). Cost of goods sold at 58% and payroll expenses at 33% are the company's largest costs as a percentage of total revenue. Notice also that Phoenix's profit margin ratio (net income divided by total revenue) is 8%.

Now you need to compare Phoenix's budgeted operating activity with its actual operating results. You tell Karen that you can customize a budgeted versus actual report to include only selected information and to change its layout from the default format that QuickBooks provides.

To create a budgeted and actual income statement comparison:

1 Click **Reports**, **Budgets**, then click **Budget vs. Actual**.

2 Select **FY2003–Profit & Loss by Account**, then click **Next**.

3 Select **Account by Month**, click **Next**, then click **Finish**.

4 Change the report From date to **01/01/03** and the To date to **03/31/03** in the Modify Report window.

5 Select **Quarter** from the Display columns by drop-down edit box.

6 Make sure that all checkboxes—**Show Actuals**, **$Difference**, and **and % of Budget**—are checked.

Figure 7.1

A Modified Income Statement
for Phoenix with a Percent of
Income Column

Phoenix Software 07
Income Statement
for the three months ended March 31, 2003

	Jan–Mar '03	% of Income
Ordinary Income/Expense		
Income		
Computer Add-ons	3,100	3%
Computer Sales	80,950	79%
Consulting Income	7,800	8%
Maintenance & Repairs	10,625	10%
Parts Income	150	0%
Total Income	102,625	100%
Cost of Goods Sold		
Cost of Goods Sold	59,170	58%
Total COGS	59,170	58%
Gross Profit	43,455	42%
Expense		
Bank Service Charges	185	0%
Depreciation Expense	688	1%
Insurance		
Liability Insurance	346	0%
Total Insurance	346	0%
Interest Expense		
Loan Interest	525	1%
Total Interest Expense	525	1%
Office Supplies	650	1%
Payroll Expenses	34,123	33%
Rent	2,400	2%
Telephone	328	0%
Utilities		
Gas and Electric	619	1%
Total Utilities	619	1%
Total Expense	39,864	39%
Net Ordinary Income	3,591	3%
Other Income/Expense		
Other Income		
Investment Income	3,500	3%
Interest Revenue	725	1%
Total Other Income	4,225	4%
Net Other Income	4,225	4%
Net Income	**7,816**	**8%**

7 Click the **Fonts & Numbers** tab, then click the **Without Cents** checkbox, then click **OK**.

8 Click the **Print** button. Make sure the **Fit report to 1 page(s) wide** checkbox is checked, then click **Print** in the Print Reports window to print the report shown in Figure 7.2.

9 Close all windows.

Figure 7.2

A Budgeted vs. Actual Income Statement for Phoenix

<table>
<tr><td colspan="5" align="center">Phoenix Software 07
Profit & Loss Budget vs. Actual
January through March 2003</td></tr>
<tr><td></td><td>Jan–Mar '03</td><td>Budget</td><td>$ Over Budget</td><td>% of Budget</td></tr>
<tr><td>Ordinary Income/Expense</td><td></td><td></td><td></td><td></td></tr>
<tr><td> Income</td><td></td><td></td><td></td><td></td></tr>
<tr><td>   Computer Add-ons</td><td>3,100</td><td>3,000</td><td>100</td><td>103%</td></tr>
<tr><td>   Computer Sales</td><td>80,950</td><td>57,000</td><td>23,950</td><td>142%</td></tr>
<tr><td>   Consulting Income</td><td>7,800</td><td>9,000</td><td>–1,200</td><td>87%</td></tr>
<tr><td>   Maintenance & Repairs</td><td>10,625</td><td>9,930</td><td>695</td><td>107%</td></tr>
<tr><td>   Parts Income</td><td>150</td><td></td><td></td><td></td></tr>
<tr><td> Total Income</td><td>102,625</td><td>78,930</td><td>23,695</td><td>130%</td></tr>
<tr><td> Cost of Goods Sold</td><td></td><td></td><td></td><td></td></tr>
<tr><td>   Cost of Goods Sold</td><td>59,170</td><td>44,100</td><td>15,070</td><td>134%</td></tr>
<tr><td> Total COGS</td><td>59,170</td><td>44,100</td><td>15,070</td><td>134%</td></tr>
<tr><td>Gross Profit</td><td>43,455</td><td>34,830</td><td>8,625</td><td>125%</td></tr>
<tr><td> Expense</td><td></td><td></td><td></td><td></td></tr>
<tr><td>   Bank Service Charges</td><td>185</td><td></td><td></td><td></td></tr>
<tr><td>   Depreciation Expense</td><td>688</td><td>700</td><td>–12</td><td>98%</td></tr>
<tr><td>   Insurance</td><td></td><td></td><td></td><td></td></tr>
<tr><td>   Liability Insurance</td><td>346</td><td></td><td></td><td></td></tr>
<tr><td>   Total Insurance</td><td>346</td><td></td><td></td><td></td></tr>
<tr><td>   Interest Expense</td><td></td><td></td><td></td><td></td></tr>
<tr><td>   Loan Interest</td><td>525</td><td></td><td></td><td></td></tr>
<tr><td>   Total Interest Expense</td><td>525</td><td></td><td></td><td></td></tr>
<tr><td>   Office Supplies</td><td>650</td><td></td><td></td><td></td></tr>
<tr><td>   Payroll Expenses</td><td>34,123</td><td>36,000</td><td>–1,877</td><td>95%</td></tr>
<tr><td>   Rent</td><td>2,400</td><td></td><td></td><td></td></tr>
<tr><td>   Telephone</td><td>328</td><td></td><td></td><td></td></tr>
<tr><td>   Utilities</td><td></td><td></td><td></td><td></td></tr>
<tr><td>   Gas and Electric</td><td>619</td><td></td><td></td><td></td></tr>
<tr><td>   Total Utilities</td><td>619</td><td></td><td></td><td></td></tr>
<tr><td> Total Expense</td><td>39,864</td><td>36,700</td><td>3,164</td><td>109%</td></tr>
<tr><td>Net Ordinary Income</td><td>3,591</td><td>–1,870</td><td>5,461</td><td>–192%</td></tr>
<tr><td>Other Income/Expense</td><td></td><td></td><td></td><td></td></tr>
<tr><td> Other Income</td><td></td><td></td><td></td><td></td></tr>
<tr><td>   Investment Income</td><td>3,500</td><td></td><td></td><td></td></tr>
<tr><td>   Interest Revenue</td><td>725</td><td></td><td></td><td></td></tr>
<tr><td> Total Other Income</td><td>4,225</td><td></td><td></td><td></td></tr>
<tr><td>Net Other Income</td><td>4,225</td><td></td><td></td><td></td></tr>
<tr><td>**Net Income**</td><td>7,816</td><td>–1,870</td><td>9,686</td><td>–418%</td></tr>
</table>

You and Karen go to Casey's office with both reports in hand. As you explain the budget comparison to him, his eyes grow large and focus on the % of Budget column.

"Wow!" he exclaims. "A 418% net income! We're doing great!"

"Not exactly," Karen interrupts. "The 418% figure means that your actual net income is 418% greater than the amount you budgeted. But since you budgeted net loss of only $1,870, any deviation in actual results from that small budgeted number is significantly magnified in percentage terms."

Karen continues to explain that the company's revenues were 125% higher than planned; but that cost of goods sold was 134% higher than planned. Because Casey is somewhat uncertain as to how to interpret this information, you suggest that analyzing the balance sheet would be likely to help him gain a more complete picture of how well the company has performed.

CREATING BALANCE SHEETS

You return to your office to create the balance sheets Casey needs for the first quarter. You explain to Karen that QuickBooks can prepare balance sheets for any accounting period you specify. Since Casey wants results from the first quarter of the fiscal year of Phoenix's activities, the two of you start by preparing a standard balance sheet. You want to keep the report simple—you'll include the main accounts from the chart of accounts and collapse the subaccounts into their main accounts. Later you'll customize the balance sheet to include a percentage column, and then you'll create a budgeted and actual balance sheet comparison—taking advantage of the budget work you did previously.

To create a standard balance sheet:

1 Click **Reports, Company & Financial,** then **Balance Sheet Standard.**

2 Change the report dates to read from **01/01/03** to **03/31/03,** then click **OK.**

3 Click the **Print** button, then click **Print** in the Print Reports window to print the report shown in Figure 7.3.

   trouble? Notice that QuickBooks includes a line item called "Net Income" in the (Owners') Equity section. Standard accounting practice does not allow inclusion of such an income statement category in a balance sheet. Usually this net income is included in the Retained Earnings account.

Next you'll create a balance sheet for the quarter with a column indicating each item's percent of total assets. For example, you'll report the percentage that cash bears to total assets, the percentage that accounts receivable bears to total assets, and so on. To do this you'll use the Modify Report button to add a new column.

Figure 7.3

Standard Balance Sheet for Phoenix

Phoenix Software 07
Balance Sheet
As of March 31, 2003

	Mar 31, 03
ASSETS	
Current Assets	
Checking/Savings	
Bank of Cupertino	80,795.51
Short-term Investments	13,225.00
Total Checking/Savings	94,020.51
Accounts Receivable	
Accounts Receivable	31,397.01
Total Accounts Receivable	31,397.01
Other Current Assets	
Inventory Asset	17,579.40
Investments	14,000.00
Prepaid Insurance	1,038.50
Prepaid Rent	800.00
Undeposited Funds	10,000.00
Total Other Current Assets	43,417.90
Total Current Assets	168,835.42
Fixed Assets	
Computer Equipment	
Cost	28,750.00
Accumulated Depreciation	−375.00
Total Computer Equipment	28,375.00
Furniture	
Cost	3,756.44
Accumulated Depreciation	−313.04
Total Furniture	3,443.40
Total Fixed Assets	31,818.40
TOTAL ASSETS	**200,653.82**
LIABILITIES & EQUITY	
Liabilities	
Current Liabilities	
Accounts Payable	
Accounts Payable	2,199.50
Total Accounts Payable	2,199.50
Other Current Liabilities	
Payroll Liabilities	11,754.36
Sales Tax Payable	7,696.88
Short-Term Debt	5,250.00
Unearned Revenue	4,162.50
Total Other Current Liabilities	28,863.74
Total Current Liabilities	31,063.24
Long Term Liabilities	
Long-Term Debt	86,775.00
Total Long Term Liabilities	86,775.00
Total Liabilities	117,838.24
Equity	
Capital Stock	75,000.00
Net Income	7,815.58
Total Equity	82,815.58
TOTAL LIABILITIES & EQUITY	**200,653.82**

Compare this to
**Net Income shown on
the Income Statement.**

To modify the balance sheet:

1 Click the **Modify Report** button, then click the **% of Column** checkbox.

2 Click the **Fonts & Numbers** tab, then click the **Without Cents** checkbox.

3 Format the Header by clicking the **Header/Footer** tab.

4 Remove the "07" from the header by clicking to the right of the 7 and backspacing twice.

5 Choose **Left** as the Page Layout, then click **OK**.

6 Click the **Print** button, then click **Print** in the Print Reports window to print the report shown in Figure 7.4.

7 Close all open windows.

Karen comments that at first she thought the percentage column was the same as the one shown in the income statement: the percentage each item is to the total revenue (what QuickBooks calls "income"). But now she sees that this column shows the percentage of total assets. For example, total cash (that is, the total amount in checking and savings) is 47% of Phoenix's total assets, and accounts receivable is 16% of total assets. She comments that it looks like a large portion of those assets came from long-term debt, as indicated by the 43% long-term debt to assets ratio.

"I wonder if this is what Casey expected for Phoenix's results as of March 31, 2003?" she asks. "Let's compare our actual balance sheet with what Casey budgeted."

To create a budgeted vs. actual balance sheet:

1 Click **Reports**, **Budgets**, then click **Budget vs. Actual**.

trouble? The balance sheet report created in the prior sequence of steps cannot be modified to include a budget column. Instead you must create a new report from the Budget menu item described in Step 1.

2 Select **FY2003–Balance Sheet by Account**, then click **Next**, then click **Finish**.

3 Change the report dates to read from **01/01/03** to **03/31/03** in the Modify Report window.

4 Select **Quarter** from the Display Columns by drop-down edit box.

5 Make sure that all checkboxes—**Show Actuals**, **$ Difference**, and **% of Budget**—have been checked as shown in Figure 7.5 on page 218.

6 Click the **Fonts & Numbers** tab, then click the Show All Numbers **Without Cents** checkbox, then click **OK**.

Phoenix Software
Balance Sheet
As of March 31, 2003

	Mar 31, '03	% of Column
ASSETS		
Current Assets		
Checking/Savings		
Bank of Cupertino	80,796	40%
Short-term Investments	13,225	7%
Total Checking/Savings	94,021	47%
Accounts Receivable		
Accounts Receivable	31,397	16%
Total Accounts Receivable	31,397	16%
Other Current Assets		
Inventory Asset	17,579	9%
Investments	14,000	7%
Prepaid Insurance	1,039	1%
Prepaid Rent	800	0%
Undeposited Funds	10,000	5%
Total Other Current Assets	43,418	22%
Total Current Assets	168,835	84%
Fixed Assets		
Computer Equipment		
Cost	28,750	14%
Accumulated Depreciation	−375	−0%
Total Computer Equipment	28,375	14%
Furniture		
Cost	3,756	2%
Accumulated Depreciation	−313	−0%
Total Furniture	3,443	2%
Total Fixed Assets	31,818	16%
TOTAL ASSETS	**200,654**	**100%**
LIABILITIES & EQUITY		
Liabilities		
Current Liabilities		
Accounts Payable		
Accounts Payable	2,200	1%
Total Accounts Payable	2,200	1%
Other Current Liabilities		
Payroll Liabilities	11,754	6%
Sales Tax Payable	7,697	4%
Short-Term Debt	5,250	3%
Unearned Revenue	4,163	2%
Total Other Current Liabilities	28,864	14%
Total Current Liabilities	31,063	15%
Long-Term Liabilities		
Long-Term Debt	86,775	43%
Total Long-Term Liabilities	86,775	43%
Total Liabilities	117,838	59%
Equity		
Capital Stock	75,000	37%
Net Income	7,816	4%
Total Equity	82,816	41%
TOTAL LIABILITIES & EQUITY	**200,654**	**100%**

Figure 7.4

A Modified Balance Sheet for Phoenix

7 Click the **Print** button, click the **Fit report to 1 page(s) wide** check-box, then click **Print** in the Print Reports window to print the report shown in Figure 7.6 on page 219.

Figure 7.5

Modify Report Window

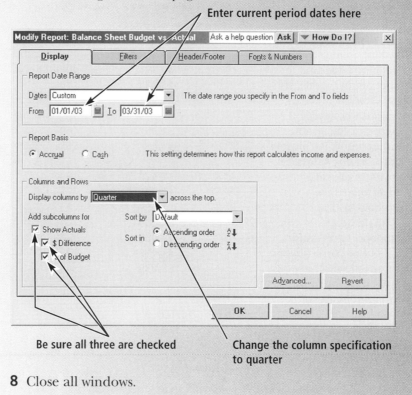

Enter current period dates here

Be sure all three are checked

Change the column specification to quarter

8 Close all windows.

Karen takes the Standard Balance Sheet and the Balance Sheet Budget Comparison to Casey.

"This is very helpful information," he comments as he quickly skims these reports. "I can see Phoenix's financial position, and how we stand in relation to where I thought we'd be. To save time, though, can I see this information expressed in graphical form? I'm afraid I might miss something when I look at this detailed report. A graph would help me see things I might miss when I look at just numbers."

Both you and Karen agree that some graphs would be helpful.

CREATING GRAPHS

In particular, Casey is anxious to know more about his product sales and expenses. It is clear that graphic representations of sales, revenue, and expenses will be helpful.

To create a sales graph:

1 Click **Reports**, then click **Sales**, then click **Sales Graph**.

2 Click the **Dates** button, and change the dates to read from **01/01/03** to **03/31/03** in the Change Graph Dates window. Then click **OK**.

Figure 7.6 A Budgeted vs. Actual Balance Sheet for Phoenix

Phoenix Software 07
Balance Sheet Budget vs. Actual
As of March 31, 2003

	Mar 31, '03	Budget	$ Over Budget	% of Budget
ASSETS				
Current Assets				
Checking/Savings				
Bank of Cupertino	80,796	23,330	57,466	346%
Short-term Investments	13,225	50,000	–36,775	26%
Total Checking/Savings	94,021	73,330	20,691	128%
Accounts Receivable				
Accounts Receivable	31,397	25,000	6,397	126%
Total Accounts Receivable	31,397	25,000	6,397	126%
Other Current Assets				
Inventory Asset	17,579	40,000	–22,421	44%
Investments	14,000			
Prepaid Insurance	1,039			
Prepaid Rent	800			
Undeposited Funds	10,000			
Total Other Current Assets	43,418	40,000	3,418	109%
Total Current Assets	168,835	138,330	30,505	122%
Fixed Assets				
Computer Equipment				
Cost	28,750	30,000	–1,250	96%
Accumulated Depreciation	–375	–400	25	94%
Total Computer Equipment	28,375	29,600	–1,225	96%
Furniture				
Cost	3,756	3,500	256	107%
Accumulated Depreciation	–313	–300	–13	104%
Total Furniture	3,443	3,200	243	108%
Total Fixed Assets	31,818	32,800	–982	97%
TOTAL ASSETS	**200,654**	**171,130**	**29,524**	**117%**
LIABILITIES & EQUITY				
Liabilities				
Current Liabilities				
Accounts Payable				
Accounts Payable	2,200	13,000	–10,801	17%
Total Accounts Payable	2,200	13,000	–10,801	17%
Other Current Liabilities				
Payroll Liabilities	11,754	12,000	–246	98%
Sales Tax Payable	7,697	8,000	–303	96%
Short-Term Debt	5,250	10,000	–4,750	53%
Unearned Revenue	4,163			
Total Other Current Liabilities	28,864	30,000	–1,136	96%
Total Current Liabilities	31,063	43,000	–11,937	72%
Long-Term Liabilities				
Long-Term Debt	86,775	55,000	31,775	158%
Total Long-Term Liabilities	86,775	55,000	31,775	158%
Total Liabilities	117,838	98,000	19,838	120%
Equity				
Capital Stock	75,000	75,000	0	100%
Retained Earnings	0	–1,870	1,870	0%
Net Income	7,816	0	7,816	100%
Total Equity	82,816	73,130	9,686	113%
TOTAL LIABILITIES & EQUITY	**200,654**	**171,130**	**29,524**	**117%**

3 Click the **By Item** button in the QuickInsight: Sales Graph window, if it is not already selected. Selecting this button causes QuickBooks to display sales in the graph by item, in this case by the hardware and the services that Phoenix sells.

4 QuickBooks generates two graphs—a bar chart and a pie chart—as shown in Figure 7.7. Study these graphs.

Figure 7.7

A Sales By Month Graph for Phoenix—By Item

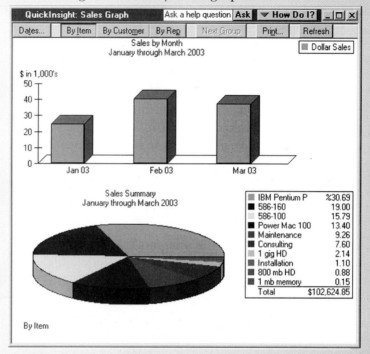

5 Click the **By Customer** button in the QuickInsight: Sales Graph window to create a graph that illustrates sales for the quarter by customer. See Figure 7.8.

Figure 7.8

A Sales By Month Graph for Phoenix—By Customer

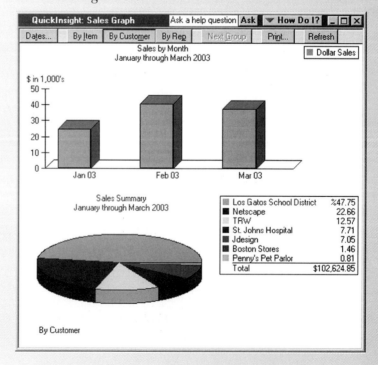

6 Close all windows.

Graphs such as these help managers interpret financial information, because they often reveal important relationships not obvious from the financial statements. For example, in Figure 7.8, sales growth by month is illustrated and the source of sales by customer is revealed. In this case Los Gatos School District represents almost 48% of sales for the quarter.

Next you decide to produce a graph that illustrates Phoenix's revenues (or "income" as QuickBooks calls it) and expenses.

To create a revenue and expense graph:

1 Click **Reports**, then click **Company & Financial**, then click **Income & Expense Graph**.

2 Click the **Dates** button, and change the dates to read from **01/01/03** to **03/31/03** in the Change Graph Dates window. Then click **OK**.

3 Click the **By Account** button at the top of the screen and the **Expense** button at the bottom of the QuickInsight: Income and Expense Graph window, if they are not already selected.

4 The graph shown in Figure 7.9 appears. Study this graph.

trouble? Your vertical axis scale might be different, depending on the size of the figure you choose to view.

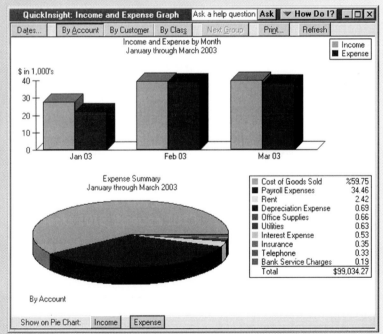

Figure 7.9

An Income (Revenue) and Expense by Month Graph for Phoenix Systems, Including Details of Expenses for the Quarter

5 Close all windows.

These two graphs help to explain revenues and expenses, but they do not provide insight into the financial position of the company as of March 31.

"Does QuickBooks have similar graphing capabilities for items such as accounts receivable and accounts payable?" Karen asks.

"Yes," you respond. "In fact, we should probably create a graph for both accounts to demonstrate how current or noncurrent our receivables and payables are. QuickBooks can create a bar chart that illustrates aging for accounts receivable and then another for accounts payable, and simultaneously identify who owes us or who we owe, respectively, at any single time, such as March 31, 2003."

To create accounts receivable and accounts payable graphs:

1 Click **Reports**, then click **Customers & Receivables**, then click **Accounts Receivable Graph**.

2 Click the **Dates** button and change the date to **03/31/03** in the Change Graph Dates window. Then click **OK**.

3 A graph appears. See Figure 7.10. Study this figure.

Figure 7.10

A Graph Illustrating the Aging of Accounts Receivable and Customer Balances

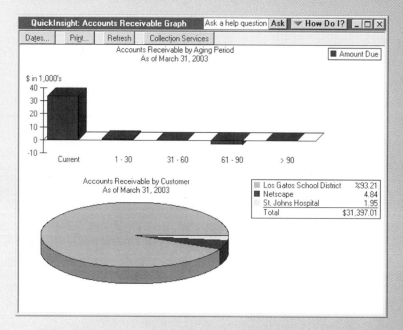

4 Click **Reports**, then click **Vendors & Payables**, then click **Accounts Payable Graph**.

5 Click the **Dates** button and change the date to **03/31/03** in the Change Graph Dates window. Then click **OK**.

6 A graph appears. See Figure 7.11 on the next page. Study this figure.

7 Close all windows.

When you show Casey these graphs, he comments that they will be very helpful. But he wants to see even more information derived from the financial statements—specifically, he wants to see reports on sales, purchases, and inventory.

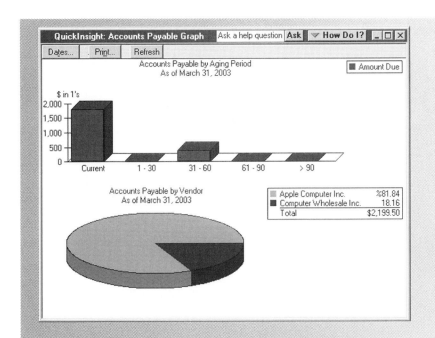

CREATING ADDITIONAL REPORTS

With QuickBooks you can generate many supporting reports for the financial statements—what accountants consider traditional support in the form of schedules.

Karen reads through QuickBooks Help and discovers two reports that QuickBooks generates that will help Casey—the Sales by Customer Summary and the Summary Sales by Item. Together you decide that the Sales by Customer Summary should identify sales for each month of the quarter so you can see to which customers you sold product or services. The Summary Sales by Item reports on the number of items sold, the average price of each item sold, and each item's related average cost. This report also identifies the gross margin (sales revenue minus cost of goods sold) amount for each item and summarizes the gross margin for all items sold during the period. Karen suggests that you produce this report on a quarterly basis.

To create the Sales by Customer Summary and the Summary Sales by Item reports:

1 Click **Reports**, then click **Sales**, then click **Sales by Customer Summary**.

2 Change the report dates to read from **01/01/03** to **03/31/03** in the Modify Report window.

3 Select **Month** from the Columns drop-down edit box, then click **OK**. The screen shown in Figure 7.12 appears.

4 Click **Reports**, **Sales**, then click **Sales by Item Summary**.

5 Change the report dates to read from **01/01/03** to **03/31/03** in the Modify Report window.

Figure 7.12

Sales by Customer by Month

Figure 7.12

Sales by Customer by Month

Phoenix Software 07
Sales by Customer Summary
January through March 2003

	Jan 03	Feb 03	Mar 03	TOTAL
Boston Stores	0.00	0.00	1,500.00	1,500.00
Jdesign	640.00	6,590.00	0.00	7,230.00
Los Gatos School District	17,125.00	0.00	31,875.00	49,000.00
Netscape	0.00	20,250.00	3,000.00	23,250.00
Penny's Pet Parlor	0.00	834.85	0.00	834.85
St. Johns Hospital	6,875.00	0.00	1,035.00	7,910.00
TRW	0.00	12,900.00	0.00	12,900.00
TOTAL	24,640.00	40,574.85	37,410.00	102,624.85

6 Select **Total Only** from the Columns drop-down edit box, then click **OK**.

7 Adjust the column width to view more of the report on your screen as shown in Figure 7.13. You may need to scroll down the report to view items sold and total sales.

Figure 7.13

Sales by Item for the Quarter

Phoenix Software 07
Sales by Item Summary
January through March 2003
Jan - Mar 03

	Qty	Amount	% of Sales	Avg Price	COGS	Avg COGS	Gross Margin	Gross Margin %
Inventory								
1 gig HD	4	2,200.00	2.1%	550.00	1,800.00	450.00	400.00	18.2%
1 mb memory	3	149.85	0.1%	49.95	119.85	39.95	30.00	20%
586-100	9	16,200.00	15.8%	1,800.00	13,500.00	1,500.00	2,700.00	16.7%
586-160	5	19,500.00	19%	3,900.00	11,500.00	2,300.00	8,000.00	41%
800 mb HD	3	900.00	0.9%	300.00	750.00	250.00	150.00	16.7%
IBM Pentium P	3	31,500.00	30.7%	10,500.00	22,500.00	7,500.00	9,000.00	28.6%
Power Mac 100	5	13,750.00	13.4%	2,750.00	9,000.00	1,800.00	4,750.00	34.5%
Total Inventory		84,199.85	82%		59,169.85		25,030.00	29.7%
Service								
Consulting	104	7,800.00	7.6%	75.00				
Installation	25	1,125.00	1.1%	45.00				
Maintenance	190	9,500.00	9.3%	50.00				
Total Service		18,425.00	18%					
TOTAL		102,624.85	100.0%					

8 Close all windows.

Karen tells you that three additional reports are commonly prepared to support the balance sheet for the quarter: an accounts receivable aging, an accounts payable aging, and an inventory status report. QuickBooks can easily generate these reports.

To create an Accounts Receivable Aging report:

1 Click **Reports**, then click **Customers & Receivables**, then click **A/R Aging Summary**.

2 Change the From date to **01/01/03** and the To date to **03/31/03** in the Modify Report window, then click **OK**. The report shown in Figure 7.14 appears. Examine this report.

3 Did you notice a negative $887.50 amount on the Boston Stores line? To investigate, double-click the **–887.50**.

Note the −887.50 amount

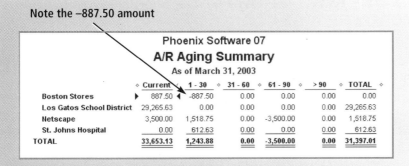

Figure 7.14

Accounts Receivable
Aging Report

Phoenix Software 07
A/R Aging Summary
As of March 31, 2003

	Current	1 - 30	31 - 60	61 - 90	> 90	TOTAL
Boston Stores	887.50	-887.50	0.00	0.00	0.00	0.00
Los Gatos School District	29,265.63	0.00	0.00	0.00	0.00	29,265.63
Netscape	3,500.00	1,518.75	0.00	-3,500.00	0.00	1,518.75
St. Johns Hospital	0.00	612.63	0.00	0.00	0.00	612.63
TOTAL	33,653.13	1,243.88	0.00	-3,500.00	0.00	31,397.01

4 When the A/R Aging QuickZoom window appears, double-click the **03/06/03** payment.

5 The Receive Payments window appears showing a payment of $2,500, of which only $1,612.50 was applied to open invoices. Now you remember that the balance of $887.50 was transferred to Unearned Revenue (a liability account) for the balance sheet disclosure.

6 Click **Reports**, then click **Vendors & Payables**, then click **A/P Aging Summary**.

7 Change the From date to **01/01/03** and the To date to **03/31/03** in the Modify Report window, then click **OK** to view the report shown in Figure 7.15.

Figure 7.15

Accounts Payable
Aging Report

Phoenix Software 07
A/P Aging Summary
As of March 31, 2003

	Current	1 - 30	31 - 60	61 - 90	> 90	TOTAL
Apple Computer Inc.	1,800.00	0.00	0.00	0.00	0.00	1,800.00
Computer Wholesale Inc.	0.00	0.00	399.50	0.00	0.00	399.50
TOTAL	1,800.00	0.00	399.50	0.00	0.00	2,199.50

8 Click **Reports**, then click **Inventory**, then click **Inventory Stock Status by Item**.

9 Change the From date to **01/01/03** and the To date to **03/31/03** in the Modify Report window, then click **OK** to view the report, which is shown in Figure 7.16. Scroll to the right to view the remaining report.

Figure 7.16

Inventory Stock Status by Item

Phoenix Software 07
Inventory Stock Status by Item
January through March 2003

	Item Description	Pref Vendor	Reorder Pt	On Hand	Order	On Purchase Order	Next Deliv	Sales/Week
Inventory								
1 gig HD	1,000mb Bengal H...	Bengal Driv...		4		0		0.3
1 mb memory	Memory modules	Computer W...	20	12	✓	0		0.2
586-100	Phoenix Pentium C...	Computer W...		1		0		0.7
586-160	Phoenix 586 160 M...	Computer W...	3	5		10	03/24/03	0.4
800 mb HD	800mb Bengal Har...	Bengal Driv...		2		0		0.2
IBM Pentium P	IBM Pentium Plus C...	IBM		0		0		0.2
Power Mac 100	Apple Power Mac ...	Apple Comp...	4	1	✓	0		0.4

10 Close all windows.

EXPORTING REPORTS TO MICROSOFT EXCEL

· ·

In QuickBooks you can export reports to Microsoft's Excel spreadsheet program.

"Why export to Microsoft Excel when QuickBooks gives us so many report options?" Karen asks. You explain that, occasionally, she may need to change a report's appearance or contents in ways that are not available within QuickBooks. Since the changes you make in Excel do not affect your QuickBooks data, you are free to customize a report as needed or even change report data to run "what if" scenarios.

Karen reads through QuickBooks Help and discovers that exporting a report to Excel is as simple as clicking a new button on the report's button bar. She suggests the two of you experiment with this feature by creating an income statement for March with a year-to-date comparison column.

To create a Comparative Year-to-date Income Statement:

1 Click **Reports**, click **Company & Financial**, and then click **Profit & Loss YTD Comparison**.

2 Change the From date to **03/01/03** and the To date to **03/31/03** in the Modify Report window, then click **OK** to view the report shown in Figure 7.17.

Click the Export button to Export Report to Excel

Figure 7.17

P&L YTD Comparison

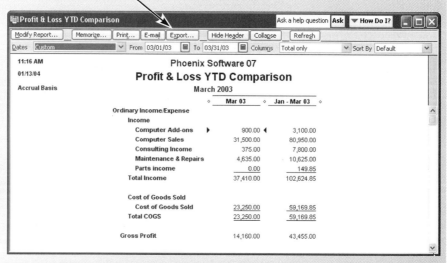

3 Open the Modify Report window again, then click the **Header/Footer** tab and change the report title to **Comparative Year-To-Date Income Statement**, change the Page Layout to **Left**, then click **OK**.

4 Click the **Export** button on the Report button bar to display the Export Report window shown in Figure 7.18. Uncheck the box which adds a new worksheet with Excel tips.

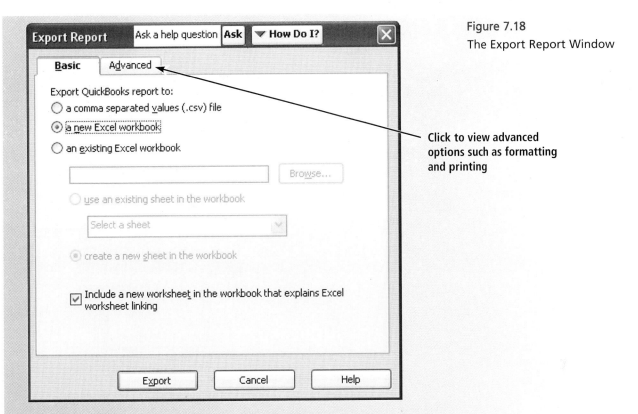

Figure 7.18
The Export Report Window

5 Click the **Advanced** tab in the Export Report window to view advanced options such as formatting and printing, as shown in Figure 7.19.

Figure 7.19
Advanced Options Window

6 Make sure the options checked in the Advanced Options window are the same as those shown in Figure 7.19.

7 Now click **Export** in the Export Report window.

trouble? To export reports to Excel you must have Microsoft Excel '97 or higher installed on your computer.

8 Select cell I10 and note that the export process has created not only a spreadsheet with values, but also one with formulas, as shown in Figure 7.20.

9 Click File in Excel, then click **Print Preview**. Note the header information is that which you modified in QuickBooks previously.

Figure 7.20
Exported Report in Excel

This box identifies the active cell you selected

Note the formula created during the export process

Select this cell

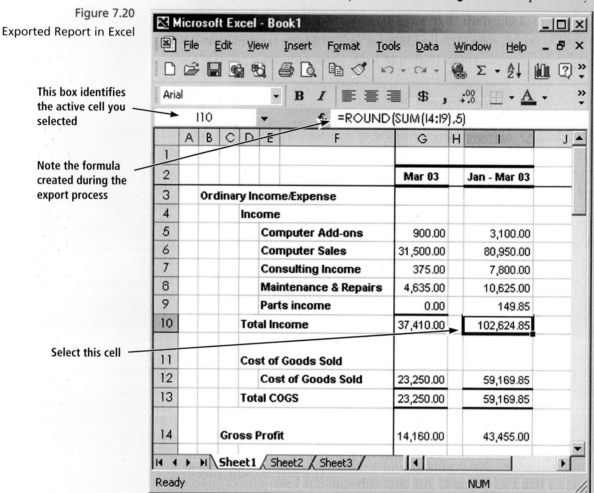

10 Click **Setup**, then click the **Sheet** tab in the Page Setup window. Place a check mark in the **Gridlines** and **Row and column headings** checkboxes, then click **OK**. (This will enable the printing of gridlines and row and column headings.)

11 Click **Print** in Excel, then click **OK** in the Print window to print the Excel document you just created. Your spreadsheet should look like Figure 7.21.

12 Click **File** in Excel, then **Exit** to quit the Excel program.

13 Click **No** to not save the spreadsheet since it will no longer be used.

14 Close all windows in QuickBooks.

	A	B	C	D	E	F	G	H	I
1									
2							**Mar. '03**		**Jan–Mar '03**
3			Ordinary Income/Expense						
4					Income				
5						Computer Add-ons	900.00		3,100.00
6						Computer Sales	31,500.00		80,950.00
7						Consulting Income	375.00		7,800.00
8						Maintenance & Repairs	4,635.00		10,625.00
9						Parts income	0.00		149.85
10					Total Income		37,410.00		102,624.85
11					Cost of Goods Sold				
12						Cost of Goods Sold	23,250.00		59,169.85
13					Total COGS		23,250.00		59,169.85
14				Gross Profit			14,160.00		43,455.00
15					Expense				
16						Bank Service Charges	75.00		185.00
17						Depreciation Expense	688.04		688.04
18						Insurance			
19							Liability Insurance	346.17		346.17
20						Total Insurance	346.17		346.17
21						Interest Expense			
22							Loan Interest	525.00		525.00
23						Total Interest Expense	525.00		525.00
24						Office Supplies	57.60		650.16
25						Payroll Expenses	11,263.84		34,122.86
26						Rent	1,600.00		2,400.00
27						Telephone	75.95		328.16
28						Utilities			
29							Gas and Electric	210.00		619.00
30						Total Utilities	210.00		619.00
31					Total Expense		14,841.60		39,864.42
32				Net Ordinary Income			–681.60		3,590.58

Figure 7.21
Printed Excel Report

	A	B	C	D	E	F	G	H	I
1									
2							Mar. '03		Jan–Mar '03
33						Other Income/Expense			
34						Other Income			
35						Investment Income	1,500.00		3,500.00
36						Interest Revenue	725.00		725.00
37						Total Other Income	2,225.00		4,22500
38						Net Other Income	2,225.00		4,225.00
39	**Net Income**						**1,543.40**		**7,815.58**

END NOTE

You've completed the reports for Casey and decide to deliver them to his office. After quickly skimming each report, Casey compliments you both on your fine work and you turn to walk back to your office.

As you walk back to your office, Karen comments, "That's the first time I've ever created financial statements without using debits and credits. How is that possible?"

"All the debits and credits are done for you," you explain. "Tomorrow I'll show you that QuickBooks in fact still keeps data in a debit and credit format and can provide the traditional general ledger, journal entries, and trial balance procedures you are more familiar with."

practice

Chapter 7 Questions

1 Explain how you can use QuickBooks to modify any report.

2 What are the optional columns available in the Modify Report window when you create a balance sheet?

3 What time periods are available for the columns of a balance sheet?

4 What options are available in the Fonts & Numbers tab for a balance sheet?

5 How do you resize a report that would normally print on two pages to one page?

6 When you create a balance sheet, what result does clicking the Collapse button have?

7 What different graphs are available in QuickBooks?

8 Discuss why percentage changes identified in the budgeted vs. actual reports need to be interpreted carefully.

9 Describe the information available in the accounts receivable and accounts payable aging reports.

10 Describe the information available in the inventory stocks status report by item.

Chapter 7 Assignments

1 *Creating Financial Reports and Supporting Schedules for Phoenix Systems, Inc.*

Use Phnx07.qbw to create and print the following reports and spreadsheets:

a. a Profit & Loss Standard report for the month ended January 31, 2003

b. the report created in item *a* exported to Excel (Be sure to enable gridlines and report and column headings.)

c. a Balance Sheet Standard report as of January 31, 2003

d. the report created in item *c* exported to Excel

e. a Profit & Loss Budget vs. Actual report for the month ended January 31, 2003

f. a Balance Sheet Budget vs. Actual report as of January 31, 2003

g. a Sales by Customer Summary report for the month ended January 31, 2003

h. a Sales by Item Summary report for the month ended January 31, 2003

i. an A/R Aging Summary report as of January 31, 2003

j.   an A/P Aging Summary report as of January 31, 2003

k.   an Inventory Valuation Summary report as of January 31, 2003

2   *Creating Graphs for Phoenix Systems, Inc.*

Use Phnx07.qbw to create and print the following graphs:

a.   sales for the month ended January 31, 2003

b.   revenue (income) and expense for the month ended January 31, 2003

c.   accounts receivable aging as of January 31, 2003

d.   accounts payable aging as of January 31, 2003

3   *Adding More Information: Central Coast Cellular*

In Chapter 6, you added some budget information to your QuickBooks file for Central Coast Cellular (CCC), a cellular phone sales, phone rental, and consulting company. Make a copy of that file in Windows Explorer, name the file CCC7, and use that file to create the following:

a.   a Profit & Loss Standard report for the month ended January 31, 2003 without cents, a revised title of "Income Statement," and a % of income column in a portrait orientation

b.   the report created in *a* exported to Excel with gridlines and row and column headings

c.   a Balance Sheet Standard report as of January 31, 2003, without cents, and a % of Column column in a portrait orientation

d.   the report created in *c* exported to Excel with gridlines and row and column headings

e.   a Profit & Loss Budget vs. Actual report for January 2003, without cents, right aligned, without the date prepared, time prepared and report basis

f.   a Balance Sheet Budget vs. Actual report as of January 31, 2003, without cents, left aligned, without the date prepared, time prepared, and report basis; collapse this report (***Hint:*** Click the **Collapse** button on the report button bar.)

g.   an Inventory Valuation Summary as of January 31, 2003 without cents, in landscape orientation

4   *Using the South-Western Home Page for More Assignments or Cases*

If you have Internet access, go to the home page for this textbook at **http://owen.swlearning.com**.

Select the **Chapter 7** section from the Additional Problem Sets, and complete the problem(s) assigned by your instructor.

Go to
http://owen.swlearning.
com

Chapter 7 Case Problem 1: OCEAN VIEW FLOWERS

In Chapter 6, you modified your QuickBooks file for Ocean View Flowers, a wholesale flower distributor. Make a copy of that file and use that copy for the following:

1 *Create and print the following reports/spreadsheets:*

    a. a Profit & Loss Budget vs. Actual report for the period January through February 2004, which shows actual results, budgeted amounts, amount over budget, and percentage of budget in total only, not by month

    b. a Balance Sheet Budget vs. Actual report as of February 29, 2004, which shows actual balances, budgeted amounts, amount over budget, and percentage of budget in total only, not by month

    c. an Excel spreadsheet from the report created in *b*

    d. a Sales by Customer Summary report for the two-month period January and February 2004

    e. an Inventory Stock Status by Item report for the two-month period January and February 2004 (print with a landscape orientation)

2 *Create and print the following graphs:*

    a. a graph of income and expenses for the months of January and February 2004 with a pie chart showing expenses by account for the two-month period

    b. a graph of sales for the months of January and February 2004 with a pie chart showing sales by item for the two-month period

Chapter 7 Case Problem 2: JENNINGS & ASSOCIATES—Financial Reports and Graphs

Now that the budget data and related adjustments have been made, Kelly can create and print the appropriate reports and graphs.

Use Kj07cp.qbw from your Data Files CD. (***Note:*** Additional transactions have been included in this file that were not included in Chapter 6. Do not use your completed Kj06cp.qbw file.)

1 Create and print the following reports or spreadsheets using proper headings:

    a. a Profit & Loss Standard report for the quarter ended March 31, 2004 with left page layout and without cents

    b. a Balance Sheet Standard report as of March 31, 2004 with left page layout and without cents

    c. a balance sheet showing budgeted vs. actual amounts with $ Over Budget and % of Budget columns as of March 31, 2004 with left page layout and without cents (***Hint:*** Display only the month of March.)

    d. an income statement showing budgeted vs. actual amounts with $ Over Budget and % of Budget columns for the quarter ended March 31, 2004 with the header in a left page layout with cents

    e. the report created in item *d* exported to Excel

    f. a Sales by Customer Summary report for the quarter ended March 31, 2004 with left page layout and without cents

g. a Sales by Item Summary report for the quarter ended March 31, 2004 with left page layout and without cents

h. an A/R Aging Summary report as of March 31, 2004

i. an A/P Aging Summary report as of March 31, 2004

j. an Inventory Valuation Summary as of March 31, 2004 in landscape view with left page layout and without cents

2 Create and print the following graphs:

a. sales for the quarter ended March 31, 2004

b. revenue (income) and expense for the quarter ended March 31, 2004

c. accounts receivable aging as of March 31, 2004

d. accounts payable aging as of March 31, 2004

Comprehensive Problem 1

Use the following information to modify a company in QuickBooks. Then create and print the reports as requested below.

Sports City, Inc. is a sporting goods store that opened for business on 4/1/04. Scott Szulczewski invested $40,000 to open the business. He has recorded various transactions in his QuickBooks accounting software but needs you to come on board and help him finish the month's accounting. Use QuickBooks to restore the Sports City.qbb file available on your data file CD and add the following transactions. (***Note:*** Be sure to enter these transactions in the proper date period):

1 On 4/16/04 the company received a bill from Office Max for $250 for office supplies purchased on account (Record as Supplies:Office, an expense, terms: due on receipt).

2 On 4/17/04 the company received items and entered a bill from Nike for a previously recorded purchase order #1 (terms: due on receipt).

3 On 4/18/04 the company received items and entered a bill from Wilson Sporting Goods for a previously recorded purchase order #2 (terms: due on receipt).

4 On 4/19/04 the company hired a new employee, Anne Franks, 112 East Fir #3, Lompoc, CA 93436, a single woman, social security number 233-89-4232. She will earn an hourly wage of $8.00, be paid semimonthly like all employees, and is subject to all payroll taxes including the training tax.

5 On 4/20/04 the company received a $400 payment on account from Cabrillo High School, which is grouped with other undeposited funds.

6 On 4/21/04 the company invoiced Buena Vista Elementary for 100 shirts and 5 footballs.

7 On 4/22/04 the company received a $600 payment on account from Lompoc High School, which is also grouped with other undeposited funds.

8 On 4/24/04 the company borrowed $10,000 from Mid-State Bank with a short-term note payable.

9 On 4/25/04 the company paid all bills due by 4/30/04.

10 On 4/29/04 the company deposited by mail all previously received but undeposited payments, totaling $1,000, to Mid-State Bank.

11 On 4/30/04 the company paid all employees for the pay period 4/16 – 4/30. Ms. Franks worked 75 hours during this period. (See tax information below.)

	Sam Snead	Kelly Flowers	Anne Franks
Federal withholding	$244.00	$147.00	$73.00
Social security employee	$90.41	$77.50	$37.20
Social security employer	$90.41	$77.50	$37.20
Medicare employee	$21.14	$18.12	$8.70
Medicare employer	$21.14	$18.12	$8.70
CA—withholding	$57.39	$40.72	$7.66
CA—disability employee	$7.29	$6.25	$3.00
CA—training tax	$1.46	$1.25	$0.60
Federal unemployment	$11.66	$10.00	$4.80
CA—unemployment	$0.73	$0.62	$0.30

12 On 4/30/04 the company recorded depreciation of $2,000 on furniture & fixtures.

13 On 4/30/04 the company recorded the expiration of $3,000 in prepaid rent.

14 On 4/30/04 the company reclassified the advance payment made by Arroyo Grande High School to unearned revenue.

15 On 4/30/04 the company reconciled the bank account. The ending bank balance per the statement is $5,333.52. The bank charged a $40 service charge. Checks for the April 30th payroll do not appear on the statement, nor does the $1,000 deposited by mail on April 30th.

16 Budget information for April through June 2004 is as follows:

Account	April 04	Following
Sales	$10,000	15% increase each month thereafter
Cost of Sales	$6,000	60% of sales
Depreciation	$2,000	Constant each month thereafter
Payroll	$6,500	$500 increase each month thereafter
Rent	$3,000	Constant each month thereafter
Telephone	$100	5% increase each month thereafter
Utilities	$200	5% increase each month thereafter

Prepare and print the following:

1   Custom Transaction Detail Report by date report for the period 4/1/04 through 4/30/04.

2   Standard balance sheet as of 4/30/04 with a % of column.

3   Standard profit and loss statement for April 2004 with a % of income column.

4   Statement of cash flows for April 2004.

5   Profit and loss budget vs. actual for April 2004.

6   Profit and loss budget overview for April 2004 through June 2004.

7   Summary bank reconciliation as of 4/30/04.

8   Export the balance sheet created above to Excel, and then print the Excel worksheet.

Comprehensive Problem 2

This is a continuation of the Pacific Brew, Inc. case from Chapter 3. The following additional transactions occurred:

Chronological list of business transactions

Date	Transaction
1/17/06	Received items and entered a bill from purchase order 1003 to Lost Coast.
1/17/06	Received a bill from Staples for $2,500 of office supplies purchased on account terms net 15. These supplies will be used over the next 6 months, thus you will need to create an Office Supplies (Current Asset) account.
1/17/06	Using purchase order 1004, ordered 1,000 of item 402, 1,500 of item 403, and 2,000 of item 404 for immediate delivery, terms: net 15 from Lost Coast.
1/17/06	Using purchase order 1005, ordered 750 each of item 302, 303, 304, and 305 for immediate delivery, terms: net 30 from Mad River.
1/18/06	The manager believes the company charges too little for its products and increases all product prices 50%. (Use QuickBooks Help to find out how to increase sales prices of items by a percentage.)
1/19/06	Using purchase order 1006, ordered 500 of each item 502, 506, and 507 for immediate delivery, terms: net 15 from Humboldt.
1/20/06	Received and shipped an order to Bon Jovi's for 200 units of item 302, 150 units of item 303, and 100 units of item 507. Invoice number 7001 was generated to bill the customer on net 15 terms. (Be sure to use the Intiut product invoice form to record this transaction.)
1/20/06	Received and shipped an order to Ocean Grove for 100 units each of item 302, 304, and 305. Invoice number 7002 was generated to bill the customer on net 15 terms.

1/23/06 Received and shipped an order to Avalon Bistro for 150 units each of item 505, 506, and 507. Invoice number 7003 was generated to bill the customer on net 30 terms.

1/24/06 Received items and entered a bill from purchase order 1004 to Lost Coast.

1/24/06 Received a bill from Verizon for telephone services for the month of January in the amount of $500 terms: due on receipt.

1/24/06 Received a bill from the City of Arcata for electrical services for the month of January in the amount of $1,500 terms: due on receipt.

1/25/06 Received payment on account from Bon Jovi's of $4,575 on invoice 7001, which will be deposited later in the week.

1/26/06 Received an advance on future orders from River House in the amount of $1,200, which will be deposited later in the week.

1/27/04 Deposit checks received earlier in the week to Wells Fargo.

1/30/06 Received items and entered a bill from purchase order 1005 to Mad River.

1/30/06 Paid bills from Verizon, City of Arcata, and Staples for a total of $4,500 assigning check numbers 110, 111, and 112 respectively.

1/30/06 Received and shipped an order (5007) to Hole in the Wall for 250 units each of item 303, 305, and 404. Payment of $7,032.50 was deposited and mailed to Wells Fargo Bank that same day.

1/31/06 Paid employees. Duarte worked 83 hours and Lopez worked 79 hours during the period. See tax information in the table below.

1/31/06 Recorded depreciation of $500 on equipment and $300 on furniture and fixtures for the month with journal entry 1.

1/31/06 Recorded the use of office supplies of $400 with journal entry 2.

1/31/06 Reclassified payment from River House to unearned revenue with journal entry 3.

1/31/06 Accrued interest expense on short-term investments of $2,000 with journal entry 4.

1/31/06 Accrued interest expense on long-term note payable of $2,600 with journal entry 5.

1/31/06 Reconciled the Wells Fargo bank account.

1/31/06 Budget information for January through March is as follows. Consulting revenue is expected to remain constant at $15,000 per month. Sales of $20,000 are expected in January, increasing $5,000 each month thereafter. Cost of goods sold of $15,000 is expected in January, increasing $2,500 each month thereafter. Depreciation, interest, rent, and office supplies expenses are expected to remain constant at $1,000, $2,000, $2,500, and $500 respectively. Telephone expenses of $450 are budgeted for January and are expected to increase $50 each month thereafter. Payroll expenses are budgeted at $8,500 for January and February and then $10,000 for March. Electric expenses are budgeted at $1,200 for January and are expected to increase by 5% each month thereafter. Interest income of $1,500 is expected each month.

Tax/Withholding	Duarte	Lopez	Patrick
Gross Pay	$913.00	$948.00	$2,083.33
Federal withholding	125.08	129.88	285.42
Social security employee	56.61	58.78	129.17
Medicare employee	13.24	13.75	30.21
CA—withholding	50.22	52.14	114.58
CA—disability	4.57	4.74	10.42
CA—employment training tax	0.91	0.95	2.08
Social security employer	$56.61	$58.78	$129.17
Medicare company	13.24	13.75	30.21
Federal unemployment	7.30	7.58	16.67
CA—company unemployment	27.39	28.44	62.50
Check amount	663.29	688.72	1,513.54

Requirements

1. Make a copy of the QuickBooks file you created for Pacific Brew in Chapter 3. Rename the file as Brew1.qbw.

2. Record the above business transactions in chronological order (remember dates are in the month of January 2006).

3. Create and print the following reports:

   a. Custom transaction detail report by date for the period 1/17/06 through 1/31/06 in landscape orientation fit to one page wide.

   b. Standard balance sheet as of 1/31/06, with a % of column, and a right page layout alignment without cents in portrait orientation.

   c. Standard profit and loss statement for the period 1/1/06 through 1/31/06, with a % of column, and a right page layout alignment without cents in portrait orientation.

   d. Statement of cash flows for the period 1/1/06 through 1/31/06, with a right page layout alignment without cents in portrait orientation. (Be sure to properly classify changes in accumulated depreciation.)

   e. Profit and loss budget vs. actual for January 2006 in portrait orientation.

   f. Profit and loss budget overview for January through March 2006 in portrait orientation.

   g. Summary bank reconciliation as of 1/31/06 in portrait orientation. There were no bank service charges. The bank statement balance was $35,673.30 at 1/31/06. None of the checks dated 1/30/06 had cleared the bank and one deposit, made on 1/31/06, was not reflected on the bank statement.

   h. Export the profit and loss statement created in *c* above to Excel, and then print the Excel worksheet with gridlines and row and column headings.

   i. Sales by customer summary for January 2006 in portrait orientation.

j. Sales by item summary for January 2006 in landscape orientation fit to one page wide.
k. Sales graph for January 2006 by customer.
l. Inventory stock status by item for January 2006 in landscape orientation fit to one page wide.

Traditional Accounting Records

In this appendix you will:

- **Prepare a trial balance**

- **Examine a general ledger**

- **Examine a journal entry used to record a business transaction**

- **Journalize a transaction**

CASE: PHOENIX SYSTEMS CONSULTING, INC.
. . . .

You and Karen have been recording business transactions for Phoenix without using journal entries or mentioning the terms *debit* and *credit* even once. This is another one of the benefits of using QuickBooks: It enables businesspeople who were not accounting majors to "do accounting." Moreover, accountants appreciate QuickBooks because they can use it with clients who want to have more control over their finances but who do not have formal accounting training.

As a user of QuickBooks, you should know that although you haven't actually used debits and credits in this book other than for adjusting journal entries, QuickBooks is based on a dual-entry or double-entry accounting system. Every transaction that you entered in Chapters 2 through 7 had an effect on two or more accounts in the chart of accounts. For example, every sales invoice increased Sales Revenue and Accounts Receivable. Every time you initiated a QuickBooks activity such as "receive payments," Cash was increased and Accounts Receivable was decreased.

QuickBooks actually provides three equivalent ways for you to record transactions using the double-entry system: You can record transactions by using business documents (what QuickBooks refers to as Forms), by using registers, or by making journal entries. In this textbook so far, you have used documents and registers. Recall that using a document involves recording a transaction by completing a business document, such as a sales invoice or a check. When you correctly complete the document, the effect(s) of the transaction on the financial statements are automatically entered. For example, when Phoenix paid its yearly insurance premium of $1,384.67 on 1/7/03, the dual effects of this transaction on the Prepaid Insurance account (increased) and the Cash account (decreased) were processed by filling out a business document, specifically a check. In contrast, using registers involves accessing a particular account's register and inputting the effects of the transaction. For example, you could choose either the Prepaid Insurance register or the Bank of Cupertino (cash) register and enter the changes (increase/decrease) as needed.

Karen asks if it is possible, however, to still use debits and credits in QuickBooks, because her formal accounting training focused primarily on journal entries as the source of every transaction. You explain that, yes, it is indeed possible, and you offer to demonstrate QuickBooks's ability to prepare a trial balance, a general ledger, and a journal entry. You point out that under normal circumstances you would begin the accounting process with a journal entry. In this case, however, you will view the steps with her in reverse order, because the process has already been completed.

TRIAL BALANCE
. . . .

The trial balance is a two-column listing of all asset, liability, owners' equity, revenue, and expense accounts. Accounts that have debit balances are listed in the debit column, and accounts that have credit balances are listed in the credit column. Although not foolproof, an equality between debits and credits generally indicates that the accounting process has been followed correctly.

With QuickBooks you can quickly create a trial balance. All you need is the date as of which you want the trial balance. Then you can use QuickBooks's QuickZoom feature to view supporting accounts and supporting journals or business documents.

To create the trial balance and examine supporting detail:

1 Open Phnx07.qbw located on your Working Disk.

2 Click **Reports**, **Accountant & Taxes**, then **Trial Balance**.

3 Change the report dates to read from **01/01/03** to **03/31/03** in the Modify Report window, then click **OK** to view the trial balance you have prepared, as shown in Figure A.1.

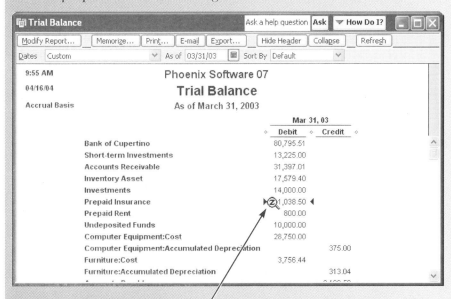

Figure A.1
Trial Balance

Double-click here to view the Prepaid Insurance account

4 Double-click on the **1,038.50 Prepaid Insurance** amount to view the Prepaid Insurance account shown in Figure A.2.

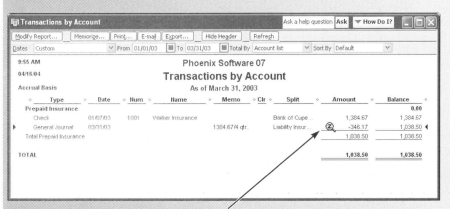

Figure A.2
General Ledger Account

Double-click here to view the adjusting journal entry

5 Double-click on the **–346.17 Prepaid Insurance** amount to view the Prepaid Insurance register shown in Figure A.3, then double-click the word **GENJRNL** to view the prepaid insurance adjusting journal entry in the Make General Journal Entries window. Recall that this adjusting journal entry increases an expense and decreases an asset.

Figure A.3
Prepaid Insurance Register

Double-click here on GENJRNL to view the prepaid insurance adjusting journal entry

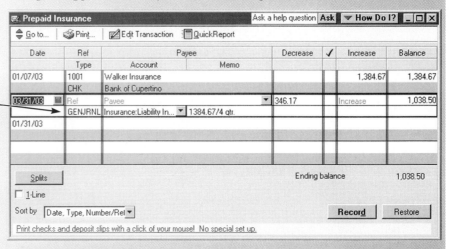

trouble?   The magnifying glass containing a "Z" does not appear when you point to GENJRNL, but you *can* double-click there to view the prepaid insurance adjusting journal.

6 Close all windows.

The journal entry shown in the Prepaid Insurance register was actually recorded by entering an adjustment to an account register. The adjustment itself was not a standard transaction entry prompted by the existence of a business source document, such as a check, an invoice, or a bill. Instead it was necessary for Casey to anticipate its recording at the end of March.

GENERAL LEDGER

The general ledger is used in accounting information systems to store the effects of individual asset, liability, owners' equity, revenue, and expense accounts. In manual accounting systems, journals are used to record business transactions, the effects of which are then posted or transferred to a general ledger. This recording and posting is compressed into one step in QuickBooks as the transactions are recorded. You decide to use a sales invoice to demonstrate to Karen how the effects of a transaction are stored in the general ledger.

You explain to her that the invoice itself is used as a source business document. Information is entered into the invoice and when you click OK, the invoice is stored and the consequence of that invoice is immediately recorded. In accounting jargon, once you enter the invoice, a debit is posted to the Accounts Receivable account in the general ledger and a credit is posted to the Sales Revenue account in the general ledger.

"In my accounting classes we usually posted all the sales for a month with one journal entry," Karen comments. "In this case, it looks like each sale is recorded individually. Doesn't that take a lot of time?"

"Yes," you agree. "But once you enter this invoice, several steps are completed simultaneously. Accounts Receivable is debited and Sales Revenue is credited. If we're selling inventory, the same invoice updates the perpetual inventory record, credits the Inventory account, and debits the Cost of Goods Sold account. Plus, the customer's account is adjusted accordingly so we know how much each customer owes and when amounts are due. Let's take a look at QuickBooks's general ledger and some underlying transactions."

To create the general ledger:

1 Click **Reports**, **Accountant & Taxes**, then **General Ledger**.

2 Change the report dates to read from **01/01/03** to **03/31/03** in the Modify Report window, then click **OK** to view the general ledger, as shown in Figure A.4.

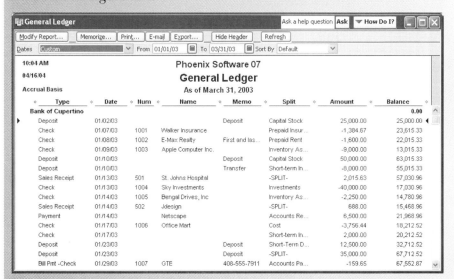

Figure A.4
Phoenix's General Ledger

3 Scroll down to display the Prepaid Insurance and Prepaid Rent general ledger accounts, as shown in Figure A.5.

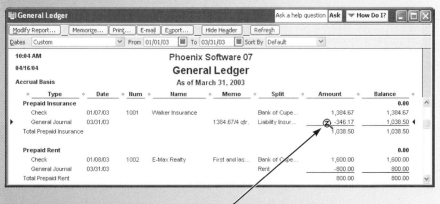

Figure A.5
General Ledger Accounts

Double-click here to view the journal

4 Double-click on the **–346.17 Prepaid Insurance** amount to view the Prepaid Insurance account, then double-click the word **GENJRNL** to view the prepaid insurance adjusting journal entry in the Make General Journal Entries window as you did before.

5 Click on **Insurance:Liabili**. Note in Figure A.6 that this adjustment includes a debit to Liability Insurance, an expense account, and a credit to Prepaid Insurance, another current asset account.

Click here first to reveal the drop-down arrow

Then click the drop-down arrow to view a list of accounts

Figure A.6
General Journal Entry

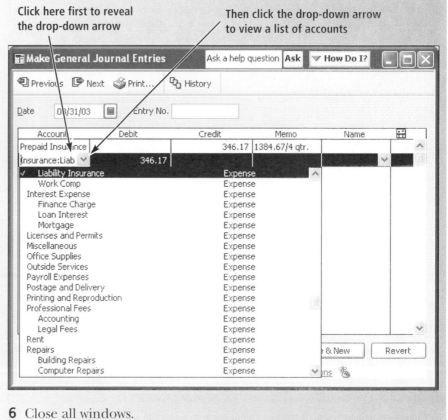

6 Close all windows.

After seeing how easy this is, you might wonder why QuickBooks—or some other similar program—isn't used all the time in business. The reason is that many companies often have their own accounting software that has been customized to their specifications. However, many smaller businesses, which often can't afford such a luxury as customized software, have found QuickBooks to be an inexpensive, yet powerful and easy-to-use alternative.

JOURNALIZING AN ADJUSTMENT

Another way to record adjustments—other than through an account's register—is to enter a transaction with a journal entry using the QuickBooks activity known as "entering special transactions." You decide to show this approach to Karen by recording next quarter's depreciation.

To record an adjustment using a journal entry:

1 Click **Company**, then **Make Journal Entry**.

2 Change the date to **06/30/03**, then enter the Journal Entry No. **101**.

3 Click in the upper part of the Account column, then click on the drop-down edit arrow to select a debit account: **Depreciation Expense**.

4 Click in the Debit column across from the Depreciation Expense account; then enter **500**.

5 Click in the Account column below Depreciation Expense, then click on the drop-down edit arrow to select a credit account: **Furniture:Accumulated Depreciation**. Note that a $500 amount is automatically entered in the Credit column across from the Accumulated Depreciation account.

6 Click at the top of the Memo column, then enter **Depreciation for the 2nd quarter**.

7 Maximize the General Journal Entry window to view the screen shown in Figure A.7.

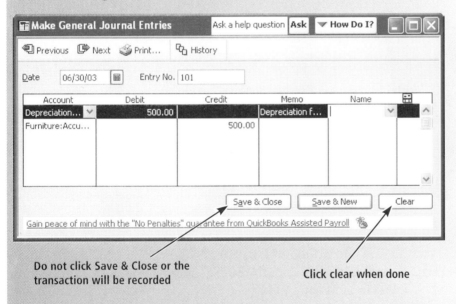

Figure A.7

Sample General Journal Entry

Do not click Save & Close or the transaction will be recorded

Click clear when done

8 Do *not* click Save & Close. Instead click **Clear**. Then close the window.

END NOTE

Many accountants prefer to use journal entries (that is the debit-credit format) to record business transactions. But Intuit Inc. designed QuickBooks for businesspeople who did not want to use journal entries. Although QuickBooks allows you to enter all transactions using the journal entry format, you then must sacrifice QuickBooks's specialized invoicing, bill payment, payroll, and other useful features. The choice is yours!

practice

appendix

Appendix Questions

1 In what order does QuickBooks list accounts in the trial balance report?

2 What QuickBooks feature allows you to access supporting accounts or journals when viewing the trial balance?

3 What happens when you double-click an amount on the trial balance?

4 Explain how a transaction recorded through an account register also creates a general journal entry.

5 Why does QuickBooks have a general ledger?

6 What advantages does QuickBooks's document-initiated recording method have over the standard journal entry method?

7 What happens when you double-click on an amount in the general ledger?

8 Explain how QuickBooks allows you to use journal entries to record business transactions.

9 What menu would you use to access QuickBooks's journal entries?

10 Explain how accounts are accessed when you enter information into QuickBooks's general journal entry window.

Appendix Assignments

1 *Creating a Trial Balance, General Ledger, and Journal Entry for Phoenix Systems, Inc.*

Use Phnx07.qbw to do the following:

a. Create and print a trial balance as of February 28, 2003.
b. Create and print Page 1 of the general ledger as of February 28, 2003 in landscape view.
c. Locate the journal entry that amortized one month's rent expense in March 2003.

2 *Adding More Information: Central Coast Cellular*

In Chapter 7, you added some reports to your QuickBooks file for Central Coast Cellular (CCC), a cellular phone sales, phone rental, and consulting company. Make a copy of that file in Windows Explorer, name the file CCCapp, and use that file to create the following:

a. Prepare and print a journal entry to accrue Utilities: Gas and Electric expenses of $250 with entry number 4 on January 31, 2003. (Debit the expense and credit accounts payable vendor So. Cal Edison.)

   b. Print a trial balance as of January 31, 2003.

   c. Print Page 1 of the general ledger in portrait orientation.

3 *Using the South-Western Home Page for More Assignments or Cases*

If you have Internet access, go to the home page for this textbook at **http://owen.swlearning.com**.

     Select the **Appendix** section from the Additional Problem Sets, and complete the problem(s) your instructor assigns.

Go to
http://owen.swlearning.
com

Appendix Case Problem 1: OCEAN VIEW FLOWERS

Use the same file you used in Chapter 7 to do the following:

1 Create and print a trial balance as of January 31, 2004.

2 Create and print Page 1 of the general ledger for the two-month period ended February 29, 2004 (print in landscape orientation).

Appendix Case Problem 2: JENNINGS & ASSOCIATES—Debits and Credits

Kelly has hired an outside accountant to review her financial statements. The accountant has asked for a trial balance and a general ledger, and Kelly asks you to prepare them.

1 Use Kj07cp.qbw to do the following:

   a. Create and print a trial balance as of March 31, 2004.

   b. Create and print Page 1 of the general ledger for the quarter ended March 31, 2004 in landscape view.